GREGORY BENFORD

Modern Masters of Science Fiction

Science fiction often anticipates the consequences of scientific discoveries. The immense strides made by science since World War II have been matched step by step by writers who gave equal attention to scientific principles, human imagination, and the craft of fiction. The respect for science fiction won by Jules Verne and H. G. Wells was further increased by Isaac Asimov, Arthur C. Clarke, Robert Heinlein, Ursula K. Le Guin, Joanna Russ, and Ray Bradbury. Modern Masters of Science Fiction is devoted to books that survey the work of individual authors who continue to inspire and advance science fiction.

A list of books in the series appears at the end of this book.

GREGORY BENFORD

George Slusser

UNIVERSITY OF ILLINOIS PRESS
Urbana, Chicago, and Springfield

Manufactured in the United States of America
1 2 3 4 5 c p 5 4 3 2 1

∞ This book is printed on acid-free paper.

Frontispiece courtesy the University of California–Irvine.

Library of Congress Cataloging-in-Publication Data
Slusser, George Edgar.
Gregory Benford / by George Slusser.
pages cm. — (Modern masters of science fiction)
Includes bibliographical references and index.
ISBN 978-0-252-03822-8 (hardcover : alk. paper) —
ISBN 978-0-252-07980-1 (pbk. : alk. paper) —
ISBN 978-0-252-09603-7 (e-book)
1. Benford, Gregory, 1941- —Criticism and interpretation.
2. Benford, Gregory, 1941- —Interviews. 3. Science fiction,
American—History and criticism. I. Title.
PS3552.E542Z87 2014
813'.54—dc23 2013023554

To Z

Contents

Acknowledgments

I wish to thank a number of people who were instrumental in bringing this book into print. I thank Bill Regier of University of Illinois Press for his interest in this project and encouragement along the way. Special thanks to Professors Paul Alkon and David Samuelson for their cogent and fruitful comments on my manuscript. Most of all, I want to thank Gregory Benford for all the help he gave me during the writing of this book. He provided me with hard-to-get materials and gave valuable input concerning scientific and literary matters pertaining to his work. It was a great pleasure to work productively with him. Finally, supreme thanks to Danièle Chatelain, my colleague and partner, for her constant support. She has convinced me that the creative force behind science fiction is science itself, and that all SF—not just the so-called "hard" variety—must answer to its criteria and method. It is that insight that drives this book.

GREGORY BENFORD

INTRODUCTION

Gregory Benford's life has been active, varied, and highly significant—a life that has generated much fiction. Born in 1941 in Mobile, Alabama, he has strong roots in the American South. But as member of a military family, he spent much of his adolescence in such far-flung places as Germany and Japan. Of this was born a cosmopolitan perspective, which gave rise to a lifelong fascination with "alien" cultures. Benford chose a career in science. He and his exact twin brother Jim—with whom he has remained close throughout his life—earned doctorates in physics at the University of California, San Diego. This was a new campus and an amazing creative environment for the study of science in the 1960s. Study there was to mark Benford's subsequent career as scientist. He received his PhD in 1967 and spent the next four years at the Lawrence Berkeley Laboratory. In 1971, he joined the physics faculty at the University of California, Irvine, where he remained until his "retirement" in 2005. His career as a physicist has been a distinguished one. Benford directed a laboratory and published well over one hundred scientific papers in the fields of particle and plasma physics, and later in mathematical physics. Benford left UC Irvine to become co-founder and CEO of Genescient Inc., a biotech firm specializing in "twenty-first-century biology" and issues of cellular longevity, based on the experiments of evolutionary biologist Michael Rose with Methuselah flies.

Benford has had a longstanding interest in longevity technologies such as cryonics. He dealt with the cryonics question in a mystery novel *Chiller* (1994, written under the pseudonym Sterling Blake, revised and republished by Benford under his own name in 2011 as *Chiller: A Scientific Suspense Novel*). Benford's move into genetics research involved mastery of a whole new discipline—indeed, a second scientific career. In this area, in fact, he has undertaken a third career as commentator on the culture and politics of science today, writing in journals such as *Nature*, as well as in his blog *Benford and Rose: Essays and Articles, the New Science* (www.benford-rose.com). He has written interesting scientific papers on ecological issues and climate change. He has always been pessimistic about mankind's ability to deal with its environment, yet he continues to propose interesting solutions.

Benford's alternate career as science fiction writer is equally distinguished, and that is the subject of this book. It was in Germany that Benford's interest in SF became manifest: here, with brother Jim, he organized a fan convention and launched the fanzine *Void*, which was later to attract SF figures such as editors Ted White and Terry Carr, the latter an important force in shaping the "new wave" of the 1960s and 1970s, when Benford began his professional writing career. His first professional sale was "Stand In," published in *F & SF* in 1965, while a graduate student at UC San Diego. Since, he has published more than twenty novels, over one hundred short stories, some fifty essays, and myriad articles. Despite his Genescient adventure, Benford has not abandoned writing science fiction. Recently he has written and published a number of books, freely exploring the new e-book format. His novel *The Sunborn* (2007), a sequel to *The Martian Race*, was his first e-book venture. The years 2011 and 2012 have seen a rebirth of Benford the writer in all formats—fiction and nonfiction, hard SF and fantasy. Today he moves seamlessly from self-published work to the bestseller list. Under the Lucky Bat e-format, he published in rapid succession: a revised version of *Chiller* (2011), a collection of short stories and novellas, *Anomalies* (2012), and a curious novella *Down the River Road* (2012), described in the promotional literature as "a backwoods fantasy in a riverland derived from mysterious science indistinguishable from magic." Electronic media allow the author to create a web of commentary around his e-publications. In this regard, see Benford's website (www.gregorybenford.com, an umbrella site with links to "recent posts," "Benford's blog cloud," and ancillary sites). One of the most successful editors in the fanzine world, Benford has mastered the new electronic form of literary dissemination.

Benford, man of many careers, has received numerous awards and prizes in all areas of activity. He has been a Woodrow Wilson Fellow, a Cambridge Visiting Fellow in physics, an advisor to NASA, and more recently to the U.S. Department of Energy and the White House Council on Space Politics. In 1995 he was awarded the coveted Lord Foundation Award, given both for scientific achievement and for promoting public understanding of science. In the SF field, he has won two Nebula Awards (awarded by a jury of his writer peers), a John W. Campbell Award, and in 1990 the United Nations Medal in Literature. Curiously, he has never won a Hugo Award; a fan-based jury, their criteria is more often popularity than literary excellence. Benford is a complex and sophisticated writer who sets before him the difficult task of writing fiction about scientifically probable worlds.

If *science* fiction is the literature that examines the impact of scientific and technological advancement on human beings and their belief systems, then Benford has the perfect background to write it. He knows science, both theoretically and professionally. He is well read in literature in general. And his life experience is active and varied. He has worked with scientists all his life. No one is more qualified to write about scientists "doing science" and to examine the social and cultural issues raised by science. In public remarks made in 1985 to a group of physics graduate students at UC San Diego, Benford laments the "lab smock image" of the scientist and sets forth the image he would like to see of scientists and their work: "I feel that we have the obligation as scientists to continually remind people that we are not the mandarins of some Byzantine, complex, non-understandable, great set of facts. Instead we are explorers trying to find what is going on."[1] The title he gives to his talk is "Why Does a Scientist Write Science Fiction?" The above citation neatly sums up his vocation as a science fiction writer. His task, in fiction, is to present the working scientist as explorer, as seeker of knowledge to be used by humans in what humanists see as the increasingly dehumanized world modern science has created. To do so, he must write an SF true to its name—fiction based on discoveries in science and on the activity of the scientist.

Benford has been pigeonholed as a hard SF writer. Yet his fascination with other cultures, and the decade in which he comes of age as a writer, make him a far more complex literary figure. He has seen SF from the "other shore," working as advisor and commentator for the TV series *A Galactic Odyssey*, prepared for Japan National Broadcasting. He did the same for the Japan 2000 series. He remains today scientific consultant to the Japan Broadcasting Corporation (NHK) network. Guided by his friendship and collaboration with Arthur C. Clarke, he has become increasingly fascinated with India. A story such as "Matter's End" (1990) seeks synthesis between Western and Eastern views of physics. Nor must one forget that Benford, by his dates, is a New Wave writer, the contemporary of Harlan Ellison, Philip K. Dick and Ursula K. Le Guin. This literary company suggests that, for Benford as for the diverse writers of his generation, science need not be the enemy of humanist culture. It is, as Benford emphasizes, its potential partner in defining the nature of the modern world.

Benford's life and work offer an extraordinary, seemingly inexhaustible display of creative energy. This study presents Benford's ideas on science and the writing of science fiction and then addresses his literary production in terms of its main categories. Rather than a survey, the book devotes ample space to the analysis of significant works in each category, in an attempt to give the reader a feel for these texts and evidence as to why they are important, both for the author's achievement and for the development of science fiction. The study hopes, by identifying direct sources and making parallels with other works and writers, to reveal the vast scope of Benford's knowledge, both of literature and of the major scientific and philosophical issues of our time. Benford's achievements are impressive, both in a general literary sense and as milestones in the history of science fiction. In his unique combination of scientist and man of letters, he is a quintessential science fiction writer. His work is of Grand Master status, and I hope to make the case as to why this is so.

CHAPTER 1

GREGORY BENFORD

The Scientist as Writer

Throughout his long career as science fiction writer, Gregory Benford has remained steadfast in his claim that science is at the center both of the twentieth century and of the form of literature he sees as its central mode of expression. What else should SF deal with than the impact of scientific ideas and discoveries on society and the individual? Remarks he made to physics graduate students at UCSD in 1985 are typical: "Science is the mainspring of this century. Historians will call this the century of science . . . because it is where it became obvious that the big driving term in the equation of society is science."[1] Clearly he sees these remarks to be valid for the twenty-first century as well, as he chose to reprint them verbatim in 2005. This is a restatement of Isaac Asimov's famous definition of "social science fiction" as the literature that deals with the *impact* of scientific and technological advancement on human beings. Benford, however, has a deeper historical sense of this process. He realizes that this impact did not begin just in the twentieth century. In his fiction and nonfiction he reveals a deep understanding of the philosophical currents born, as early as the Western seventeenth century, from the impact of scientific discovery on conventional worldviews. This engenders profound changes in the way—if we play by the new rules of science—in which we see the world. The literature that responds to these changing worldviews must of necessity be an *experimental* one, perhaps the only really experimental form of literature modern mankind has. Science has radically altered conventional ways of seeing space, time, and mankind's relation to the physical world; so must it do for narrative forms as well. Benford imagines physical environments in which human activity becomes radically problematic, if not unthinkable, and thus unnarratable in terms of conventional fictional structures, governed by a Newtonian stability. His writing faces technical challenges other writers, even many SF writers, habitually avoid. This is because he insists on writing "with the net up," strictly adhering to the laws of physics rather than conveniently "suspending disbelief." He is, in perhaps all the history of science fiction, the one writer who most successfully synthesizes the often-contradictory demands of science and fiction. Common wisdom today tends to oppose science and literature as having opposite, even antagonistic, goals. This makes Benford's synthesis all the more interesting. The problems he wrestles with as writer, given his sense of the ideas and world models that issue from scientific inquiry, are fundamentally philosophical rather than social. His work is philosophical fiction of the highest order.

SCIENCE AND FICTION

Benford is extremely well read in the history of science, and he often reveals his sources. In many other instances, however, it is clear that he is dealing with concepts whose basic source is unmentioned but which remain underlying problems for science today. As well, Benford is one of the rare writers who seeks to anchor the origins of science fiction in the origins of scientific thought. Science fiction has taken a long time to define itself, to gain a clear sense of its generic identity. Benford sees this problem, historically, as having much to do with the difficult relation between the two terms that have come to describe it: science and fiction. Both terms, as we know them today, came into being in the seventeenth century. The new methods and vision of the scientific revolution were codified in the work of thinkers and writers like

Descartes and Pascal. In their work, the vision of the new science challenges the conventional worldviews—religious and moral—that were, and remain, deeply imbedded in human fictions and stories. The works of a Pascal are not science fiction as we know it. But they do offer mini-narratives that suggest the *possibility* of a literary form that deals with Asimov's *impact* of scientific and technological *advancement* on *human beings*. The idea is profoundly simple. But it took a long time in Western literary history for this definition to yield a clearly identifiable literary *genre*. Part of the problem involves the nature of the scientific method, which is experimental, tentative, and open-ended by nature. Science's findings increasingly contradict the classical human-centered worldview. Science then, for Benford, is the scientific method. Applying this to human situations is the defining element of a "science fiction." His abiding concern, over his long career, has been to bring science and fiction into a creative, ever-evolving dialogue. True to the objective method of science, the consistent purpose of his fiction has been to *explain* (and not simply to justify) the ways of an increasingly alien nature to man.

Benford's task goes far beyond just bridging a "two-cultures gap." In English culture the antipathy between science and the conventional worldview of fiction goes back as far as Chaucer's Canon's Yeoman, in the age of alchemy. We see it in the punishment of scientist-overreachers from Dr. Faustus to Victor Frankenstein. In the eighteenth and nineteenth centuries, science and fiction (at least in England) seem to follow alternate paths, until technology and the shock of evolutionary theory forced a science-born worldview—with the force of Wells's Martians invading Earth—on a literary culture now seen to be dying. Matthew Arnold, in his speech "Science and Literature" (1883), delivered to an American audience, sees scientific materialism triumphant. Its note of defeat, however, was quickly challenged by critics like F. R. Leavis, whose "great tradition" hearkens back to Dr. Johnson and his defense of a literature based on cultural conservatism and stylistic and formal elegance. In the American twentieth century, this same vision was adopted by the cultural and academic establishment, associated with the Ivy League East Coast. Given this, it is no accident that American science fiction emerged in very different geographical and cultural regions—the immigrant backroom New York of Asimov's Futurians; the Midwest of writers like Philip Jose Farmer, Wilson Tucker, Clifford Simak, not to mention Bradbury and Heinlein; the

West Coast of Philip K. Dick's L.A. and Stan Robinson's Pacific Shore. Finally, there is Benford's Deep South. Science fiction in the United States grew up in these ghettos, rejected by critics and academics alike. But in the same way Arthurian legends captivated the medieval mind, the feats of science and technology are today the stuff of popular legend, generating hundreds of thousands of space epics and new and parallel worlds. Working with this popular material of wonder, science fiction became the dominant cultural, if not literary, form of the second half of the twentieth century. The problem here is science driven, and Arnold's proposition was an either-or one—the future of science or the past of humanism. Benford's science fiction, on the other hand, follows Pascal in *confronting* mankind's humanist, and religious, past with the challenges of science's future. He moves beyond Pascal, however, in considering the possibility of mankind's surviving and changing in that future. In the midst of theories of the universe in which we seem to take no part, he asks: Can some part of *us*, something "human," remain and evolve in even the strangest of futures, worlds beyond Pascal's imagining? If this question seems to lurk beneath every Star Trek episode, it is best examined by a scientist-writer like Benford, who possesses sufficient scientific knowledge of what this alien future might be like to speculate how something human might fit into it.

Benford frequently describes his creative activity as working with a scientific paper on one side of his desk, and a science fiction story (or novel) on the other. This lets him move back and forth, negotiating between the strictures of scientific method and the freedom of fictional speculation, allowing the "what if" to resonate with the "must be." The scientist's task is to state the cold equations of nature; the task of the speculative scientist-writer is to seek, and hopefully affirm, the role of organic (and perhaps human) life in science's cold future. In the epigraph to his novel *Across the Sea of Suns*, Benford lets poet Wallace Stevens state mankind's science-fictional strength: "After the final no there comes a yes / And on that yes the future world depends." The use of these lines (from "The Well-Dressed Man with a Beard") is characteristic of Benford's desire to mediate between conventional and new worlds. They are the opening lines of a poem that subsequently retreats into private enigma. But for Benford these lines become a call to action. They express the need for mankind to spread its "yes" throughout the mysteries of the cosmos.

Benford is usually classified as a "hard" science fiction writer. This designation, however, pigeonholes his work, places it in unfair opposition to the antiwar, antitechnology ideology of post-Vietnam found in other of his "New Wave" contemporaries. To Ursula Le Guin, for example, the designation "hard" means male domination via technology and science. These are the forces responsible for machines, aggression, destruction of nature; their soft opposite is return to "community," by which she means Indian and other tribal cultures. For her, the result of Benford's hard science is egomania, war, conquest—all characteristics of the "male" culture of technology and the aggressive, Cartesian "self." But this simplistic division misses the point that science is first and foremost a *method* of knowing, a particular type of cognitive activity. When Benford says "yes" to an expanding future for mankind, and for organic life in general, he demands that we seek to understand the physical forces that might govern that future. For him, this is the fundamental requirement for a *science* fiction. It must obey a material imperative that requires we take literally, as physical facts, any and all events that happen in its science-fictional world, future or otherwise. If mankind would have some aspect of its being survive in this future, this must be done on nature's terms; there is no deus ex machina, nor the logical and mathematical sleight of hand of Pascal's thinking reed, claiming to preserve the role of human reason at the center of physical infinities whose very existence deny any such centrality. For Benford, "hardness" means refusal of all such wishful thinking, however scientific it appears to be.

The term "hard science fiction" is often associated with interplanetary or cosmic engineering feats. Paradigmatic examples are Arthur C. Clarke's terraforming in *The Sands of Mars* and Larry Niven's artificial planet Ringworld. The idea behind both is to build an environment according to the laws of physics, and to "get it right." Niven's mode of creation is to present a working model to an audience of engineers and scientists and then refine it as details of its functioning are examined and corrected. Fans often place Benford's works at the far creative end of this cosmic engineering spectrum. For example, the July 31, 2009, entry on the blog "Fred's Place" (freds-ramblings .blogspot.com) marvels at Benford's conversion of cosmic strings into a massive planet-mining machine in the novel *Tides of Light*. It is clear, however, that Benford, although past master at this sort of cosmic engineering, is seeking to create in the vast reaches of spacetime an "ecology" in the original sense of this word—the search for a "home" or suitable habitat for some possibly or impossibly evolved form of humanity.

Benford's "exo-engineering" derives from the tradition of Larry Niven, and of Hal Clement's planet Mesklin and its Mesklinites in *Mission of Gravity*. Its reach is even vaster. But its purpose is quite different. It is closer to Clarke in its insistence on placing the human element at the center of its engineered alien futures, always exploring the link, however tenuous, that ties us to "it." In this sense, it is instructive to compare Benford's work with a novel that combines unsurpassed environment building with skillful engineering of a means of communication between humans and beings adapted to a physically alien environment: Robert L. Forward's *Dragon's Egg*. Forward both creates a plausible life form adapted to the extreme physical conditions of a neutron star, and works out a way for his "Cheela" to interface with human beings despite their incredibly accelerated chemical processes and infinitesimally short duration of their individual lives. The critic John Clute hailed this work as "a romance of science." This perhaps is a backhanded compliment for a novel whose characters are little more than counters. Forward, in fact, initially saw his role in this project more as scientific consultant than as writer. He was simply to design this world, and Niven or Pournelle were to write its story. They had other commitments, however, and Forward (with much guidance from his editor) went on to write the novel.

Like Benford, Forward is a professional scientist. But unlike Benford, Forward sees the *whole* goal of writing SF as getting the science right. He describes *Dragon's Egg* as "a textbook on neutron star physics disguised as a novel." In his essay "When Science Writes the Fiction," he describes his writing method: "I don't even write science fiction. I just write a scientific paper about some strange place—and by the time I have the science correct—the science has written the fiction."[2] Forward openly mocks "human-bound stories." He makes statements like "humans don't count, intelligence does," which promise bold, extrapolative reach beyond the anthropocentric worldview of conventional fiction. But he does not deliver on this promise. As it turns out, the superior aliens of *Dragon's Egg* worship the orbiting human ship as if it were a cargo-cult god. Humans are scientifically inferior to the Cheela. But they are physically larger, and their hosts, despite their scientific superiority, immediately agree to share their technology with humans. The scenario has not changed since Murray Leinster's benchmark story "First Contact." Benford's fictional worlds easily rival Forward's in the sophisticated modeling of scientifically plausible aliens. But Benford does not "do science" for science's sake, nor do his aliens display crude anthropocentrism once the veil of science is lifted. His fiction is anthropocentric only in the sense that the nature and limits of human experience is its abiding theme, and that its narrative voice is necessarily human. Unlike Forward, Benford is both a scientist and a writer. As such, his science fiction pushes the envelope of human experience, as the stuff of fiction, into realms of increasing scientific wonder. He extrapolates alien beings and worlds from cutting-edge discoveries in astronomy, physics, and biology. He does so, however, not to display his theoretical ingenuity but to test the limits of mankind's capacity to relate to, and possibly communicate with, uniquely alien life forms. If science "writes the fiction" here, it is only to the degree that scientific exploration opens an ever-expanding field of human endeavor, full of strange beings and physical forces beyond human capacity and perhaps comprehension. If Forward's human characters lack depth and believability, Benford's protagonists (necessarily human because his stories are all about humans moving "against infinity") are strong, complex presences. The use of such figures allows fiction, in turn, to rewrite the science, insofar as their actions redefine possible human roles and purpose amidst a landscape of physical and evolutionary wonder.

Benford's evolving sense of mankind's place in the material universe owes an acknowledged debt to philosophically inclined writers from Pascal to Robert A. Heinlein. From Pascal, he derives the terror of infinity. Western culture has never recovered from this sense of mankind's nothingness in contrast to the infinitely expanding vistas of modern physics. Here, things we thought permanent, such as matter, may also have their end, opening new vistas on infinite terror and mystery. Benford refers frequently to Pascal. He also mentions early evolutionist thinkers and writers, such as Olaf Stapledon and J. D. Bernal. He shares with them the idea that, ultimately, it is neither human reason nor Forward's "intelligence" that "counts," but sentience and Life in general. Thus he imagines, and chronicles, the struggle across universes and galaxies, not just between sentient and nonsentient beings, but between various upward-striving forms of sentience: organic, mechanical, silicon clay, and possibly beyond. But, however much these entities evolve and acquire intelligence, what seems to lack in all of them, for Benford, is the "human element," by which he means the dynamism and uncertainty generated by human beings with their vast ambitions and short life spans. Benford shares this vision with the benchmark writer of SF's Golden Age, Robert Heinlein. As with Heinlein's humans, Benford's explorers spread across vast reaches of spacetime. Yet they remain ever conscious of the necessity to create a home, a place where they can protect their original biology and identity, where they resist the possibility (and the temptation) of becoming something nonhuman.

Whatever debt Benford's vision of mankind owes to Pascal—and to the evolutionists, with their cold and often terminal sense of things—he ultimately turns to Heinlein for the dynamic element in his fiction. Heinlein revives the dynamic optimism of Huck Finn and the American frontier tradition. He proclaims that mankind's evolutionary edge comes from its short life span and its irrational desire to throw that short life away in pursuit of some larger sense of human destiny. Heinlein's upward-striving monad incarnates Stevens's "yes" in the face of nature's terminal "no." This vision informs his highly influential "juvenile" novels. Of this series, the most notable in expressing Heinlein's philosophy is *Have Space Suit, Will Travel* (1958). Its archetypal figure Kip, a typical young Midwestern boy who dreams of space and keeps a spacesuit at the ready, is snatched up by an alien spacecraft and, after a number of adventures, finds himself before a cosmic panel of "judges," a group mind that has been observing humans and finds their individualistic, often violent behavior a danger to universal harmony. These judges propose to "rotate" all of Earth and humanity, destroying it. Before doing so they convoke some sample humans before the bar of judgment to plead the cause of humanity. They choose a Neanderthal, a Roman centurion, and Kip and his girl companion PeeWee. Kip rejects the group mind that would judge them. He defiantly proclaims, in the face of cosmic strictures, that humans "have no limits." And when his defiance causes his judges to condemn humanity, he affirms this human otherness by demanding to die with the rest of humanity. Because his judges cannot grasp such absurdity in the face of cosmic law, they ask for time to ponder. They give Kip (and humanity) a reprieve, sending him back to his Midwestern home, where he is free to prepare some future assault on these judges. For Heinlein, the green hills of Earth remain the dynamic springboard for all human expeditions into the unknown. Likewise, Benford's seekers across seas of suns preserve their human identity by building human habitats—akin to Heinlein's "freeholds"—in intergalactic environments Heinlein could never imagine, nor Niven build.

Unique among hard SF writers, Benford draws upon a wide variety of sources, both in literature and in the philosophy of science. He is conversant with Descartes, Kant, and other figures in the history of Western science. If many of his scientific colleagues reject the mind-matter duality in favor of strict materialism, Benford, at the heart of his speculative universes, continues to wrestle with the question of the human mind and its claims to uniqueness. Though a physicist, Benford is intimately familiar with the evolutionary model that evolves from Darwin and remains today the central paradigm of biology. Benford the scientist is an internationalist, and his sense of the history and problems of science has broad international scope as well. Yet despite this, his literary and cultural roots remain undeniably American. In this, he remains a writer in the lineage of SF's Grand Masters. Bradbury's grotesques derive directly from those of Sherwood Anderson and Edgar Allan Poe, whom Benford refers to as the first great Southern writer. Behind Heinlein's solipsism we detect the Midwestern isolation of Sinclair Lewis's Main Street. Likewise, in Benford's narrative voices we hear echoes of the labyrinthine interior monologues of Faulkner. Finally there is deep at work in Benford, as in all these other American SF Grand Masters, the strong rhythms of Emerson's power and form, the undulating dynamic that sustains the self-reliant Man. In his novels and stories, it is always the dynamic human center that generates its own circumference. It is this same dynamic that drove James Fenimore Cooper's Pathfinder, Natty Bumppo, to explore the vast frontier forests, the same quest for power and form that drove Captain Ahab, that caused Whitman to seek a passage to more than India. It is the dynamic that informs what Hemingway called the "great American novel," *The Adventures of Huckleberry Finn*, to which Benford's protagonists refer again and again as their roadmap to the stars. His protagonists all claim one or more of the traits of Huck Finn, notably his ability to adapt to, and master, new and increasingly complex situations, improvising and surviving as he is inexorably carried down the river. Benford's river is now the Great Sky River of evolutionary and relativistic spacetime. Yet his heroes remain ever ready to catch a ride on the timeboat. Their edge against the universe is always Huck's tilt forward, his ability and ever-restless need to light out for the territories, wherever and whenever these may be.

It is fascinating then that Benford's central and enduring spacetime Huck Finn is an Englishman—Nigel Walmsley. Walmsley's career spans Benford's career as writer, and that of the Galactic Center epic that is central to it. Walmsley's first appearance, in *In the Ocean of Night* (1972), places him in the world of a near-future NASA. Episodes in this novel date from 1999 to 2019. In the subsequent novel, *Across the Sea of Suns*, Nigel is on a spaceship in 2056, exploring the moons of a planet eight light years from Earth. The novel ends with Walmsley, in 2064, "sliding out" of this astronaut world, commandeering a starship and lighting out for strange new territories at the Galactic Center. After a thirty-thousand-year hiatus, our British Huck Finn returns in the form of a series of temporal manifestations in the sixth and final book of the series, *Sailing Bright Eternity*. Here Nigel-Huck is still navigating, this time within a bizarre spacetime structure that exists at galactic center. Nigel's gradual advancement in the first two novels, moving by cautious increments into the future, coupled with his miraculous return in the final work, points to the influence of the British writer Arthur C. Clarke and the space adventures of Bowman in Clarke's *2001: A Space Odyssey* series. Huck Finn may be the perfect incarnation of Emerson's open-ended dynamic of power and form. But for Clarke it is the classical figure of Odysseus, whose exploration of the unknown is simultaneously a voyage of homecoming that embodies what seems a uniquely British dynamic, one whose first SF incarnation is Wells's *The Time Machine*. Wells's protagonist travels to the end of evolutionary spacetime on Earth. But his voyage, at the same time, is presented as a return to the primal seas from which now dying life once began. The Traveler stops at the year 802701 and then goes on to witness the end. His subsequent return, to his comfortable home in 1895, is more or less to the exact moment from which he began his odyssey.

In terms of origins then, Benford's paradigmatic protagonist Nigel is a cultural hybrid who combines two very different visions of the nature and limits of scientific investigation. On one hand, like Huck, Nigel establishes new bases of operation as he advances in spacetime, from which, ever tilting forward, he hopes to launch new explorations. On the other hand, he appears to enact the same "odyssey pattern" Clarke presents in all of his space adventures. In the initial *2001*, a first Odysseus, the prehistoric Moon Watcher, is hurled like Wells's Traveler many thousands of years into humanity's future, where he morphs into Dr. Haywood Floyd, seated in a space shuttle with all the comforts of home, traveling to the moon to investigate a strange "monolith." We inch forward in the future as Bowman (an all-too-obvious reference to Odysseus) and Poole head toward Jupiter, tracking the signal sent by the monolith. Then, near Jupiter, there is another big leap: Bowman enters the Star Gate and is projected through infinite spacetime. Yet his journey ends in a familiar place, this time in the famous eighteenth-century white room that appears to embody human classicism, that stable center where mankind forever remains the proper study of man. Clarke's sequels continue this pattern, as (in dated sequence) mankind appears to progress toward a transhuman or even posthuman condition. But even so, each of these new odysseys, predictably, results in a new reinvesting of mankind's original home. Strikingly, in *3001: The Final Odyssey*, future advancement follows a clearly elliptical path that turns back to the initial starting point of the entire *2001* adventure—the moon of the seminal story "The Sentinel." The original monolith that signaled the initial journey has, in 3001, become a powerful engine of future change, one that is physically capable of transforming Jupiter into a new sun. As it does so, the monolith appears to lose its resemblance to the human form, a property it carried with it for a thousand years. But this is not simply exo-engineering in the manner of Niven or Forward. For what remains after this transformation, kept intact in the myriad small rectangles that reform after this explosion, is the classic *human proportion*: 1:4:9. Supposedly guiding the monolith's future actions is a new transhuman entity—Halman, Bowman's flesh fused with HAL's machine intelligence. Yet this Halman, because it is a cybernetic entity, can be stored on a "petabyte memory tablet." This in turn is an object that a future Poole can return to its original home on the Moon, there to await some future awakening to new encounters with the monolith. As with Odysseus, it seems that mankind does not achieve longevity by further exploring the future, but rather by securing its home base, by staying within a radius where the oars of human tradition may still be recognized.

Benford, then, in his dual allegiance to Heinlein and to Clarke, stands between two worlds, two modes of interpreting mankind's scientific adventure.

It is perhaps because he occupies this position that Benford is able to offer a possible solution to the mind-matter duality that science continues to engage, and that fiction seems unable to solve. True, evidence has increasingly come down on the side of matter. Mind, now seen as a finite network of circuitry and electrical charges, can no longer pretend to metaphysical uniqueness. The human form itself, vehicle of that mind, seems little more than an evolutionary way station. There appears to be, contrary to the Dow Chemical ad, no specifically "human element" in chemistry's table of elements. And yet despite this, in both science and fiction the Cartesian ghost abides, if only as a sign that the human mind could, or should, somehow, occupy a unique place in the universal order. To this question of how and in what ways human beings "matter" in this ocean of matter and time, science fiction offers two responses, each of which appears to resonate with Benford in different circumstances. One is the American vision of Heinlein. Here what survives is not the rational but the dynamic self, the self-reliant individual as generator of energy capable of establishing a power base that projects its own circumference, no matter where or under what conditions. The danger here is the monstrous solipsism we see in figures like the Lazarus Long of *Time Enough for Love*, or the Johann Sebastian Bach Smith of *I Will Fear No Evil*, where this single individual, mind *and* body, extends its own being in an attempt to encompass the entire spacetime universe. The other response is Clarke's "odyssean" vision. Clarke writes in the lineage of Olaf Stapledon, where no matter how far humanity evolves, its goal remains ineluctably tied to its origins—last and first *men*. Clarke's other mentor is J. D. Bernal, who sees mankind's future as a "dimorphic split," wherein if part of humanity transcends itself, becoming a new form of life devoted to unsteadily groping after the unknown, the other part remains behind to secure the original home, now a "well-tended zoo" awaiting mankind's eventual homecoming. Clarke perfects this vision in novels like *Childhood's End* and the *Space Odyssey* series, works that have, as author Benford testifies, had an enduring effect on his sense of the endgame of science.

Benford's science fiction, as it pursues the rigorous trajectory of scientific investigation, moves naturally into the area of philosophy. More than once in his work, Benford cites poet Wallace Stevens. To paraphrase the latter, one can see Benford's work, in its deepest sense, as exploring the metaphysical streets of hard SF's physical town. Up till now, I have mentioned writers and thinkers who have had a direct influence on Benford's method and vision as scientist-writer. These are influences documented or admitted to by the writer himself. His stated goal as science fiction writer, however, has antecedents. Most notable among these is a scientist-philosopher of a previous century and a different scientific culture: French physiologist Claude Bernard.

Claude Bernard was a contemporary of Jules Verne's. Unlike the latter, he did not write "extraordinary voyages." But in his writings on science he did what Verne's early SF claimed to do: mediate between the complexity of the new experimental sciences and the general public. His book *Introduction à l'étude de la médicine expérimentale* (1865) was a landmark attempt to clarify the general understanding of modern science by defining its method and addressing the cultural and philosophical issues involved in doing scientific experiments. Likewise Benford, a century later, sees the same goal for both science and science fiction. In the above-mentioned 1985 speech to his former UCSD classmates, he admonishes: "I would say you all ought to be communicators of science. . . . They [the general public] can't understand the difference between the surface complexity [of doing science] and the simplicity underlying it. . . . Simplicity is the only way we are going to reach people."[3] This is precisely what Claude Bernard did—set forth a statement of basic scientific method that cuts through the "surface complexities" of positivist science to allow the general reader and scientist alike to see the potential of empirical scientific experiment. More than any writer in his century perhaps, Claude Bernard defines a simple path both for doing science and for writing the sort of science fiction Benford will later produce. Science, to Claude Bernard, is the unending pursuit of a physical unknown we will never fully grasp. But what those who pursue this unknown have is the terrors and joys of the experimental chase—the scientist's encounters with what Benford calls the "ineffable," which, for science and SF alike, becomes the much daunted (and derided) "sense of wonder."

Like Benford, Claude Bernard was a significant experimental scientist; he discovered the role of the liver's glycogenic function in human diabetes. Opposing the official method of Comtean positivism, which focused on observing and systematizing facts rather than seeking their causes, Bernard proposed an experimental method in the empirical manner of Bacon—observation, hypothesis, verification. He describes science's pursuit of the material unknown—in terms much like Benford's scientist-protagonists later do—as something arduous, austere, thankless, Sisyphean in its never-ending travails. His description of this process has uncanny echoes in Benford's numerous accounts of the work of the scientist: "The experimental method is impersonal; it destroys all sense of individuality in the act of bringing together and sacrificing the single ideas of each person . . . for the benefit of a general truth established according to experimental criteria. . . . It advances slowly and painstakingly, and because of this it will always appeal less to the mind."[4] Benford describes this slow and painful advance of the working scientist in blunter terms: "Watching scientists work is on a par with watching paint dry."[5] Yet for both Claude Bernard and Benford, the scientist is neither a drudge nor a classifier. He or she does not merely seek order, subsuming facts under some unified field theory. The experimental scientist is on a quest. And if that quest is for truth, this truth, for both Claude Bernard and Benford, is an existential experience rather than an act of cognition. Benford would concur entirely here with Claude Bernard's statement: "The scientist moves ever upward in pursuit of the truth, and if he never finds the whole truth, he nonetheless finds important fragments of that truth, and it is precisely these fragments of the general truth that constitute science" (307).

Science, then, for both men, is a human enterprise. Its message for mankind lost in the infinities of matter is to seek a truth it will never wholly find, but only glimpse. And yet it is precisely because this scientific unknown is forever out of human reach that the scientist's pursuit of these fragments of truth is so important. What is glimpsed is partial and fleeting. But it is the "wonder" of the glimpsing that spurs the scientist to seek further. As Claude Bernard describes it, this experience, if not religious, is certainly an aesthetic one. As such, it is an eminently fictional experience: "He who has never known the torments of the unknown can never know the joys of the discovery. . . . And yet, because of some caprice in our nature, this joy of discovery we so seek and desire vanishes the minute we find what we were seeking. It is merely a flash of light that briefly shows us new horizons toward which our unslaked curiosity carries us with ever more ardor. And so it is that in science itself the known loses its attraction, while the unknown always remains full of charm" (307). Claude Bernard is exactly describing what Benford and his Golden Age forebears call "sense of wonder." And as with Claude Bernard, this flash of wonder, in Benford, comes in the midst of doing the daily work of science.

Benford exhorts his UCSD scientist audience: "I think scientists should try to write fiction." And had Claude Bernard written scientific fiction from his perspective, he (instead of Jules Verne) might have been the "father" of the genre, and its course a very different one. Benford, however, a century later is taking SF in the very direction Claude Bernard foresaw. As a scientist, Benford is aware that science has been "writing the fiction" for a long time, and that the challenges of newly discovered scientific world views have turned fiction itself into an experimental mode, the culminating form of which is SF. He also knows how heavily science has come to rely on fiction. He knows that modern science, pushing the envelope of the unknown, freely uses such fictional terms as Claude Bernard's "charm" in its attempt to describe the actions of subatomic particles that lie beyond tangible experiment. Benford, like Claude Bernard, is against philosophical systems (or any kind of system) co-opting experiment, be it scientific or literary. Even so, if the experimental scientist and SF writer alike reject philosophical systems, he or she must ultimately embrace what Claude Bernard calls "l'esprit philosophique." This he simply defines as "the eternal yearning of human reason towards the understanding of the unknown" (307). This describes not only the cutting-edge science Benford wields with ease, but also the near-sacred sense of the act of *doing* science, which informs his science fiction. The Claude Bernard parallel provides a means of understanding what Benford's science fiction, at its deepest level, is striving to accomplish. It also shows us that scientific science fiction—the kind that Heinlein, Clarke, and Benford write—needs a redefinition. Such science fiction is not simply a scientific paper or an engineering feat. Claude Bernard calls for the scientist to participate actively in the search for cosmic truth. Following this precept, hard SF, in its truest sense, must be seen as the chronicle of science's exercise of this "l'esprit philosophique" in the endless pursuit of the unknown.

CHAPTER 2

BENFORD IN HIS OWN WORDS
Toward a Craft of Science Fiction

Gregory Benford has written much nonfiction commentary over his long career, both on his own fiction and on that of others. He has also written on philosophical, cultural, and political issues that concern science fiction. These writings are essential to understanding Benford's science fiction, for in their aggregate they define his science fiction as a literature of action. The purpose of his SF is not to describe possible futures or to predict them (this for Benford is nonscientific, for there is no way to verify predictions). Instead, science fiction *engages* the future, and in doing so it gives mankind an active role in creating that future. As Benford puts it, the science fiction writer should aim to be *ahead of the future*, rather than simply flow with it. Over the years, Benford has written criticism and commentary in many forms and venues—for the diverse fan audience in fanzines and "sercons" (serious and constructive criticism), in science columns in SF magazines (Ted White's *Amazing Stories*), in general interest magazines, and in blogs. He has written scripts for television series, as well as prefaces and commentary for numerous nonfiction compilations, such as the recent *Popular Mechanics* series, with titles like *The Amazing Weapons that Never Were* (2012). But he has also, surprisingly, written extensively in academic journals such as *Extrapolation* (1969 to the present), *Foundation* (U.K., 1972 to the present), and *Science-Fiction Studies* (1973 to the present). He is also a member of the editorial board for *Science-Fiction Studies*.

In all of these venues, Benford has produced a vast amount of commentary, both on science fiction and on the culture of science. What I propose—as means of seeing clear in the myriad texts—is to focus on the series of essays Benford wrote for UC Riverside's Eaton Conference. I do so for several reasons. Benford was one of the founding contributors to this conference, which began in 1979 with the participation of a number of UC faculty. He remained active as a core contributor to the Eaton Conference, which in its initial format ran from 1979 to 2008. In 1979, science fiction was a field rarely if ever addressed in academic circles. The idea was to generate an ongoing series of forums, each tightly focused on a single important aspect of the genre (for example, science fiction and fantasy, the theme of immortality). The format was to bring together writers, prominent fans, scientific professionals, and editors, along with teachers and academic scholars. Conferences were small, only the best papers were accepted, and everyone listened to everyone else's paper. Discussion was lively. Graduate students presented ideas before noted writers like Brian Aldiss, Theodore Sturgeon, and Gregory Benford, academics like Harold Bloom and Leslie Fiedler, and scientists like Marvin Minsky. Much as with the French colloquia at Cérisy-la-Salle, polished essays from presented papers, along with recorded commentary, were shaped into published volumes, each focused on its single topic. Over the history of the conference, thirty-two volumes, one per conference, were published in academic presses. The result was a formidable body of criticism that, collectively, served to define the genre.

From 1979 to 2009 Benford published a series of essays in these Eaton volumes. Because they were conceived in the demanding and focused context of the Eaton Conference, all of these essays are tightly reasoned, their main points carefully argued. They are classic works in the true sense. Essentially, Benford presented an essay whenever a conference topic coincided with his preoccupations and writer's concerns of the moment. They are, therefore, a testament to the growth of the writer's mind and craft. The abiding concern of Benford, as science fiction writer, is the ways in which scientific methods and ideas might interact with narrative structures to create a genuinely *science-generated* fiction. As the conference evolved, Benford had a hand in isolating the themes and concepts deemed essential to defining science fiction and thus in setting the conference topics. As he addressed these topics in succession, grounding his observations in novels and stories he was writing at the time, a core of critical thought gradually developed in organic fashion. If these Eaton volumes, taken collectively, generated a poetics of science fiction, Benford's essays, within them, set forth his own personal craft of fiction. His vision from the outset is a broad one. He sees modern scientific discovery through the eyes of Pascal, who saw its infinite vistas dwarfing the pretensions of rational mankind. But at the same time, he sees science challenging mankind to imagine and explore new vistas, liberating it from the restraints of closed belief systems.

His constant concern, beyond science, is the fundamentally philosophical one of defining mankind's role in science's expanding universe. The writer, however, must find ways to *tell* this story. Benford turns naturally to reflections on how to *write about* this new, scientific mankind and its gropings. He asks himself how writers might use fiction's Aristotelian conventions to narrate our alien encounters in newly imagined contexts, such as the incalculable forces swirling around a black hole. In these essays, Benford constantly raises questions of style, of narrative form, of substance and rhetoric. He calls himself an amateur critic, yet his remarks on the genre and craft of science fiction are both compelling and insightful. He asks basic questions other critics, comfortable in their theories, often avoid. Benford's Eaton essays offer a string of years and changing, evolving positions on science and science fiction. What I hope to do here is to set forth the writer's personal vision by connecting the various threads of these essays.

The topic of the inaugural Eaton Conference in 1979 was "Bridges to Science Fiction." At the time, in academic circles, few scholars were attempting to build bridges to this form of literature. Benford's essay bears the title "Aliens and Knowability: A Scientist's Perspective." Benford asserts, in manifesto form, that science and science's quest to know the alien is central to SF. He begins by citing J. G. Ballard, who states that "one of the problems of science fiction is that it is not a literature won from experience."[1] For Benford, science fiction's futures cannot be "experienced" in Ballard's sense, because we have not yet been there. He knows that, though we may not "win anything" from the alien encounter, we *can* strive to experience the truly alien, and in doing so test the limits of knowability. He enumerates different categories of anthropocentric aliens in science fiction—the alien as enemy, as "analog human," or simply as mirror image of ourselves. Ballard and Benford alike find such aliens inadequate, but for different reasons. Ballard simply rejects the search for the alien as futile. Benford urges us to look beyond the stranger next door, to use science to locate an alien that is fundamentally unknowable in its "essential strangeness." Such unknowable aliens, for Benford, are Clarke's Rama or the Overmind in *Childhood's End*. He warns us, however, that "size alone is not all that significant . . . let us remember that some of the most bizarre aspects of reality appear at the subatomic level" (56). Ultimately, for Benford, the real issue is not knowing the alien, but *communicating* with it. Do we, like the rationalist skeptic Stanislaw Lem, simply assert that true aliens are fundamentally unknowable? Or do we, as with quantum and mathematical physics, push the question of knowability aside and look for ways to *contact* the alien?

Benford revisits Ballard's term of "experience" from the point of view of the "intuitionist" school of natural philosophy. He gives a personal example of intuition at work in "chicken sexing," comparing it with quantum mechanics, where deciding whether a chick is male or female replays, on a pragmatic level, the wave-particle experiment. The chicken-sexer is acting beyond the rationalist logic of either-or, moving in a realm where intuition and participation are more important than creating models or boundaries: "One might say that the world of the quantum is made up of models that fold into one another. When one simple picture fails, one goes to the next. . . . The notion of enfolded models [itself] is fading, being replaced by the elaborate waltz of mathematics with data" (61). Benford admits that too few science fiction works see alien encounters—in light of modern (in other words, circa 1979) science's principle of uncertainty—as intuitive acts of communication, for to do so the writer must approach its inherent strangeness by inventing and using nonclassical modes of description: "My own instincts as a theoretical physicist and a writer lie with the intuitionist school. I think that anyone who participates in science comes to realize that, by expanding our categories and using the most universal of descriptions (and languages—that is, mathematics), we can make ourselves something greater. We can, in other words, *ingest the alien*" (60–61, emphasis added). Benford warns the followers of Ballard and Lem that modern science has taken a Gödelian turn: "Yet we know from Gödel that the analytic sense of knowledge will forever escape us" (63). He places the scientist-writer at the "Einstein intersection" Samuel Delany's character Spider articulated ten years prior to his essay: "And I want a Gödelian, not an Einsteinian, answer. I don't want to know what's inside the myths, nor how they clang and set one another ringing, their glittering focuses, their limits and genesis. I want their shape, their texture, how they feel when you brush by them on a dark road, when you see them receding into the fog, their weight when they leap your shoulder from behind."[2]

In this inaugural essay, Benford lays the scientific and philosophical groundwork for his own SF at the time, whose central theme is this process of alien *ingestion*, a process he explores literally in a story written in 1979, "In Alien Flesh." Alien encounter is less a cognitive act than a participatory exercise, in the manner of mathematical physics. Thus, when he describes the SF protagonist's participation in the physical universe as a "philosophical pursuit," he means something different from existentialism: "Perhaps such philosophical pursuits can lead us finally to a deeper sense of what it means to be logical and fragile and human" (63). Pursuit of the alien unknown will guide mankind's cosmic quest in the later Galactic Center novels. In terms of size and force, human beings remain Pascal's reed. But for Benford it is not by "reason" alone that we secure our place in the universe. Instead, we survive and thrive because we know our own fragility. This drives us to "ingest" the other, to become part of the vast unknown process science hopes to engage. Benford thus redefines Pascal's concept of the human condition. He chooses to clarify his scientist's idea of the human condition in the fifth Eaton Conference, a forum on the idea of hard science fiction, in a paper titled "Is There a Technological Fix for the Human Condition?"

In light of his earlier essay, we see that his title is a rhetorical question at best. For just as there is no rationalist "fix" for the human condition, there is no technological fix either. In terms of Benford's quantum thinking, the hard-soft dualism that informs the conference is untenable. This conference (1983, published volume *Hard Science Fiction* [1986]) covers many aspects of the hard-soft dichotomy. The lead essay, Dr. Robert Forward's "When Science Writes the Fiction," sees writing science fiction as nothing more than an exercise in applied physics. Critic Robert Scholes exhorts the literary establishment to adopt a new literary model that favors "ideas, . . . and events beyond ordinary experience" over conventional settings such as depth of character and verisimilitude. Author Norman Spinrad defines hard SF as an aspect of tone rather than content: a "feel" of "hard-edged, materialistic, deterministic reality."[3] Benford's essay passes in review these reasons for the hard-soft dichotomy—the presence (or absence) of plausible science, the use of science as symbol for a non–man-centered worldview, rhetorical devices such as tone and narrative focus, appeal to different types of readers (the psychology of reading), and finally class and political-ideological divergences. In contrast, he sees hard SF as one that presents human beings striving to participate in an unknowable, perhaps forever inaccessible, physical universe. This is the activity of the modern scientist. Thus, hard SF must be that which deals with scientists doing science. For Benford, SF must present real scientists, trained to follow the strict rules of scientific research. Their setting may be the everyday reality of mundane lab work, but their hope is breakthrough to contact, finding a window into the mysteries of matter.

Benford's essay seems to address an incident that occurred two years earlier between him and Ursula Le Guin, concerning this centrality to the genre of the scientist doing science. The bone of contention was an article by Benford published in the British journal *Foundation* as number 22 in their series "The Profession of Science Fiction." The article is entitled "A String of Days" (*Foundation* 21, February 1981). In the subsequent issue of the journal, Le Guin published a short satire on Benford's piece, "A Day of Strings." Her response is a frontal attack on what she sees as "hard" traits in Benford's description, which revolves precisely around a portrait of the contemporary scientist doing science. Le Guin has a radically different idea of what issues SF should address and what sort of human beings should be the focus of an SF novel. She contrasts her ideal SF protagonist with a satirized portrait of Benford's scientist-writer, taken from his self-description in "A String of Days." The ensuing controversy is central to what is to be a looming struggle for the heart and soul of the SF genre.

The 1970s were arguably Le Guin's most productive years in terms of science fiction. But by the time of *The Dispossessed*, Le Guin felt alienated from the worldview behind the space adventure and heroic fantasy modes in which she first chose to write. In a 1979 article entitled "American SF and the Other," she equates "American" with "hard" SF. She sees it as "parochial" and "power worshipping." It is itself the alien, a force at odds with every possible form of "community"—sex, society, culture, race.[4] Hard SF is the legacy of John W. Campbell's male elitism, rendered more odious yet in the ruthless male power fantasies of a Jerry Pournelle. None of this bears any resemblance to Benford's vision as he articulates it in "Aliens and Knowability." But "A String of Days" came along, and Le Guin seized the opportunity for polemic, reacting to the author's somewhat smug tone in the *Foundation* piece, a tone absent from his soberly argued Eaton essays.

Nevertheless, the portrait of the artist Benford paints in "A String of Days" is useful in understanding (despite its smugness) how doing science and writing fiction interact in the day-to-day life of a busy university professor and lab director. The creative process described is purposely opposite from the (Romantic) myth of the creative artist as inspired and disorderly dreamer. What drives Benford's string of days is not *angst* but a balanced metabolism. Creation is not the result of personal suffering but of broad interests, vitality, and discipline. The author describes a busy and carefully balanced schedule, right down to the 3,500-plus calories needed daily to fuel the machine. He rejects the garret for the stock market and investment strategies; money is necessary to maintain the mobility needed for his creative activities. He speaks of his writer's days as "some scraps of memory, a few bits of fiction, cancelled checks and tax returns," a life where one must trade high style for banter and shop talk. Driven by the course of his days, the creator's task is to control and balance the multiple strands of his personal spacetime continuum. Posing as a modern Leonardo, Benford presents his string of days as a model that allows the scientist-writer to navigate his particular field of activity, which as scientist he sees steeped in movement, change, contingency—"life whole."

In his "Technological Fix" essay, Benford moves beyond polemics and, sure of his vision of hard science fiction as the only logical form of fiction that has science in its name, proceeds to outline the narrative and rhetorical devices needed to achieve what he calls that "falsely quiet" moment when the practicing scientist senses the possibility of alien encounter. He describes the need for "constraint" and "verisimilitude," by which he means sticking to scientific fact, to currently accepted laws of physics—"playing with the net up." At the same time, he envisions what can only be called a rhetoric of sense of wonder—a technique of instilling moments of awe and perhaps terror through the surprise discovery of an unanticipated facet of some momentarily glimpsed future. Likewise he envisions, where necessary for effect, strategic violations of his constraint imperative. An example is Poul Anderson's classic *Tau Zero*, where visible contradiction between physical fact and fictional outcome results in a powerful effect. In 1983, Benford is about to launch his Galactic Center epic into deep spacetime. Here he will push both his alien creations and his sense of human capacity beyond previously known limits. Mankind cannot know or function in such a world by reason alone. His mode of apprehension, in this new world beyond strangeness, must involve contradiction, intuition, awe, and wonder.

In this essay, Benford reflects on the kind of human mind and voice he would see operating on the far edge of scientific possibility. He reviews past models of narrative voice and tone. He analyzes Arthur C. Clarke's ability to modulate from the "cool analytical tone" of scientific description to one of "cosmic mysticism" in a work like *Childhood's End*. But he also invokes "the wiseguy insider" tone patented by Heinlein in his novels of the 1950s. These are fast-talking, fast-acting characters who use their intuitive, pragmatic brand of "scientific" reasoning to "get the job done." This, increasingly, will become a facet of Nigel Walmsley's personality, a gestalt in elaboration at the time of this essay. In subsequent Galactic Center works, Benford will alternate between the high voice of scientific law, the collective patter of science, and the human voice of the crafty actor, Huck Finn seen through the intergalactic eyes of Heinlein. The interaction of these various voices in a same narrative creates a powerful effect. If Le Guin hears only one voice in hard SF—that of inhuman technology echoing inhuman science—Benford's narratives offer a polyphony of voices. The high voice of scientific law, for example, speaks as the exemplar of a higher logic and scheme, "to which humans would be well advised to respond with a mingling of scientific interest and mystical devotion" (87). For Benford this voice functions as a powerful rhetorical device: "I suspect such vast perspectives fight feelings of powerlessness by putting the reader at one with the universal scheme" (88). In opposition to this, the human voice, as Benford sees it, must be that of a being who displays, both in words and deeds, "a conspicuous ease with large matters." It is this character who dares sail those seas of suns ordained by the high voice of science.

Benford gives short shrift to those who claim that hard SF appeals only to "convergent personalities," or that it is the expression of some disenfranchised "sci/tech" class. He resolutely rejects the idea that hard or scientific SF is simplistic because its focus on machines rather than people renders it incapable of irony or depth of character. If hard SF is conservative, it is because science itself is conservative. Following science's conservative process, the nature of science fiction is to seek out and propose solutions rather than simply to detect problems. Seeking solutions to mankind's place in nature, Benford asserts, requires ingenuity, an intuitive sense of nature's laws and ways, and the will and desire to pursue this quest into alien realms at the farthest reaches of the universe. Benford responds to the attacks of Le Guin and others by asserting that the real SF protagonist is the scientist who both does science and fully lives the doing, equally at home in the laboratory or in a starship sailing the galaxies. For Benford, his presence defines scientific science fiction, and this, he asserts, *is* science fiction. And if this kind of SF has scientists as its primary readers, that is fine, because all of us, in the world today, need to begin seeing with the eyes of science. Looking through these eyes, a reader will not see SF as "a literature of hardnosed technophiles and adolescents . . . but as an expression of the bittersweet truths emerging in our century, an echo of man's progressive displacement from a God-given center of creation, so that mankind's perspective is now forever, like science, provisional and ambiguous and evolving" (98).

Benford's next significant Eaton essay appears in the volume *Aliens: The Anthropology of Science Fiction* (published 1987, conference held 1986). If the scientist-protagonist occupies one pole of Benford's galvanic circuit, pursuit of the genuinely alien is the other pole—the outer limit of human scientific investigation. Benford's essay in this volume, written at the moment in his career when he was launching humanity's great quest to *fuse with* the cosmic alien at the Galactic Center, is key to understanding his evolving fictional worldview. He prefaces his essay with lines from Kingsley Amis, British author of a pioneering study of SF, *New Maps of Hell*. These lines stand as his response to Le Guin:

> Their light of pocket torch, of signal flare,
> Licks at the edge of unsuspected places,
> While others scan, under an arc-lamp's glare,
> Nursery, kitchen sink, or their own faces.

Amis's "unsuspected places" makes a crucial statement about the role of the alien in science fiction: "There is probably no more fundamental theme in science fiction than the alien. The genre reeks of the desire to embrace the strange, the exotic and unfathomable nature of the future. Often the science in SF represents *knowledge*—exploring and controlling and semi-safe. Aliens balance this desire for certainty with the irreducible unknown."[5]

By the time of this essay, Benford speaks with authority, as a science fiction *writer* for whom "the most interesting problem set by the alien is in *rendering* the alienness of it" (14, emphasis added). Comparing safe knowledge—that which domesticates the alien—to an intuitive approach that seeks to participate in *extremes* of alien strangeness, Benford engages the question of "plausible" aliens and how to create them. He sets a scale that runs from anthropomorphic to totally other. On one extreme, aliens are us. Thus for Soviet SF writer Ivan Yefremov, any advanced alien that humans encounter *would have to be just like humans* (that is, like Soviet socialist humans) because we represent the highest form of sentient life achievable for any chemical life form in any universe. On the other extreme, the alien is fundamentally unknowable. For Benford, it is not that aliens are unknowable, but that unknowability is the central narrative and rhetorical problem of science fiction. Benford begins his essay with philosophical and cognitive questions but moves swiftly to reflections on how writers might use the alien in SF to achieve a maximum effect of scientific wonder: "For me, the most interesting problem set by the alien is in rendering the alienness of it. This is a central problem for SF. Very seldom has it been attempted in full, using the whole artistic and scientific arsenal" (14). Again, the SF writer is not faced with an either-or situation. He or she does not have to choose either scientific description or "literary" style. Instead, the way to approach the ineffable is to employ both, so as to define the crucial moment when fact shades into mystery.

Indeed, Benford is adamant that the scientific imperative apply in the rendering of the alien. The writer must remind the reader that the alien is a literal "thing," lest it slip into metaphor: "By the rules of 'realistic' fiction, aliens can't be real. SF insists that they are—and that important issues turn upon admitting alien ways of knowing" (15). The SF alien, then, is neither a figure of speech nor simply (as with Forward) a scientific description, a well-conceived blueprint for an otherwise nonexistent entity. For Benford, the alien in SF is primarily an *experience*: "When SF works, it gives us an experience of the *style of knowing something*. . . . This means that the prime virtue in depicting the truly alien is expressiveness, rather than 'content.' . . . We don't read *The War of the Worlds* for its views on Martian biology or psychology, but for the *sensations of encounter*" (15, emphasis added). Benford makes cogent suggestions as to how the SF writer achieves these effects.

Benford the scientist is convinced we can approach the truly alien, even experience forms of contact, though we may never know it in any cognitive sense. He passes in review theories that posit the possibility of some form of language communication between us and the alien. He rejects what he calls "the gospel of the universal language": "Language can't simply refer to an agreed-upon real world, because we don't know if the alien agrees about reality" (17). He considers that, if evolutionary models fail, perhaps mathematics can furnish such universally translatable ideas. We may try to use mathematics to communicate with an entity that is a "thing." But this may not lead to knowledge, for mathematics, Benford reminds us, "allows us to describe 'things' accurately and even beautifully without ever knowing what they are." He cites Feynman: "The glory of mathematics is that *we do not have to say what we are talking about*" (19, original emphasis). But if for Benford the possibility of communication with the alien remains oblique, this obliquity can yield aesthetic effects, as with the "beautiful" figures of mathematics. In this regard, the author points to what he calls the "trapdoor moment" in a story like Terry Carr's "The Dance of the Changer and the Three," where "the core of the story is that *sideways lurch into the strange*" (21, emphasis added).

Benford's conclusion is clear. At the "supreme moment" of alien encounter, the SF writer must abandon science for aesthetic effects: "We cannot know the true deep substance of the totally alien, but we can use conscious and conspicuous style to suggest it" (21). In the section of this essay titled "Modernist Aliens," Benford details some concrete stylistic devices that describe his attempts to "eff the ineffable" in his Galactic Center novels. SF must adapt the stylistic techniques of "modernist" writers, such as Joycean or Faulknerian "stream of consciousness." In mindbending situations, SF can use these techniques "to undermine consensual reality and achieve a more personal, dislocated view" (22). SF can use run-on sentences and verbal flow as a means of rendering "the scientifically *unknowable*—or, at least, unfathomable by humans. The blizzard-of-strangeness motif is a persistent notion, even among hard SF types" (22, original emphasis). His own "blizzard of strangeness" is often a blizzard of prose effects that invades and overwhelms mundane description. In his later Galactic Center novels, he presents aliens that are both scientifically plausible *and* beyond human scale and comprehension. The approach to these aliens occurs at moments when prose itself, the vehicle of scientific description, becomes unhinged, murky. The reader, caught up in this stream of words, is brought closer to contact with something that (as the turgidly unclear prose makes clear) cannot be defined by words. Benford ends his essay with a statement both sweeping and highly personal, which can stand as his *profession de foi* as scientist-writer: "Rendering the alien, making the reader experience it, is the crucial contribution of SF. [Its] tales can argue over communication, spring trapdoors, inundate the reader with stylistic riverruns—all to achieve the end of a fresh experience. That's what the alien is really about" (25).

Throughout these essays, Benford the scientist consistently uses philosophical terms such as "unknowability." In his essay on the alien, he frequently uses Pascalian absolutes such as the "truly alien." Pascal was the seventeenth-century scientist, mathematician, and writer who first formulated—with an implacable geometry of extremes—mankind's absolute insignificance in relation to material science's newly discovered "infinities." In a short paper presented at the 9th Eaton Conference (1987)—and in an expanded essay published in the volume *Mindscapes* (1989) as "Pascal's Terror"—Benford pays homage to his great French predecessor. He sees Pascal as creator of what remains today the ultimate landscape of science fiction—infinity. In Pascal, there is no place for alien encounter. Rather, mankind itself, by virtue of its position in the universe, is now seen as the alien, the rational mind now alone and alien between the infinitely large and the infinitely small. Pascal's question still resonates in science today. For what would be the consequence if there were no aliens "out there" to communicate with? What if there were only emptiness, void, silence? This Benford calls Pascal's terror, the silence of the infinite. Benford sees Pascal's universe, beyond the

Greek sense of a mathematical infinity, as a genuinely infinite *physical* universe. Pascal hoped beyond hope that, even though his infinities were physical, *res extensa*, that behind them there remained a "hidden God," the *deus absconditus*. Mankind's terror, then, came from this God's silence, His refusal to "tip His hand." Pascal's infinity remains, for Benford the scientist and SF writer, a place of "*portentous* silence." It is thus the ultimate setting for scientific and fictional exploration.

Pascal's terror is augmented by modern astronomy, for astronomy has thrown open a window that cannot be shut again. Henceforth, "our imaginations cannot avoid infinite classes of things, and our telescopes report equally terrifying vistas."[6] Such vistas run opposite to mankind's fundamental desire for limits, its "cultural agoraphobia." For Benford, the middle ground of realistic fiction cannot escape the infinite by going indoors. In Pascal's world, if we shut out the stars, the floor beneath us opens onto the yawning gulf into the infinitesimal. Benford uses the example of Pascal to prove that the modern schism between SF and mainstream fiction is a bogus one. For it was Pascal who first saw that any and all fiction, in the new age of modern science, must face, as central to its very being, this same problem of the silence of the infinite. Science fiction openly shows us that "black holes pack infinite mass into infinitesimal space," and "a singularity is an infinity you can hold in the palm of your hand." Mainstream fiction, however, must cope with these terrors as well. He gives as examples Borges's discovery of the Aleph in the basement of a Buenos Aires apartment, or the famous "Hilbert Hotel," infinitely large yet always full, where a room can still be had by moving the guest in room #1 to room #2 and so on infinitely "down the line." In terrifying manner we discover, in this banal hotel, that 1 + 1 = infinity. As Benford puts it, behind such intimations of the infinite, there lies the "fear at the idea of a quicksand universe that went on and on, into which I sank" (272). In reaction, Benford detects in humanity a deep "urge to diminish nature's scale." He finds this urge in much science fiction. For instance, Verne's famous moon rocket is a "subverting strategy, filling the infinities with people" (274). This same need drives SF's fascination with cosmic empire, its need for tyrants to rule galaxies that, once in their pockets, become grains of sand. Even Heinlein, for Benford the apostle of the space frontier, could not resist this desire to fill the void with the human form. In novels from *Time Enough for Love* (1972) to *Number of the Beast* (1980), Heinlein seeks to fill Pascal's vacuum with myriad humans all spawned from the genetic material of a single man—from the fictional Lazarus Long, and finally from author Heinlein himself. For Benford, all of mainstream literature, and much of SF, abhors the vacuum of infinity. The same is true for science—examples are Roger Penrose's "cosmic censorship hypothesis," which denies the existence of a "naked" singularity as hole into the infinite, and Stephen Hawking's attempts "to dethrone that primordial singularity by finding a probability function that describes the various states the universe could be in—a 'wave function' of the universe" (274). In all of these efforts, Benford perceives "the desire to find a deeper essence, a truer key that persists smoothly, that banishes the realm of infinity" (274). Science has not gotten beyond Pascal's comforting yet absent God.

Benford qualifies such abstruse scientific theories as having "the quality of mankind making a deal with infinity, allowing it limited expression" (275). So it was with Pascal's famous *pari*, where we must bet on something (God), because if we don't, we are certain to lose everything. Even so, this infinite universe is not empty for Benford; it is filled with *something*. In this context he restates the alien problem on an infinite scale. Benford feels that SF should address the problem of infinity. For if conventional fiction simply broods about it, SF needs to devise ways—again stylistic and rhetorical devices—that allow us to "creep up" on it. One way of doing so is "the construction of great artifacts." These can be vast monuments like pyramids, or titanic engineering feats such as Niven's Ringworld, a world so vast "that you cannot plausibly explore it in a human lifetime—yet a world you can *see* all in one glance, hanging in the sky" (276, original emphasis). Such artifacts embody Benford's concept of "deep time," mankind's constructing a monument *against* infinity, as means of communicating across stretches of geological, evolutionary, and relativistic time. The idea of investing infinity also explains the author's fascination with India: "Many modern Anglo-Saxon texts evade the promise of strangeness and immensity of, for example, other cultures (the infinity of human facets), especially of the richness of India" (274).

Concluding this short but provocative essay, Benford the scientist asks: "Should we feel dwarfed by infinity? Physically, perhaps. But our imaginations, both in mathematics and physics, have transcended our bodily limitations" (277). He now speaks with the voice of the SF writer, for whom narrative devices and stylistic effects must ultimately replace physics: "And in literature? The essence of enormity must be attacked indirectly—by leaving in the narrative a feeling for the noncentrality of humans themselves. And by finding fresh expressions for the prospect that unlimited space and time promises more, finally, than our ultimately futile attempts at closure and domestication" (277). Again, the creation of such narrative "feelings" and "fresh" expressions is the work of the mid and later novels in Benford's Galactic Center series, where mankind learns to operate on the edge of a naked singularity.

Papers from the 11th Eaton Conference, held in 1989, were published as *Styles of Creation: Aesthetic Technique and the Creation of Fictional Worlds* in 1992. Benford expanded his initial essay for this event, "Style, Substance, and Other Illusions," during the time he was at work on his final Galactic Center novels. Style and rhetoric were a constant concern in his earlier essays. Here he offers something akin to a formal, if loosely structured, treatise on the uses of literary style, both in SF in general and in his own writing. The author restates his holy grail as writer—the use of stylistic effects in order to come as close as possible to "effing the ineffable." At this point in his career, however, Benford sees this goal as "illusory." Pursuit of the scientific unknown remains the motor of SF. But actually "grasping" this unknown, he now sees, is at best an evanescent experience, a "spot of time" or Proustian "miracle" that issues from those rare instants where style and substance fuse. Here is Benford's description of such moments: "Authors often concentrate their themes into stylistic turns. You can see the story implicit in the manner of telling. Substance dances with style, and the dance is what we see, seldom the dancers. To separate them is to falsify the reading experience."[7] Despite this new pessimism, we do see that, for Benford, style remains a "hands on" activity. The author's role, still, is to allow substance to *dance* with style. Style remains the best tool an SF writer has for active exploration of the unknown.

Benford argues that because a writer's style "tells us matters beyond their conscious control," it is not only an important element in SF, but "can be crucial in determining matters the author cannot say any other way." This is especially important "in this supposedly analytical, science-based literature, its rational underpinnings so often displayed for all to see like a lady's scarlet bloomers" (48). Benford rejects the claim that science fiction must have a "styleless style." The idea that science must use a plain, factual language and eschew rhetoric and stylistic flourishes goes back to Bishop Thomas Sprat and his admonitions to the Royal Society to adopt the "merits of a plain English prose style, uncontrived and unadorned, devoted to a bare recital of the facts."[8] Benford respects the style of Buffon, just as he does the cool, analytical voice of Arthur C. Clarke. But he finds the argument for such a style specious: "No style is in fact transparent except to a certain kind of reader, with whom it shares plenty of assumptions" (49). On the contrary, Benford sees SF's brushes with the ineffable demanding a "hot" style, what he calls *stylistic blowout*. Referring to the style of his collaborative novel with Gordon Eklund, *If the Stars Are Gods,* Benford describes how the authors used "stylistic immersion" to overwhelm the reader with a mindbending experience—in this case alien beings physically merging with their divine sun: "Overpower the reader with adjectives, throw apparently incompatible analogies at him, mingle senses ('he sounded green down the analytic corridors,' to make up one on the spot). Give him rushes of prose, quiet pauses of apparent contradictions, tweaks and allusions to ideas he already knows but will find topsy-turvy here" (50).

In this substantial essay, Benford speaks openly, autocritically, about his own use of style in specific works. For example, he sees his reliance on "modernist" devices as often obsessive: "I use style unremittingly, trying to get at elements not approachable with any of the tones I listed for the hard SF writer. . . . I used Joycean rhythms and methods in an early novel, *In the Ocean of Night*, though for different purposes and without actually having read much Joyce" (53). Benford marks an important difference between the style of a Faulkner and that of the SF writer: "We really *do* talk about the grandly discordant, the truly alien. Stream of consciousness is now a technique that, taken over into a wildly different SF context, can mean very different things—the choice is up to the writer, who can trim his stylistic canvas and sail before these mainstream winds. That I have tried to do" (53–54). Benford may enforce SF's material imperative, its mandate that fictional situations conform to the physical laws of science, not to the desires and fears of human beings—yet in terms of science fiction *writing*, Benford sees literary form as the means of negotiating this rigor: "No matter how much an SF text may insist on humankind's trivial role in the universe, its fall toward a valueless limbo is arrested by the perfectly stretched safety net of literary form itself: which argues perpetually for meaning" (57). These are worthy pronouncements. Yet one suspects that, for Benford, the "safety net" of style is just that. For no matter how much one desires to ballast the human condition with words and effects, the facts of science's increasingly indifferent universe confront the writer today with a formidable version of Dr. Johnson's stone.

As the topics of subsequent Eaton Conferences necessarily become more specialized, Benford's essays tend to be more topical and practical, less inclined to address big questions of science and philosophy. At the special Eaton forum on cyberpunk, held at the University of Leeds in July 1989 (essays published as *Fiction 2000: Cyberpunk and the Future of Narrative*), Benford offered a paper titled "Science Fiction, Rhetoric and Realities: Words to the Critic." The change of focus is immediately clear. By "rhetoric" here, Benford means the hype surrounding cyberpunk, the claims of its proponents that it is the future of SF, indeed of fiction in general. The focus of this conference was the work and influence of William Gibson as prime practitioner of the form. Benford gives Gibson's work credit for having an impact on SF comparable to that of Arthur C. Clarke's vision of space exploration, expressed in his writing and in his memoir *Astounding Days*. Yet he regrets that we no longer have a "fresh, central vision of the future that is at once a powerful metaphor and a scientific possibility."[9] But absent that grand vision, there are still some who "expect science fiction to abide by the constraints of science and to look beyond the claustrophobia of the present" (223). The "some" Benford refers to here are a diminishing number of scientifically inclined SF writers. Looking to explain why this number is diminishing, he singles out the role of the personal computer "in our lives in this decade." Yet he does not accept the cyberpunk vision "of the coming world ruled by the impact of computers" (224). He dismisses cyberpunk as something equivalent to the contemporary French "cinéma du look": "Thus we get film noir and pulp plots against a background taken mostly from the glossy aesthetics of magazine ads" (224). Generally laudatory of modernist "mainstream" writers, Benford rejects cyberpunk as a "literature of surfaces," with little underlying meaning. He now turns to the SF critics themselves. He urges them "to concentrate on what the SF genre makes, not merely what it reacts to, what emerges from it, not what it mirrors" (224). Benford denounces the iconic film *Bladerunner* as "driven by a visual aesthetic and a postmodern need to revisit and recycle the tropes and mannerisms of earlier fiction" (225). The conclusion he draws from comparing Gibson to Clarke is that cyberpunk is a literary attitude and form driven by the world, whereas Clarke's vision of space travel *drove the world*.

Benford uses the cyberpunk phenomenon to decry what he sees as the disturbing rise of fantasy as a cultural phenomenon. As opposed to scientific fiction, fantasy "suggests a program of managing the world through acts of personality—will and virtue rather than intellect" (225). The rise of horror fiction, to Benford, is even more disturbing. Even so, he finds positive SF trends developing in the 1980s. He applauds "the advances in sheer writing ability by people as diverse as Stan Robinson, Connie Willis, Vernor Vinge, and Lucius Shepard. It also seems to me," he says, "that hard SF has strengthened noticeably at the hands of Haldeman, Bear, Brin and others" (226). He sees as well new advances in science leading his own thought and fiction in new directions: "I feel that we may be entering a postliterate era, in which information is best conveyed by tagging it to recognizable personality complexes. All this underlies the ideas I am struggling with in *Great Sky River, Tides of Light* and beyond" (227). Further, Benford predicts that science and fiction alike, over the next decades, will be "driven more strongly by biotechnology." And to the degree that cyberpunk grapples with issues raised by biotechnology, Benford praises it for showing us that fiction in this new age has "reached the point at which reflection on our own pace and hectic momentum is worthwhile" (227). This, however, is faint praise. For Benford, the central problem of cyberpunk is not its superficial and ephemeral nature, but the fact that it preaches a vision of progress based on quick technofixes. As he puts it, one cannot address the "deep cultural reality" of the Third World with criminals and console cowboys. Benford is fond of formulating laws. Here he offers his "law of science fiction," which states that the aim of the SF writer is not to be with the future, but ahead of it. One concludes from this essay that Benford is deeply disturbed by the critical acclaim of cyberpunk. And so he ends his piece with a challenge to the SF critic: "Work out new methods of dealing with fantastic literature that do not rely on the old habits of mind. Such approaches are needed to fathom what's already been done, and they will certainly be essential for navigating through the literature of the century approaching" (229). Looking back from our new millennium, it is far from certain this has been accomplished.

In his cyberpunk essay, Benford sees a link for this "literature of surfaces" running from Ballard to Gibson. He thus suggests a British influence in SF's shift from a future based on scientific extrapolation to a "claustrophobic" one. Ballard is a leading figure in the British New Wave. Benford, in terms of generation, is himself a New Wave writer. And if he seems frankly critical of cyberpunk, his take on the New Wave is more nuanced: "I find cyberpunk less interesting than the New Wave because it exhausted quickly, didn't play into many fruitful streams. It was more interesting as a marketing strategy using the idea of literary progress" (226). The link however between cyberpunk and the British New Wave is clear in his mind. In his essay for the 12th Eaton Conference (held in 1990, paper published in *Science Fiction and Market Realities*, 1996), titled "In the Wake of the Wave: The British Science Fiction Market," Benford elaborates on this link by addressing the larger question of the influence of the British New Wave on the course of anglophone SF and on the SF marketplace in general. Embedded in this conference topic are issues of literary "canons" and of "establishment" versus "popular" publishing and reviewing venues. These issues arise as competing forms of literature and SF vie for control of the critics and trendsetters who decide what will dominate the marketplace. The span of six years between the initial presentation and the published paper allowed Benford to refine his arguments and broaden the context from simple consideration of "market realities" to matters of literary politics. The broader phenomenon of the British New Wave brings him to ask what kind of books actually sell in the post–New Wave 1980s and 1990s and why they sell.

This cross-cultural perspective, in the case of British SF, is important for our understanding of Benford's work. Benford is clearly a writer in the American tradition of Mark Twain. But he has lived in the United Kingdom, as a fellow at Cambridge, and worked alongside scientists like Roger Penrose and Stephen Hawking. One suspects that, as a Southern writer, Benford harbors a secret empathy for his English ancestors. His paradigmatic hero, Nigel, is and remains an Englishman; his freethinking rebelliousness has a British accent. And, via the work of Arthur C. Clarke, the British vision of evolution and space exploration has remained an important influence on Benford's work. Finally, Benford's most lauded novel, *Timescape* (1980), juxtaposes two scientific laboratories—one in La Jolla, the other at Cambridge. Their two approaches to the problem are "science with the net up," again simply with different accents. Benford is addressing SF in general in this essay. But specifically it is U.K. science fiction "in the wake of the wave," the SF that evolved *as a consequence of* the British New Wave of the 1970s. Tracing his link back from cyberpunk, Benford sees this SF as turning its back on space and modernism, reverting instead to a dreary form of the novel of manners. He chooses to discuss this trend in terms of the marketplace, for by the 1990s it was clear to Benford, always the astute marketer of his literary products, that these fictions and their cyberpunk avatars were not selling as well as once hoped.

Benford delineates the differences between British and American SF as they appear in the 1990s. His overall sense of the difference is this: "There certainly is in British SF a studied lack of interest in how the world works. Mechanism does not seem to animate its authors; they care more for what the world *is*. And their reaction to it is often a pervasive sadness."[10] He sees two "literary facets" that typify the difference between British and U.S. science fiction. One is "landscape." British SF abandons space for realistic venues, which he sees as a refurbishing of the world of the nineteenth-century novel, a world that opposed a blighted rural England to the ravages of the Industrial Revolution—"Hardy's Wessex heath and Charlotte Brontë's bleak moors" (151). Benford sees its technophobic return to "roots" as a challenge to a perceived rootlessness of American SF, its conviction that the land is "malleable." The other facet of post–British New Wave fiction he identifies is a renewed focus on "character," which to Benford marks a return to a static worldview now cloaked in "kitchen coziness": "U.K. critics often assume that higher standards in SF entail greater fidelity to the bourgeois novel of character, without wondering whether such concerns may undermine what SF can achieve" (152). In their poking fun at American "materialist" science fiction, U.K. critics and writers may be "avoiding the unsettling strangeness that is central to SF" (152). He sees British writers enacting a "we're Athens, you're Rome ritual," touting as antidote to American "expansionism" an anachronistic fidelity to character and manners. More centrally, he deplores the doom and gloom of the British "entropy lovers," and is quick to point out that "recent explorations of self-organizing structures in physics and cellular biology contradict [such] easy oversimplifications" (158). Benford's essential beef with post–British New Wave SF is that it has turned its back on scientific extrapolation, wallowing instead in postcolonial remorse and guilt. Benford produces figures to show that by the 1990s, this sort of SF, in the wake of a waning interest in its American analogue cyberpunk, no longer sold books. Tolling its demise, however, may have proven premature. For, at least in terms of ideology, this form of fiction now appears to dominate the first decade of the new millennium. And sales figures may have risen, as New Wave postcolonialism mutates into more commercially viable forms such as "steampunk."

Yet however harsh Benford's recriminations are (he is correct in seeing this "wave" as his ideological adversary), he finally admits that he "[does] not see that much difference between the countries" (153). He correctly identifies the nontechnophobic strain in British SF—from Clarke through John Brunner to recent writers like Stephen Baxter. Nor is all British SF criticism doom and gloom or ideologically slanted. He cites Colin Greenland's *Entropy Exhibition* as a book about the New Wave that "shows how diverse it really was" (155). And for all his talk of "kitchen coziness" of character, he gladly integrates both character and domesticity into the depiction, in *Timescape*, of his British world of 1999. Benford himself in *Cosm*, a novel he may have been working on as he revised his "Wake of the Wave" article, elaborated his own form of "scientific novel of manners." Benford finally admits the influence of the British New Wave on American hard SF and on this own fictional development: "The outstanding, digested legacy of the New Wave in the United States . . . is two-fold: first, an increased literary sophistication used by many of our best writers, from adroit dinosaurs like Frederik Pohl to newer, hard-edged people like Joe Haldeman. This is indeed a positive force, often underrated. I felt the influence of British SF strongly in the early 1970s, when I began to think earnestly about writing" (156). But he speaks here of early New Wave. If this legacy was positive, that of this "new" New Wave has been a disaster, especially for post-1970s British writers themselves. As he sees it, what was bequeathed to these writers is a restricted technophobic worldview, a focus on "atmospherics (interior landscapes, as it were)," and an "arts-graduate posture about surfaces rather than content," all of which has convinced publishers that they are "noncommercial writers" (156). Rather condescendingly, Benford announces a gradual evolution in decades to come that is away from "postures" fixated on the fall of empire. This, he predicts, might "repair the damage done to British SF in the marketplace by the New Wave hangover" (159).

Benford speaks here as voice for the "neo-Campbellian" revival of hard SF, as anthologized by David Hartwell and Kathryn Cramer in *The Hard SF Renaissance* (1994). But his prediction of stagnation, of fiction wallowing in New Wave angst, did not see the coming of the British hard SF renaissance that took shape in mid-decade with writers like Ian McDonald, Paul McAuley, and Australian Greg Egan. This strain mutates further into original works such as Charles Stross's *Accelerando* (1996). Given this, it is certainly an exaggeration to see "New Wave assumptions still [casting] their long blue shadows" over British SF (154). What is more, for this reader, the ideological divide (Benford speaks of the British market "dominated by technophiliac stories written with an American accent" (154) is not as impermeable as Benford presents it. For example, when he speaks of the British journal *Foundation*'s "slow slide . . . into a posture of wan literary-fiction boredom" (154) due to its editorial policies, he minimizes the open and varied nature of the journal in the 1980s and 1990s. For example, the journal gave much space to articles and commentary by Gary Westfahl, which raised the hackles of many British readers and created some exciting intercultural commentary. As late as 1994, in a special edition of *Foundation* guest-edited by the same Gary Westfahl (Spring 1994), I published "The Politically Correct Book of Science Fiction: Le Guin's Norton Anthology," which drew lightning from the "technophiliacs" but stirred up healthy controversy on both sides of the Atlantic. And, of course, there is Benford's own "Profession," Le Guin's parody, and a subsequent string of pro-and-con letters to the editor over several issues. This is proof that the Anglo-American SF dialogue, on the criticism front, is more complex than Benford claims. But even though Benford stands his ideological and creative ground in this essay, he offers many nods toward dialogue, describing a situation that is by no means black and white.

Around this same time, Benford wrote a short essay, "Suffering Fools, Not Gladly," for a special Eaton forum, *Genre at the Crossroads: The Challenge of Fantasy* (essays compiled circa 1990, publication delayed until 2003). His remarks were in response to a position paper, "The Ghost in the Canon: 'High Culture' Repressions of Science Fiction." The question asked was: Who's afraid of science fiction? Benford's answer is: everybody, and most notably the East Coast "mainstream" literary establishment that steadfastly refuses to consider SF as a "serious" literature, despite the fact that SF remains the proverbial 800-pound gorilla in their ivied halls. Benford goes for the jugular here. SF represents the new and the future—things that *scare* the mavens of high culture, whom he accuses of commissioning endless "literary muggings" in elite magazines like *Harper's* and *Esquire*. He decries their official mandate that fiction be about character and style, and not about situation and setting, as "Babbitry," the work of "limousine liberals," the increasingly irrelevant elite who spend their time lamenting over the ascent of science and demise of literature. The positive side of all this, in Benford's eyes, is the fact that current SF is pushing "lit" books out of the market. He ends his essay by calling on these critics to do what they promise—an impartial critics's "job of work." Ultimately, for Benford, their persistent rejection of SF as literature raises serious questions about the limits of narrative itself. Why, he asks, must it be so difficult for a writer "to do 'characterological studies' in science fiction's deliberately strange surroundings?"[11] Must SF situations always be "more than passing strange?" If so, then what difficulties ensue when a writer seeks to narrate them? He offers these interesting thoughts in passing, though the bulk of the essay is polemical. Benford is clearly exasperated, for in his eyes the high-culture exclusion of science fiction has gone on far too long. In his earlier essays, he accuses "soft" SF of pandering to the pundits in order to achieve recognition, if not book sales. Here he simply laments the ongoing fact of SF's literary rejection.

The last Eaton Conference of the twentieth century, whose theme was the "two cultures" question, took place in 1999. Due to various problems, the essays from this conference were not published until 2009. Benford did not give a paper at this gathering but did contribute a short essay to the published conference volume *Science Fiction and the Two Cultures* (2009) with a rather sibylline title, "A Creature of Double Vision." Benford again turns to larger philosophical issues, this time examining the limits that beset scientific "speculation." He takes this term literally, in the sense of mirrors and optics. Mirror and glass were one before the invention of the telescope and microscope, which science hoped would let us see beyond ourselves. Yet, with uncharacteristic pessimism, Benford implies in this essay that such seeing may be nothing more than a mirror adjustment, for no matter how large or small the frame, we still see ourselves in the mirror of ourselves. This is science's N = 1 problem. Benford gives a Pascalian twist to this. Pascal said that Man's dilemma was that he could not remain alone in a room for half an hour. For Benford, mankind, gazing at itself in the new mirrors of science, can do little more than abhor the feeling of being alone with itself. The search for the other, in scientific disciplines such as artificial intelligence studies, chimpanzee studies, and the search for signs of extraterrestrial intelligence, are all expressions of mankind's anxiety as it faces its solitary image in the various mirrors and glasses of its creation.

Benford is not addressing the two-cultures gap in his essay. Instead, he explores what has been, implicitly, a constant theme throughout his work—the gap between us and the other. Speaking as the scientist, Benford returns his reader to another favorite theme—the rationalist's assertion that the human mind is alone in the universe. He sees this consideration still alive today in scientific experiments that probe the brain, looking for its Cartesian "ghost": "Scientists today probe into our brains, or build projects to engineer thinking into computers. These are all experiments to fill that gap left between us and the Other. We have invented angels and devils, gods and aliens—all to give us someone to talk to."[12] Given this dilemma, is it possible for mankind to see beyond its mirrors? For an answer, he turns once more to "intuitionist" science, giving the example of Maxwell, who used intuition, "honed by a sense of mathematical aesthetics," to move beyond the cramped mirrors of his time, in order to arrive at a verifiable "revelation": "that the speed of electrical circuitry gave the same velocity as that of light." Beyond this, Benford envisions a realm of otherness outside ourselves that would seem to lie in Emerson's realm of "experience." "Our minds seem limitless, blithe spirits, flying higher than a bird" (231). Benford's analogy is taken from our experience of animals, who would remain fundamentally unknowable, were it not for our capacity to intuit their deeper being. Likewise the unconscious mind functions in a realm we somehow experience but do not know: "Commonly we just 'have' ideas, whereas it might be better to say that they have us." (231) Both the maxim-like pronouncements in this essay and its focus on an intuitive, experiential faculty beyond reason tend to corroborate what for me all along was an intuition—that the deep influence on Benford's view of mankind in nature comes from Emerson. Emerson's vision, and the essay form he uses to express that vision, is mobile, ever probing and striving. Benford himself, in this essay, begins to sound like Emerson when he makes statements like "Immersed in life, we miss its over-arching features." The point he makes is an Emersonian one: it is because we are "immersed" in life that we can join intuition to reason and engage in a scientific quest that leads us to employ—instead of sight as the sole organ of reason—new glasses of "mathematical aesthetics" in hopes of moving beyond our mirror condition. Benford is unique among science fiction writers in engaging in such philosophical meditations on the scientist's job of work.

The Eaton Conference is now history. But Benford, in more recent writings, has not abandoned his call for exploration, his desire for sense of wonder. In step with the times, his recent focus has shifted from philosophy to practical matters, notably the need to keep the dream of space exploration alive in a time of political dickering. An example is his article in the February 2012 issue of the libertarian magazine *Reason:* "Science Fiction Faces Facts: NASA Has Fizzled, but Wernher von Braun's Exuberant Vision Lives On." Benford revives Clarke's *Astounding Days* by evoking von Braun's "sales campaign" for a Mars expedition in *Collier's* magazine in the early 1950s. This led to Von Braun's heading up the Apollo Program and to the great space feats of the 1960s. But Benford sees NASA in later years, with the International Space Station, becoming a "jobs program, not an exploratory agency": "The station was about camping in space, not living in space. . . . A school bus route writ large." Benford bemoans the demise of the space program, and of the old visionary SF of Heinlein and Clarke. Still, he sees a glimmer of hope in the spirit of new writers like Geoff Landis, Allen Steele, and the British writer Stephen Baxter, all of whom seems to revive von Braun's vision, and with it the true SF: "Much of the passion in science fiction springs from a deep-rooted human need: to reach out, to prefer movement to stasis, to understand." Benford urges NASA today, at its crucial crossroads, to make Nigel's choice, that is, "to swing for the bleachers or die." This article may seem an exercise in Golden Age nostalgia. But it is also a strong restatement of Benford's "profession of faith," which remains the key to understanding his work.

CHAPTER 3

FICTIONAL DIRECTIONS
The Makings of a Scientist-Writer

Gregory Benford is a writer who came up through the science fiction pathway, but he, like many of his generation, had ambitions to break out of the SF ghetto, to write literature. In Benford's case, the goal from the outset was to write serious fiction about the new world that science offered to mankind, and to present, in fictional works, the scientist's role in shaping and understanding that brave new world. Like so many SF writers, Benford wrote in fan publications, then moved to publishing stories in science fiction magazines. From there, he began producing novels, and a successful writing career was launched. He published his first novel in 1970. The decade that followed, from the early 1970s to the early 1980s, was a formative period of intense creative activity for the author. During this period, Benford produced two masterpieces: *In the Ocean of Night* (1976), and *Timescape* (1980). Both are set in the author's near future. But the former novel leads directly toward high space adventure at the Galactic Center. The latter work occupies the here and now;

it offers but a fleeting glimpse of future promise, Benford's famous sideward tilt, his sudden "trap door" into infinite vistas. These are the two directions Benford's subsequent fiction will take. Yet they intertwine in subtle ways. In order to understand the nature of this interweaving of fictional directions, it is necessary to examine other early works, works that are excellent in their own right but have been overshadowed by these two novels. By exploring the byways of Benford's fiction, I hope to see how the author came to explore these disparate-seeming fictional possibilities, and how both, at the beginnings of his writing career, find their common focus in the defining of a single character type—the scientist, or person of scientific vision, at work doing science.

In the Ocean of Night and *Timescape* will be discussed in later chapters devoted to the fictional works they generate. In this chapter, I propose to focus on two "bookend" novels, works that offer the opening and closing statements of this formative decade. On one hand, there is Benford's first novel, the space opera *Deeper than the Darkness* (1970). On the other, there is *Against Infinity* (1983), a work that seems to stand alone yet is crucial to our understanding of the many faces of the Benford mono-hero and the many directions his quest must take.

Deeper than the Darkness springs directly from the matrix of science fiction writing. What that matrix was during Benford's first years as a writer needs to be elucidated. His first piece of published fiction was the story "Stand In," which appeared in *The Magazine of Fantasy and Science Fiction* (June 1965). Given its initial orientation, *F&SF* seems an odd initial venue for a writer of scientific background. Yet by the mid-1960s, this magazine had evolved into a meeting ground of diverse tendencies. Under the editorship of Ed Ferman (1966–1991), the magazine, now in digest form and rebaptised *The Magazine of Fantasy and Science Fiction*, published a varied and heterogeneous slate of works, from Heinlein's "Starship Soldier" (novel *Starship Troopers*) to works by Fritz Leiber, Kurt Vonnegut, and Walter M. Miller's Canticle novellas. Its long-running science column was written by Isaac Asimov (1958–1992), the apostle of "social science fiction." Benford returned to *F&SF* in April 1969 with a novella, "Deeper than the Darkness." Ace Books published an expanded version in 1970, the 190-page novel *Deeper than the Darkness*. This work has its origins in the various and often contradictory currents outlined above. In its attempt to synthesize them, it is a curious and fascinating work.

A few words about Ace Books is in order. Benford's first novel is, by virtue of its cover art and packaging, "space opera." But it is an example, somewhat belated, of the transformation of space adventure fiction that took place in the Ace Doubles series, from the mid-1950s through the mid-1960s. During this period, editor Donald Wollheim put back to back some surprising combinations of new and old variations on space opera: Philip K. Dick's *Solar Lottery* paired with Leigh Brackett's *The Big Jump* (1955), Dick's *The Cosmic Puppets* with Andrew North's [André Norton's] *Sargasso of Space* (1960), and Samuel R. Delany's *Empire Star* with Tom Purdom's *The Tree Lord of Imeton* (1966). The careers of many New Wave writers (and other new writers of the same period)—Delany, Dick, Le Guin, Thomas Disch, Harlan Ellison, Robert Silverberg—were launched in these quintessentially pulpy Ace books. Benford is on the young side of this generation. In 1964, Benford's fanzine partner Terry Carr became editor at Ace. His Ace Specials published instant classics like Le Guin's *The Left Hand of Darkness* (1965). Benford's first novel was a product of this exciting pulp cauldron.

After its initial publication, Benford extensively revised his first novel, re-presenting it as *The Stars in Shroud* in 1977. By this time, the author had published several other works that were important in the sense that they affirmed future directions in his fiction. First, there is *Jupiter Project* (1975) (story magazine publication, *Amazing Stories* [September, 1972]), an homage to the Heinlein juvenile. Heinlein's novels are a refinement on the space opera. Beginning with *Rocket Ship Galileo* (1948), Heinlein's novels transform space opera into narratives of initiation, where a young protagonist grows up under the pressures and hardships of space adventure. The obvious model for Benford's work, because of its setting on Ganymede, is Heinlein's *Farmer in the Sky* (1953). Yet because Benford's novel does not take place on *ganymede firma*, but instead more plausibly on an orbiting space station, the other inspiration for young Matt's adventures seems to be Arthur C. Clarke's *Islands in the Sky* (1953), a classic British take on the novel of space *Bildung*. Here is an early example of a characteristic of Benford's fiction—the propensity of novels to generate sequels. Both *Jupiter Project's* Ganymede setting—now on the surface of the moon—and its main character will return in the novel *Against Infinity* (1983). Rather than sequel, the phrase "development-in-continuity" seems a better description. Characters move from novel to novel, but new thematic and generic parameters develop around them. For example, in Benford's second Jupiter novel, young Matt is now "Old Matt." He is the guiding presence behind a new initiate. But in this work, initiation takes place in a radically different context, and with a much different purpose and goal. The technology involved is no longer that of creating a space station—an activity that harkens back to Chesley Bonestell's 1950s covers on *F&SF*—but of terraforming a hostile environment, this time one that harbors a vast alien mystery at its core.

The landmark Clarke-Kubrick production *2001: A Space Odyssey*, with its revolutionary refocusing of the space adventure trope, appeared in 1968 but seems not to have been fully digested by Benford until the mid-1970s with the creation of Nigel Walmsley. For Nigel, a NASA scientist and astronaut, the aliens encountered are now Clarke-like artifacts, left on Earth and its Moon by visitors from eons ago. Planet Earth is overpopulated and polluted. As in *2001*, devastating war is on our horizon. The scientific challenge is now one of deciphering the alien message, and deciding whether or not to probe its origins—and our destiny—in outer space. Benford will keep Space Captain Ling Sanjen from *Deeper than the Darkness* as protagonist in *The Stars in Shroud*, the revised version published one year after *In the Ocean of Night*. But the transformation of Ling in the new version owes a debt to the intervening creation of Nigel Walmsley.

The same decade saw Benford embarking on a number of collaborative projects. The collaboration with Gordon Eklund, "If the Stars Are Gods" (*Universe* 4, 1974) won its authors a Nebula Award for best novelette. An expanded version was published as the novel *If the Stars Are Gods* in 1977. Benford published another collaborative effort with Eklund in 1980, *Find the Changeling*. The "changelings" in question are body snatchers intent on sowing chaos. They are being hunted on an alien planet, inhospitable to humans, by a team of bounty hunters and a genetically altered dog capable of sensing the changelings behind their disguises. The hunting scenes here look forward to the hunt for the Aleph in *Against Infinity*. Benford collaborated with artist and photographer William Rotsler on another 1980 novel, *Shiva Descending*. In the afterword to the 1991 reprint of the novel, Benford describes the book as one he and Rotsler wrote in response to a decade of what Larry Niven calls "Big Rock Hits Earth" scenarios. These novels were a popular variant on the fictions of nuclear disaster that flourished during the Cold War. They harken back to Wells's "The Star" and Philip Wylie and Edwin Bulmer's 1933 novel *When Worlds Collide*. The George Pal 1951 film *When Worlds Collide* emphasizes the "space arc" aspect, where select survivors of a doomed Earth leave for a new life in the stars.

Benford and Rotsler's novel uses this well-worn scenario to develop themes and situations that are already familiar in Benford's opus. "Shiva" is an asteroid on a collision course with Earth. Government and the scientific bureaucracy prove ineffectual. But bold individuals—scientists of the Nigel Walmsley sort—devise a plan to detonate atomic weapons near Shiva, deflecting its path so as to miss Earth. In the wake of this menace, religious fanaticism of the fundamentalist Christian variety runs rampant. The authors here explore an issue that Benford has raised in earlier works and will revisit throughout his career—the conflict between science and religious intolerance as hindrance to doing science. By naming their asteroid Shiva, Benford and Rotsler invoke a god who is both destroyer and preserver, hoping to offer a more complex model that leads humanity to a more balanced view of mankind's relationship to the sheer power of the physical universe. The focus on Indian deities, as symbols of a more sophisticated cultural attempt to mediate between science and society, will also be a constant aspect of Benford's work. It is subtly treated in *If the Stars are Gods* and is given a fascinatingly complex development in *The Stars in Shroud*. In fact, the origins of Benford's interest in this intersection of science and religion are to be found in his first novel—*Deeper than the Darkness*.

The issues developed in Benford's first novel—and reworked in the masterful *The Stars in Shroud*—are similar to issues raised by other writers involved in the Ace transformation of space adventure. Writers like Le Guin (from *Rocannon's World* to *The Dispossessed*), Dick (from *Solar Lottery* to *Martian Time Slip*), and Delany (*The Ballad of Beta-2* to *Triton*) have each found their unique paths from pulp space opera to personal issues such as antiwar protest, cultural deviance, or the metaphysical looniness of a novel like Dick's *Galactic Pot Healer*. Unlike these contemporaries, Benford chooses not to break with the space adventure tradition or to use its conventions as the means of parodying or attacking what is seen as an underlying ideology of galactic empire. Instead, he chooses continuity. His path will remain that of Clarke's and Heinlein's explorers of outer space. But it will be augmented and deeply nuanced by a theoretical plasma physicist's knowledge of the possible behavior of such phenomena as electromagnetic structures and wormholes. Unlike a Le Guin or a Delany, Benford refuses to view space adventure as a prop. Instead, he sees it as the probable and even possible means of creating and exploring a unique human experience at the far reaches of massively a-human forces, forces that are, if at all, describable only in mathematical terms. But math and theory are not enough. For Benford, space remains a lived experience, one whose "feel" is conveyed to the reader by means of the "blizzard of strangeness" prose he describes in his nonfiction writing. Space adventure, as Benford develops it over this decade, is *not* to go where no man has gone, but rather to go where man probably will never be able to go. Physically, that is. For Benford proposes to use narrative and stylistic devices—the language that strives to go beyond language he describes in his critical statements—to convey the wonder we might experience were we actually to go there.

This is a big order. But *The Stars in Shroud* takes a huge step in this direction. Here Benford, working from a base provided by Clarke and Heinlein, begins to elaborate his own view of man the seeker, the scientific adventurer. We discover the author's growing sense of space as a personal adventure, as the lived experience of a scientist in a culture that asserts and then renounces its dreams of space. The creation of Ling—in his two manifestations across the seven years that separate *Deeper than the Darkness* from *The Stars in Shroud*—allowed Benford to develop a rich and complex vision, both of the space-faring hero and of mankind's potential role in the cosmic scheme of things—a scheme that already includes vast physical forces and the evolution of alien life forms on a massive, nearly incomprehensible scale.

In *The Stars in Shroud,* Benford turns the extroverted form of space opera into a literary form that explores the internal motivations and intuitions of his scientist-hero. In *Against Infinity*, the author looks outside science fiction in order to explore the possibilities of adapting what he calls "modernist" narrative and stylistic innovations to the particular challenges of science fiction. As literary form, science fiction offers a new physical terrain for innovation. As a truly scientific fiction, it offers myriad new, literal spacetime frontiers that challenge the writer to render them in words and narrative. Both novels are stylistic experiments. The former works from inside the conventions of the genre in order to transform them; the latter is a dialogue between science fiction and mainstream literature. Two very different currents of what Benford calls "modernism" are present as inspiration. One current is American and regional. The long hunting episode with young Manuel and Old Matt has distinct echoes of a Southern storyteller's yarn. The other current—at the antipodes of Southern primitivism—is the mathematical internationalism of Jorge Luis Borges. Benford's settlers on Jupiter's moon encounter an alien they call the Aleph. In mathematics and in Cabbalistic lore, the aleph is a point in space that contains all other points, an infinite set of numbers. In Borges's story "El Aleph," his protagonist discovers the Aleph in a mundane Buenos Aires basement. Benford transposes this encounter to (in terms of cosmic spacetime) an equally cramped space on Ganymede. Benford's writing, as it evolves over this formative decade, reveals at one and the same time an awareness of the cultural and philosophical issues created by science, and of the Western literary tradition in its broadest sense. On one hand, Benford probes the gap between space science and a culture that rejects it. On the other hand, in his literary experiments, he seeks to bridge the gap between SF and mainstream fiction. He not only demonstrates that he is very well read in literature and the philosophy of science, but he also, by incorporating ideas and techniques from a variety of literary sources, shows the reader that science fiction is a form of literature, period.

THE STARS IN SHROUD

The differences between the 1977 novel and its early version, *Deeper Than the Darkness*, are both obvious and subtle. The first obvious change is in the role given to protagonist Ling Sanjen's wife Angela and their two children. The initial setting of both novels is the same. We are in a distant but undetermined Earth future, where a Mongol empire, by means of a tachyon drive, has spread through outer space. The Asian races and cultures rule. Protagonist Ling is an *ofkaipan*, a racial and social outcast: "My mother was a Polynesian and my father a truly rare specimen: one of the last pure Americans, born of the descendents of the few who survived the Riot War. That placed me far down in the caste lots, even below Australians."[1] Captain of a supply ship (not a warship), Ling makes a seemingly routine run to planet Regeln, where he discovers a horrific scene. Humans on the planet have succumbed to a Quarn

Plague, which has ruptured the social fabric and caused each individual to retreat, in an extreme attack of agoraphobia, into foul underground warrens, where each lives and dies in terminal isolation. Ling's Executive Officer, a Japanese aristocrat named Tonji, wants to evacuate these people and bring them back to Earth. Ling rightly senses that they are in fact vectors for the Quarn Plague and refuses to contaminate Earth. He is overruled by Tonji and cashiered. Predictably, the Plague infects Earth, seat of the Empire. Warrens, called "slots," are built for the victims. Ling and his wife and children are infected. But Ling spontaneously gets better: "When their agoraphobia grew worse and mine got inexplicably better, we separated for 'medical reasons': I realized I had to, one day when I looked up from the routing schedules that were boring me to distraction, and saw three strangers living with me in the rancid stench of the Warrens. Their eyes were dead to me. I don't think they knew what was happening to them, or even if they particularly cared" (43). In what seems good space opera tradition, family is now an obstruction to further adventure, hence expendable. Ling subsequently secures a new command, assigned to a post as "Fleet Control Director" on the apparently insignificant outpost planet Veden. This planet has been colonized by people of Hindu descent, down the caste ladder yet still "Asians." Here he finds a new mistress, Rhandra, who becomes his companion on further adventures with the Quarn. There seems no possibility of turning back.

All these situations remain in *The Stars in Shroud*. In *Darkness*, however, the actions are thinly motivated, if at all. We see clearly, in the rewrite, that Benford has passed through the experience of writing *In the Ocean of Night*. Both Ling's family relationships and the Tonji episode are greatly developed. The former is now seen as a personal conflict for a man involved in managing an extended family; the latter becomes a vicious bureaucratic rivalry of the sort Nigel Walmsley will experience throughout his career. The Angela episode is now recast as a domestic issue, with two people drifting apart over matters of respect and ways to raise children. The Quarn Plague is present, but its effects are greatly amplified by Angela's gradual alienation from a once-loving husband, who has been humiliated by society. Ling is now a much deeper character than the stock space adventurer of the earlier version. We are now privy to his internal struggles and reflections, which lead him to desire to stay with his family. His spontaneous cure still takes place; physically unable to tolerate the claustrophobic warrens, he is driven out into the open streets. Earth administration now actively seeks specimens in remission like Ling, and he is rounded up. His arch-enemy Tonji, now a high-ranking official, learns of this, summons Ling, and offers him a new captaincy, which sends him again to Veden. This assignment, however, is now a deathtrap, for the only way a spaceship can access Veden is to be "flung" at it, a more sophisticated physics that involves hurling his ship down the gravity well of a planet twinned with a neutron star. Ling proves able to navigate and escapes this trap. But he will again encounter Tonji when he later returns to Earth on a mission ostensibly to rescue the Patanen (the spontaneously cured)—a mission he later learns is directed by the alien Quarn in order to destroy these dangerous humans. Tonji has anticipated Ling's coming and has sequestered Angela and his children, all now among the cured. Benford inserts a whole new episode devoted to Ling's rescue of his family, and to his humiliation of Tonji. And when Ling's son, during the rescue, asks for a gun and is denied it, we catch a glimpse of the father-son dynastic rivalry that will inform the Killeen-Toby relationship in the later Galactic Center novels. At the end of the novel, Ling and Rhandra effectively destroy the Quarn Master, foiling his plans to dispose of the Patanen. Unlike the straightforward, no-turning-back space adventure of the early version, Ling now returns to Angela. There is possible reconciliation: "'Angela,' I said, 'let's try to talk again.'"[2] And there is the formation of the type of composite family Nigel Walmsley creates in *In the Ocean of Night*, wherein two women gravitate around a single male, one a woman of domestic leanings, the other a woman of action. A Heinlein hero of space adventure, like Max Jones in *Starman Jones* (1953), openly rejects domesticity. Benford, on the other hand, is a product of the 1960s and its communal sexual experiments. If this is meant to be a sign of space opera "growing up," it is a shallow one.

The augmented role of Tonji, in contrast, allows the author to deepen the portrait of his protagonist, and in doing so Benford elaborates other character traits he will use in later space adventures. This new Ling develops in the shadow of Nigel Walmsley. Yet he remains more the man of action than the communicator with aliens. As such, Ling confronts challenges that look forward to figures like Killeen and Toby (in the later Galactic Center novels), who must confront and in a sense defeat entities like the Mantis that act on their deepest psychic identity. The introduction, for example, in *Stars in Shroud* of the alien Quarn "mind," seen as acting on deep zones of the human psyche, allows Benford to create a situation where external action is at the same time an exploration of the protagonist's inner self. The shift in focus from the earlier novel to *The Stars in Shroud* is reflected in the epigraphs for each book. *Darkness* is prefaced by the following lines:

> The Hand upon them,
> Strangled shout,
> No rest or solace,
> Black despair and doubt.
> Rising to the Scepter,
> They struggled all the more,
> And were cast down into darkness
> Far deeper than before.

The reference to Lucifer, God's divine "hand," external damnation, and the Fall of rebel angels is inescapable. As obligatory sword-and-sorcery window dressing, it locates the action in the realm of good and evil. But in the revised novel, the reader, seeking causes and answers, is sent in a very different direction. There is an apocryphal Goethe "quote": "Know thyself? If I knew myself, I'd run away." This suggests that the well of darkness, the place of heroic activity, lies in fact within the self, inside a mind and body that but slenderly knows itself. Until the evolutionary sources of the human mind are known, these will remain prone to alien manipulation by those such as the Quarn, whose claim to have "made us" gives them license to attempt to control us. And where such origins and causes remain obscure, our sole choice is not to run away but to act. The second epigraph has a very 1960s source—Bob Dylan's "Subterranean Homesick Blues": "Don't follow leaders; watch the parking meters." The plague Ling wrestles with remains, for him and for all humanity, a form of subterranean homesickness. But in order to solve this plague, Ling must determine where, in our evolutionary past, is home. If exploration of the psyche reveals "no direction home," then the only way to go is forward to the future. Even so, the lesson learned from Tonji's Empire and the Quarn Master is that, in exploring the human condition within the self, you must not follow leaders. Like the rolling stone in the song, you are on your own. And if you are to survive, you have to watch seemingly irrelevant things like parking meters.

In *Stars in Shroud*, protagonist Ling is much given to reflecting on the evolutionary nature of the human brain. This he sees as the key to understanding how the alien Quarn are able to disrupt human equilibrium: "Without something—rituals, the Sabal Game, wise ministering of the guru—a man could slide into the weak fragmentation of the Plague. So went the conventional wisdom. Solidarity through ritual. Man's mind divided into three separate houses—reptilian, lower animal, and cerebral cortex. Society had to govern each, the history of Earth had proven such. Otherwise, there would be massive loss of phase" (91–92). The reference here is to Carl Sagan's *The Dragons of Eden: Speculations on the Evolution of Human Intelligence*, published the same year as Benford's revised text (its key ideas were already well known from earlier venues, such as the Bronowski Memorial Lecture at the University of Toronto given two years before the book's publication). Sagan's theory (based on research as early as that of Paul Broca [1824–1880], who first identified the limbic area of the brain) is that each human brain, in its successive layers, carries with it its evolutionary history. The outer, neo-cortical area controls the higher functions—sense perception, motor commands, spatial reasoning, conscious thought, language. Enfolded beneath this lies the limbic lobe, the area that directs emotional responses, which we share with other mammals. The innermost area is the R-complex, the reptilian brain, our evolutionary Eden. The Sabal is the Mongol Game, resembling the patterning rituals in Le Guin's Earthsea novels, intended to weave order from dynamic diversity. But its sense of community, such as that formed around the gurus and Master of the Hindic peoples of Veden, is disrupted by the Quarn, who reach into the limbic area and prey on the individual human's ancestral fear of the Other. They tap a zone of primal fear, when early humans, like other mammals, were agoraphobic, huddling at night in trees, in terror of what marauded below in the dark.

But who are these Quarn? Ling, the *ofkaipan* outcast of Earth, believes he has found inner peace and unity on Veden with the Master, a sense augmented when Ling learns the Master is itself a Quarn. The Master plays on Ling's growing sense of his human condition. He is told that "Man was not meant fully for community," that "a continual tension existed between Man the social animal and Man the individualist" (133). If for Ling this tension is the source of mankind's resilience and strength, for the Quarn, who exploit it, it is the means of destroying mankind from within. Ling at one point is led to believe that the Quarn's mission—despite the fact that its Plague has cost millions of lives—is to heal this division, to provide a higher form of harmony: "I looked slowly at us all, four humans and a Quarn, the cloth vaulting hanging softly above us, and seemed to see it all from a vast new perspective. I saw that we were one and the same. So did a journey end, and another begin" (138). He is thus persuaded to take a spaceship to Earth, to gather up all of the Patanen—humans that "naturally," through evolution, have overcome the division the Quarn Plague has wrought in their brains—and take them to a new home on some new planet: "A fragment of your race will survive. I did not understand this when you first came" (135).

Ling wrestles with this possibility: "I nodded. The Patanen were the most valuable people in the Empire now, a last crucial healthy sample of mankind. Perhaps we could indeed make a new start with them . . . perhaps. 'Master . . . ' An edge in me teetered near. 'I . . . I am unsure" (137). He soon learns that the survival of humanity is not what the Quarn intend. As the Master will reveal in their final encounter, the Quarn themselves, as artist-gods, are themselves the product of "bad art." The reader is reminded of Heinlein's story "The Unpleasant Profession of Jonathan Hoag" (1942). Benford's "artists" come from the "halo stars," a place of cosmic winding down, which they see as "the true center, the sum." Their claim is that they "made us," but that the making was a botched job, an error that now must be erased: "We erase the errors made by our passing. We leave no blemish smudged upon the galaxy" (203). Yet they admit that humans have grown to be a dangerous threat to their sense of "harmony": "The neutron star was infested. The ancients timed that star for *our* use. You had begun to spread. To have festered so, to take our works and turn them to a purpose we had planned for ourselves. . . . We knew then that the legacy we had planned was rotted. Spoiled. You—our children—were now rivals" (201). Explaining why they must destroy the Patanen of Earth, these bad artists admit that, in fact, they are not true gods, but themselves fallen angels: "They were the remaining part of you who would survive. It is a measure of our fall that only with difficulty can we snuff out our ancestor's dark legacy" (203). In the end, it is because their "work"—us, beings whose dynamic tensions cannot be contained in their circle of perfection—is flawed, that we are ultimately able to defeat them. Ling overcomes his inner conflict and thus is able to shoot the Master and thwart the attempt to destroy the Patanen. In the end, Ling views them much as Heinlein's Kip views the cosmic group mind that would judge and "rotate" all of humanity—as an entity not only oblivious to whatever mass suffering they cause, but also ultimately incapable of understanding humans: "If you go out to the halo stars, I think you'll find their works. Their art, their libraries, all carefully preserved. All the things they wanted to be remembered by. Libraries—not us. They never understood us. And they were so sure they did" (212).

But in *Stars in Shroud*, it is Ling himself whom the Master does not understand. In *Deeper than the Darkness*, things are seen from the outside; we remain at the level of action, and it is Rhandra who fires the shot that kills the Master. Here, in *Stars in Shroud*, it is Ling who fires the shot; it occurs only when Ling finally overcomes the power of the alien to use mankind's own mental evolution against it: "I had sent Rhandra to search the Master's suite, remembering the black device in his hand, to find polytonal inducers, subliminal flicker screens, a host of devices. Probes into the depths of our competing three brains. Paths to enlightenment, surely; I knew that. Paths to a prison, just as certainly" (206). Ling refers to the idea of the "triune brain" here. Yet if the moment of the shot is a moment of breakthrough, underlying this act is another evolutionary model, one that specifically describes the development of the human *mind*: the bicameral mind. The Quarn have misunderstood the nature of this mind. They see but another dualistic trap, when in fact it is this bicameral mind that allows mankind to break free from the prison house of language and rational thought: "Tongues speaking without form, of days before we became encased in words . . . cutting across the filmy bonds the Master had laced around my bicameral mind, lefthand-rightbrain ancient . . ." (209). The reference is to Julian Jaynes's *The Origin of Consciousness in the Breakdown of the Bicameral Mind* (1976). Bicameralism is an evolutionary condition where cognitive functions are divided between one part of the brain that "speaks" or orders, and another part that listens, obeys, acts. It is described as a nonconscious state, allowing one to act without any "meta-reflective" ability of accounting for *why* one acts—"tongues speaking without form." Jaynes sees this as a preconscious state in human development. For Ling, however, it provides a way out of the induced breakdown of rational societal control represented by the Sabal Game. Another detail added to *Stars in Shroud* is significant in this context. In the raid to free his wife and children, Ling's *left hand* is blown off. In terms of bicameralism, the left brain controls logic and language, the right brain creative intuition. The left brain however controls the right hand, the right brain the left. Ling confronts the Master without a left hand. The "filmy bonds the Master had laced" around his bicameral mind tell him that, because this hand is gone, the intuitive half of his mind has no outlet to act. Yet Ling is able, without his physical hand, to bridge this dichotomy. Even though theoretically cut off from access to his right brain, he nonetheless is able to act by intuition just as the Master's "black device" is about to immobilize his seat of reason, its waters "encase" him: "My left arm. Sheets of pain lanced up. Clouds thinned. Left hand. Right hand. Voicesvoices—hand—swelling tension—Something within me clenched my fist. My hand—Orange carved the night. The Master toppled . . . Left hand spoke. Right hand answered. We would not go meekly into their vast night" (203). Later, he will use his right hand to fire the laser that destroys the program controlling the spaceship's inner workings, thus preventing the Master's men from jettisoning their cargo of human Patanen.

At one point, Ling makes what seems a strange remark about himself: "No Prometheus, I—more like Epimetheus, the hindsighted and thick-witted brother (never mentioned in the Fleet mythology) who always learned too late, hadn't been pinned to a rock, and made a dumbbell error with Pandora. But mythology was, like history, simply aged gossip . . ." (130). In describing his heroic nature thus, Ling is linking Hesiod to Heinlein. Hesiod, in his *Works and Days*, sees Epimetheus accepting Pandora, the poisoned gift of the Gods to mankind, and siring a daughter with her. Pandora is a secular myth of the Fall; her actions condemn mankind to this life of toil and misery. Yet, despite this, it remains an open-ended myth—for there remains the possibility of children, and thus of hope, the one thing that remains in Pandora's box. Prometheus stays chained to his rock; this could be the fate of sole scientific reason, unique and alone in the universe. But Epimetheus represents community in the sense of family—the "dull-witted" drive of intuitive humanity forward. As Ling puts it, "While Angela hatched me a responsibility in her stomach, and then another, I flapped my wings and failed to rise" (130). But in the end, he remains free to take his now-extended family, along with those few chosen humans whose evolutionary mechanism made them immune to the Quarn plague, to a new world: "The galaxy was open. We had fuel, reaction mass. We would explore" (211). Ling reminds the reader of another Heinlein protagonist, Ted Randall in "The Unpleasant Profession of Jonathan Hoag." At the end of this novella, the "art critic" Hoag prepares to "erase" the "bad art" of the Sons of the Bird, humans who have corrupted a Chicago where Ted and Cynthia Randall have always felt out of place. Hoag spares them, not only because they helped him find his real identity, but because they remained faithful to each other. As they drive south out of the city, Ted rolls down the car window—and sees the void. Rolling it up, he sees a familiar street scene. He learns from this experience what all Heinlein heroes learn: that though they may flap their wings and fail to rise, they remain free to move on. They see that in the end survival is the ability to roll the window up and down at will, to control the bicameral mind. Here is Ling's final challenge to aliens and humans alike: "We were no simple assembly of 'the seat of reason,' 'the seat of emotion,' Tinkertoy parts. A man was more than a mere man could know" (211).[3]

AGAINST INFINITY

In the elaboration of *The Stars in Shroud*, Benford moves from space opera to a pure example of scientific fiction. Though a physicist "by trade," Benford wields with ease scientific theories of the evolutionary development of consciousness. In doing so, he redirects the space opera plot inward, creating a highly sophisticated portrait of mankind's specificity in the face of a world controlled by an alien creator-surrogate. Benford has learned the lesson of Clarke's Bowman, whose odyssey is ultimately one into the mind of mankind itself. But this is not simply what mainstream critics call "psychology." Benford has created (in the wake of Clarke) a powerful work of literature that, at its core, is a *scientific* exploration of the unique nature of human consciousness and how it *might evolve* in this space-adventure future. The subtext of the next novel, *Against Infinity*, is mainstream literature itself. For this novel Benford again chooses a stock SF venue—Ganymede. Again he uses a conventional SF landscape as a place to explore the working of the human mind. But now what is explored is specifically the cultural and literary mind of humanity itself as it confronts the challenge of the unknowable alien. Ling explores his own consciousness; young Manuel in *Against Infinity* explores a cultural unconscious, that of Benford's literary America—the wilderness experience of writers like William Faulkner and Robinson Jeffers. Benford here makes a useful distinction between "frontier" and "wilderness," between space and cultural territory. Yet Ling can only probe the space frontier once he has probed his own mind. The wilderness of Ganymede has deprived Manuel of his cultural roots; he must rediscover these in reenacting rituals from his cultural past in order to confront the unknown alien future.

The narrative form of *Against Infinity* appears very different from that of *The Stars in Shroud*. The latter, as space epic, involves expansive action. We have a collapsing Earth empire, intergalactic warfare, a hostile alien culture, and a lone human adventurer who will take a Noah's ark of Earth survivors to a new destination among the stars. *Against Infinity* is a "hunker down" story of human pioneers, a small band enduring the hardships of life on a barren and hostile moon of Jupiter. An overpopulated Earth, having depleted its resources, is forced to adopt Marxist socialism. But Marxism has learned here that, in order to survive, it must encourage unbridled capitalism in the outer frontier worlds: "Socialism is a historical necessity that arises when you get a certain density of population . . . [but] the dynamics of economics drives them to adopt individualist, capitalist measures."[4] The protagonists of *Against Infinity* are Earth emigrants. They replay the Old World–New World scenario but face physical hardships many times greater than those encountered by settlers on the American continent. For antecedents, Benford has Heinlein's early Luna City stories and the radically libertarian Moon colonies of *The Moon Is a Harsh Mistress* (1966), which finally declare war on an equally over-managed and socially stressed Earth. Benford's young protagonist, Manuel Lopez, echoes Heinlein's flamboyantly multiethnic Manuel Garcia O'Kelly Davis. The hardships Benford's Ganymede colonists endure, however, are more in line with the space realism of SF works from Edmond Hamilton's "What's It Like Out There?" (1952) to Geoffrey Landis's *Mars Crossing* (2000). We have a world of methane ice, massive quakes, and long Jupiter nights. Rather than a frontier, we have an American wilderness experience more in tune with Benford's South. Beyond the cities, his characters live primarily by bounty hunting. Again and again, as they begin to approach material security and economic prosperity, natural forces intervene to wipe away these gains. City dwellers on Ganymede may be innovators with future technology such as hydroponic farming, or synthesizing organic foods in a landscape otherwise in the grip of inorganic forces. Yet the main livelihood for Manuel's family comes from hunting down and weeding out the endless spontaneous mutations that arise among the various bio-organisms mankind has devised to transform Ganymede into an oxygen-based environment, capable of sustaining human life. Civilization sits but lightly on these swamps of ice.

Benford's novel is about the adventures of a young boy who grows into a man. In this sense, it follows the interplanetary "juvenile" novel of formation pattern elaborated by Heinlein in works such as *Red Planet* (1949) and *The Rolling Stones* (1952), which deals specifically with asteroid mining. Yet Heinlein's novels of space initiation remain "sanitized" replays of the American experience. There are easy parallels: for example, the spaceship to Ganymede in *Farmer in the Sky* is named the "Mayflower." In contrast, Benford's novel taps into a deeper current in American literature. His space frontier extrapolates from the vision of Fenimore Cooper's Natty Bumppo, born of white parents but immersed in the Indian world of primeval forests. Even closer to Benford's roots, it plunges into the world of the Southern swamps and woods, the world of primitive racial and cultural memory that, in the stories and novels of William Faulkner, lies just beyond the towns and cities, just below the veneer of civilization that masks the cultural unconscious of a people. The first two-thirds of Benford's novel is essentially a hunting yarn, and the author has described it as a re-telling of Faulkner's story "The Bear." As with Faulkner's storyteller, Benford's is a focused third-person narrator speaking to a narrative audience of his "own people" in their colloquial manner, thus assuming the role of historian and repository of their cultural memory.

The debt to Faulkner is obvious when we compare the opening paragraphs of Faulkner's story "The Bear" with those of *Against Infinity*. Here is Faulkner's narrator describing the experience of young Isaac "Ike" McCaslin:

> He had listened to it for years: the long legend of corncribs rifled, of shotes and grown pigs and even calves carried bodily into the woods and devoured, of traps and deadfalls overthrown and dogs mangled and slain, and shotgun and

> even rifle charges delivered at point-blank range and with no more effect than so many peas blown through a tube by a boy—a corridor of wreckage and destruction beginning back before he was born, through which sped, not fast but rather with the ruthless and irresistible deliberation of a locomotive, the shaggy tremendous shape.[5]

And here is Benford's narrator describing young Manuel "Manny" Lopez on Ganymede: "The boy was thirteen. He watched it all with wide eyes. For five years now he had waited and listened to the talk of the ice ridges and ammonia rivers of the melting land, quick and treacherous under the feet. Hunkered down around a heater, evening after evening, he had listened, not knowing how much to believe but wanting to trust it all for fear of forgetting anything he might need later, for he knew even then that everything you learned came to use if you waited. What he knew most deeply was the bigness of the wilderness they now crawled into, bigger than any of the puny human Settlements, vast and powerful and with a reason and logic to itself" (9).

Benford's novel is closely modeled on Faulkner's story. There are frequent intertextual references to the source. For instance, the author transplants to his interplanetary outpost (quite illogically, as his future Earth is now said to be homogeneous and egalitarian) characters with specific titles such as *Colonel* López or *Major* Sánchez. There is no reason for this, except to remind the reader of *General* Compson or *Major* de Spain in Faulkner's story. With their titles, Faulkner's characters gesture backward toward the South's military history and defeat, the same murky cultural unconscious that Ike will explore as he digs into the McCaslin history of slavery and miscegenation. This is a past of deep, mysterious ties between man and nature, the same world Ike and his companions pursue in their obsessive hunt for the mythic bear—Old Ben. The protagonists' names in Faulkner's story reflect this racial and cultural mixing: the "half-breed" Sam Fathers, Boon Hogganback of obscure origins, the permutating name McCaslin (McCaslin Edmonds, Carothers McCaslin) that points to the possible incest that lies in its past. Likewise embedded in its surnames, Benford's Ganymede colony reflects its own obscure Earth history—old settlers like Petrovich, or the Spanish or Latin American origins, never elucidated, of López or Sánchez. There are as well figures whose history is purely interplanetary, like Sam Fathers's homologue Old Matt Bohles (who is the young Matt Bohles in *Jupiter Project*): "*He had no share, no fraction of a Settlement*, Manuel would think then. *There were children, his own from decades before, but all of them scattered to other outposts or even back Earthside. That part of him was dispersed*" (129).

These parallels provide an important subtext in *Against Infinity.* They not only remind the reader that he or she is dealing with an extrapolation in the literal sense; they also oblige the reader to rethink the idea of the hunt in the context of scientific advancement. Faulkner asks us to consider why we humans so passionately seek to hunt down and destroy a thing—the Bear—so naturally powerful and marvelous, why we give our best to an act that, in the larger picture, may be destructive, and reveal humanity to be meddlers in an order of things we are fundamentally incapable of understanding. In comparison, Benford may be saying that mankind's pursuit of scientific and technological advancement is itself a hunt of a different sort, one not merely for knowledge but for what Descartes calls "mastery" of that extended world which he declared by fiat to be made up of "things," animals hunted down as nonthinking machines. In a very real sense, what Descartes severed—scientific mankind's organic ties with nature—Faulkner's hunt seeks to restore, even if it must do so by means of violence and bloodshed. In Benford's novel, the outer planets and their moons have become mankind's new hunting ground. Ganymede may be a different, and much harsher, environment that the pine forests and swamps of the American South. But like these swamps, it has a severity that has somehow kept pace with—"pushed back" against—the advanced technology used by future humans to exploit the land.

Faulkner's Old Ben is a legendary creature that has wreaks havoc and destruction on human settlements, who has survived to the point of seeming invincible if not immortal. Benford's "bear" is openly an alien being. Yet in relation to those who hunt it, the Aleph occupies the same position as Ben the Bear. Young Manuel, at the beginning of his hunting adventures, knows this alien only by its mysterious name and reputed actions: "They called it Aleph. Some Jew had given it that, a blank name that was the first letter of the Hebrew alphabet: a neutral vowel that bespoke the opaque nature of the blocky, gravid thing. . . . A neutral name, and yet it was the source of a long legend of domes cracked open and rifled, of walkers and crawlers and even whole outposts caught up and crushed and trampled as it moved forward on its own oblivious missions" (12–13). Mankind here has neither time nor leisure to seek to know what this creature is. For this alien, on its own terrain, seems locked in an openly Darwinian struggle for survival against the humans who have invaded its territory. Seen through Manuel's eyes, it is a "vast, immemorial alabaster shape," "always seeking materials men also needed . . . and thus were forced to futilely defend against the legend that came for metals and rare rock, the Aleph making no distinction between what men held and what the bare plains offered . . . the alien absorbing all and giving nothing, shrugging off the puny attempts of men to deliver death to it" (13).

But if there is a heavy presence of evolutionary theory in *The Stars in Shroud*, the Faulkner subtext prevents *Against Infinity* from having the least overtone of evolutionary didacticism. As with Faulkner's Ike, there seems no clear path to vision for Manuel, but rather a sense that, in the shadow of the Aleph, evolution and devolution are inextricably intertwined. As in Faulkner's story, Manuel and Old Matt act upon obscure motives and desires, and they muddle through the hunt and apparent destruction of the Aleph. They remain condemned by their cultural and racial past to experiencing destiny and eternity from a middle position between mind and nature.

In Faulkner's story, as civilized man enters the wilderness in search of Old Ben, he finds he must enlist forces that point in the opposite direction from his claim to master nature through reason. Ike learns the true lore of Ben from the half-Indian Sam Fathers. No ordinary trained dog will do to track Ben, and the hunters deploy Lion, a wild mongrel upon which they bestow a name above its species rank, in clear violation of any chain of being. Ben, who has proven impervious to the technology of the gun, is cornered by the savage Lion, and finally killed by a knife, as Boon Hogganbeck, the savage hunter, leaps on the bear's back in an attempt to save the wild dog that has become his sleeping companion. Lion and Sam are killed as a result of the attack and are buried in a primitive gravesite to which the adult Isaac, fleeing the promise of a land-owning life, will inevitably return. Benford's novel offers a homologue to Lion: the "deffie" to which the name "Eagle" is given. A "deffie" is a human being, injured beyond functional repair, that has been "servo'd," placed in a mechanical casing that allows it, mind and consciousness abiding at the heart of the machine, to perform heavy labor. Because of their human center, the deffies are not slaves. Manual is drawn to one such being who appears particularly untamed and unbeaten: "It was a hodgepodge of parts attached to a gunmetal-gray carapace, bigger than any servo'd animal he had ever seen and powerfully made, bristling with heavy motors and big treads and bulging manifolds. He could not imagine a man or woman deep down inside the thing, tapped into the metal world that swallowed it whole, raging in an awful silent pocket somewhere" (76). Old Matt, in the role of Faulkner's Sam, wants to "run" this ferocious being in the hunt. Manuel feels an affinity with the creature, and intuits the possibility of communication. But in order to have such, he must reach the residue of its humanity deep inside: "And then he noticed the hunched-down form tapping against the bars with its head, *ding, dingding*, a pattern that varied but seemed intentional. He saw suddenly that it was a code, maybe a way for the thing inside to talk. He rapped his glove against the bars in response. It answered, *dingdingding. ding*. Manuel reached down and knocked a patient rhythm on the burnished steel skull. The huge head tilted up . . . Manuel felt something pass between them, something that tightened his throat. If there was still a human fragment left in there, if he could talk to it" (81).

There are clear parallels between Boon's and Ike's relationship with Lion, and those of Old Matt and Manuel with Eagle. But whereas the drift of things in Faulkner's story is backward and downward, Benford attempts to give them a forward nudge. The lesson Ike learns from the deaths of Lion and Old Ben goes against what humanity sees as "civilization." His growing to maturity is marked by his refusal to take up the McCaslin inheritance. The reason he gives, learned from his experience with the hunt, is that the land cannot be owned. He steps down and goes to town to take up the carpenter's trade, embracing the ways of Christ. The idea of the Fall hovers here, and the reader finds a parallel with Rousseau's "Discours sur l'inégalité," where the fall of mankind is linked to the sense of property and ownership: "This is mine." Ike refuses to make this claim but discovers there is no way back to a natural world before the fall. He returns to the hunting camp. But there he finds a different Boon, one blindly eager to shoot animals. The land itself has been sold to loggers and developers. In this new world, Ike may declare himself grandson to the old snake. But he is not free. He can neither rid himself of his past nor face a future where those like him have less and less place.

Benford's science fiction narrator retells Faulkner's tale but does not replay its cultural pessimism. In its sense of mankind's relation to its possible destiny, his story taps a different current of individual liberty in American culture. Unlike Faulkner's Southerners, none of the Ganymedans is fatally weighed down by history or by their Earth past. They bear the names and titles of that past, but that is all. Neither Manuel nor Old Matt have ever seen an eagle. To them in their alien land, this is only a name and a legend. In this sense, their ancestor is more someone like Ichabod Crane in Washington Irving's "Legend of Sleepy Hollow." Chased out of his sleepy "Eden" by the Headless Horseman, Ichabod makes sure he has enough money in his pocket to start over elsewhere. He is the ancestor of Twain's Huck Finn, whose journey down the big river is a one-way trip, at the end of which he sees only one way to go—out to the territories. Benford the storyteller makes these American legends the motor for future space adventure. We see Manuel moving in this direction. For example, his glimpsed moment of possible communication with the human part buried within Eagle's servomechanism does not kindle a hope of retrieving some lost human quality. He is not mourning a paradigm lost—here that of the human form—but instead celebrating the fact that this spark of life cannot be extinguished, even within a predominantly machine entity. Manuel's sense of things follows a clear lineage. It runs from Aristotle's *entelechy*, the vital force directing life, through Leibniz's striving monad, to Emerson's vision of power and form, where each single being generates its own circumference according to the amount of physical energy it can summon. The protagonists of Heinlein's juveniles revolt against machine eternity, opposing to its "perfection" mankind's short, dynamically unpredictable, yet creatively unique existence. And so Benford's evolved entity Eagle, however supremely adapted to its new environment on Ganymede, is important to young Manuel because it still retains this upward striving force of Life.

To Old Matt, Eagle is a product of natural selection. But if on one hand it is a "superdog," Matt senses it is more, something defined by a quality shared by animals, humans, and hybrids alike. At first, Matt does not want to name the creature: "You give them a chance, most things name themselves" (82). To name is to classify, to subject a being to a pre-determined category. Figures like Odysseus and Captain Nemo preferred to glide through life as "nobody." Only after Matt sees this being in action, does he propose a name: Eagle. Even so, to these settlers who have never seen an eagle, the name remains an open slot. No image goes along with the name, simply a set of properties, and these do not seem to fit: "But [why] Eagle? It can't fly. Not even with air could it fly" (85). Matt's only option is to fill this blank with a quality shared by life forms as opposed to machines, a quality that this future human civilization has all but destroyed: "The important thing with the eagle was not its flight, but its heart. That was why it died out, I remember. It would not give in, become a barnyard thing" (85). In the final run, when Matt and Manual bring down the Aleph, we witness Eagle's courage, going up against its mighty force: "It coasted, ghostlike. Eagle reached it then and drove in without pausing. The running thing looked slight and insubstantial as it leaped at the ponderous mass above. Eagle's claws grasped at the alabaster ribbing, scratching—and a chunk came away. . . . The boy stopped. He had never seen that before—seen a mere mortal thing rip the Aleph that way" (122). Eagle is swallowed whole. It is thought dead, but it reemerges from the ponderous mass, mortally wounded: "The black eyes peered out. . . . It studied the far hills, not with the ferocity it had shown before, but as if it wanted to be sure the broad, stretching wastes were still there, still lying beyond the ring of human faces. Manuel watched it then, sensing its adamant refusal to compromise, to give any sign of what lay wounded inside. Eagle was not of man and could not be reconciled with man, but was out of Earth, and knew that, too. It had done its job, a task in the end self-imposed, and was now free. It died at noon" (137). I hear here echoes, not of Faulkner but of another American "primitivist"—Robinson Jeffers in his poem "Hurt Hawks":

> I gave him the lead gift in the twilight.
> What fell was relaxed . . . but what
> Soared: the fierce rush: the night-herons by the flooded river cried fear at its rising
> Before it was quite unsheathed from reality.[6]

There is in both stories—Faulkner's and Benford's—the hunters and the hunted. In both, the hunters are the same: old mentor, young boy, magnificently courageous "animal." But in each case, what exactly is being hunted? On the first page of his story, Faulkner's narrator describes Old Ben as incarnation of the terrors of a "doomed wilderness": "the land where the old bear had earned a name, through which ran not even a mortal animal but an anachronism, indomitable and invincible, out of an old dead time, a phantom, epitome and apotheosis of the old wild life at which the puny humans swarmed and hacked in a fury of abhorrence and fear, like pygmies about the ankles of a drowsing elephant; the old bear solitary, indomitable and alone, widowered, childless, and absolved of mortality—old Priam reft of his old wife and having outlived all his sons" (1). Neither young Manuel nor his companions would know who Priam was. They would not know that he was a being with a past but no future. They, like Benford's narrator, have forgotten one past (Earth) and cannot know the other (Ganymede). They are between a world dead, and another, this time not powerless to be born, but simply not yet born. The Aleph on the other hand is both past and future, everything and infinity. It is something they can only define in terms of how it functions in their present: "It was bigger than five walkers together and used many things to move: quick, strong leglike extrusions, electromagnetic repulsors that sank fields into iron-rich meteor fragments and hurled them behind it; . . . treads on one side; levitating fields—all used when needed" (14). All they see is an entity going about its inscrutable business, and they remain as powerless to invent its past as to predict its future: "The Aleph was beyond them and they invented a theory that it was a mindless marauding thing . . . fulfilling no function beyond naked existence, left over from the millennia when the still-unknown aliens came. The aliens had built a mechanism for seeding Jupiter with simple, edible life—reworking whole moons, laying down a foundation for some future use that had not yet come" (14–15). The narrator's sense of their condition is clear: "They were alone at the rim of the human universe, pressed against an infinity that did not bear contemplation" (15).

But what, then, is this Aleph—this being the settlers would like to kill in order to give them a trophy, a legend, a past, and which the scientists hoped "would simply wear down and die and become a safe numb object for study, like the rest?" (15). Young Manuel's world is not that of the paleontologist. He, as focus of the narrative, is the striving monad, and confronting the Aleph is the defining moment in his coming of age. Thinking he has killed it, he will learn that it cannot be killed. He will also learn that, in relation to his existence at the rim of the human universe, the Aleph is not a being of theory. It is not the All rolled into the One. Instead, it acts as a power that draws mankind toward ever-new futures, forcing it to act *against* the possibility of infinity. For the first two-thirds of the novel, Manuel, like Faulkner's Ike, hunts the Aleph and believes that he, Old Matt, and Eagle have finally killed it. Matt's remarks, however, qualify this deed: "A man, an animal, then a gun. Now we have all three. Either it is enough or it will never be enough" (105). And in this vein, the death of Eagle teaches Manuel a valuable lesson about the "never enough" of Life in its largest sense. From this, he learns to comply with the badly wounded Matt's request not to live confined to a bed but to die "outside," facing *against* mankind's unknown future: "I'm telling you I want to see the eclipse one more time, from outside. Not on some damned screen, which is the way I'll be looking at it once they patch me up" (156).

Manuel's actions provoke a fatal rift between father and son. Manuel (like Ike) renounces the wilderness for the city Hiruko, where he lives in anonymity until called home to Sidon Settlement by his mother after his father's death. On the train, he meets Piet, an Earth scientist, part of a team studying the Aleph. Once at Sidon, Manuel decides to visit the site of the Aleph, where he again meets Piet. In a previous conversation with Piet, Manuel refused to provide details on the life of Matt Bohles, where he came from, who he was: "He taught me things, that's all." Likewise, for Manuel, the Aleph is not a thing to be studied; it is a personal event, a fact and an experience: "'Look, it's *dead*. Let it alone. Or at least let *me* alone.' 'Why are you so sure?' Manuel blinked. 'Sure?' 'That it is dead.' '*Look* at it. We killed it, Old Matt and me.' Piet smiled broadly. 'Yes, do look at it'" (225). Piet invites him to enter the Aleph. Manuel distrusts him, but he senses that Piet may lead him to a new, vaster sense of the Aleph, that this may the final step in his initiation into understanding his place in the universe.

In the first section of *Against Infinity*, Benford extrapolates from the hunting adventure at the heart of Faulkner's "The Bear." In the second section, with the introduction of Piet, Benford makes reference to another writer and work he admires: Jorge Luis Borges's "El Aleph" (1942). At the beginning of the novel, Manuel attributed the name "Aleph" to "some crazy Jew." Piet returns to this naming, but now from the Borgesian viewpoint of mathematics and Cabbalistic mysticism: "'The interesting point is that it means quite a few things in the sciences. For instance, in geometry it is written so . . . and means a point in space that contains all other points. All angles, all perspectives. And in another branch of mathematics, the number denoted by alpha null'—he wrote the sign—'is the basic transfinite number from Cantor's *Mengenlehre*—a number that has the curious property that any part of it is as large as the whole'" (231). To Manuel, such an explanation seems "crazy." But Piet invites him to enter the structure and experience for himself. During the "final" combat with the Aleph, he, Old Matt, and Eagle had all found themselves briefly taken inside the Aleph, only to be ejected. Now, floating inside the structure, he comes across the replica of a being that is Matt and yet not Matt: "Old Matt was not in helmet and suit, the way Manuel had seen him inside the Aleph before, but rather in loose-fitting coveralls" (232). He comes across another form: "In a fog of light he could tell this form was less detailed, blurred like a hazy image from only a fraction of a holographic print." Now, as Piet ties together past and present experiences, Manuel's revelation opens out to inscrutable mystery: "'You saw something like this before?' '*Sí*. something. After we shot the Aleph, while I was inside it, I thought I saw Old Matt, but when I got outside. . I . . .' He stepped back again, mouth rigid, grimacing. 'That other thing. That's *me*.'" When Piet offers his "explanation," it seems as grossly inadequate as that of Lieutenant Gregory in Stanislaw Lem's *The Investigation* (first English trans., 1977), who saw the random displacement of bodies from cemeteries all over England as a possible "resurrection": "Consider—you are a Christian, are you not? Consider how closely linked the idea of preservation, of arising again in a similar but transmuted form—how closely linked this is in your culture. It is the Christian vision of resurrection and salvation. Also, it is the image of horror at the walking dead, the zombie" (233). Manuel turns down another corridor in this internal labryinth, only to encounter another, this time monstrous image: "But that thing, where's it from?" How, he asks, can all things fit in a space this size? "Ah, but what *is* its size? That which appears to us from the outside? Or what we measure from the inside? A geometry containing other geometries . . ." (234). This description of the Aleph recalls Heinlein's story "And He Built a Crooked House," where an earthquake collapses the four spatial dimensions of a "tesseract house," and architect Homer Bailey and his clients, trapped inside this new geometry, find that doors and windows open onto different spacetime locations. One window opens onto absolute Nothingness.

All these explanations remain analogies, shadows of guesses, other people's attempts to "eff the ineffable." At this point, comparison of Benford's

Aleph with that of Borges is instructive. In Borges's story, the Aleph is discovered in the basement of a Buenos Aires house owned by a poet named Argentino Daneri. It is described as a single place where one can see everything in the universe from every angle. But there is no question, as in Benford's novel, of the observer entering *inside* the Aleph. On the contrary, in Borges's story each protagonist perceives (and conceives) infinity from his own unique angle. The narrator—"Borges"—not only mourns the death of his beloved Beatriz Viterbo, but he constructs a world around her memory and himself: "The universe may change, not me." The poet Daneri has a different (but analogous) vision of each man in his mediacosm, each allowing an entire world of images and electronic stimuli to revolve around him. The Dante subtext is obvious: Daneri is a conflation of "Dante" and "Aligheri," just as his vision seems a modern version of a Divine Comedy—a closed universe with the self as "pilgrim" within it, and with his beloved Beatriz as the goal of its pilgrimage. Borges's sense of the Aleph, then, is governed more by relativity than simultaneity. It is a place where each individual, from *its unique angle of vision*, constructs its infinity. But in order to contain what otherwise would be purest sequency, Borges must resort to positing a relationship between the one and the all that merely perpetuates the closed universe of the dualist, where mind is now endlessly called upon to master *its own* world.

Benford's Aleph, on the other hand, seems the incarnation of a sequency-simultaneity paradox—an entity always changing, yet always permanent. On one hand, if this Aleph is a transfinite entity, humans can never grasp the nature of its totality. Piet, for instance, is forced to reject the idea that it is simply a machine that makes its own parts, for in the way it remakes itself, it transcends any sense of a machine existence: "But the molecular forms, we have found, readjust because the *atomic* structure alters. And the atoms change because the particles constantly shift and move and change identity. That is it—the steady conversion of matter into other forms, like something restlessly remaking itself, forever discontented" (228). Piet continues to probe its ever-changing structure, moving to deeper levels of force and attraction and beyond: "Down at the nuclear level, and even below that, the forces *themselves*. There is a thing called the electro-weak interaction. Several numerical parameters describe it—parameters we thought fixed since time began, since the big bang started the universe. We now know, because of the Aleph, that they were not fixed. Here, they change. Always. Nothing remains, nothing is held constant" (229–30). Piet is forced to pursue this sense of change-in-permanence beyond the closed system of Dante's universe, beyond the laws of God and of matter, into unknown territory: "Somehow, it knows how to *make* laws. . . . Our fundamental constants of today will not always remain so. So natural evolution does not apply only to life—it applies to the laws of the universe as well." At this level of apprehension, we have something that is infinite because it cannot be subsumed under any human duality. To attempt to do so is to discover a universe that is at one and the same time circular and infinitely regressive: "But suppose that there was something that created *laws.* What does that? How"—he seized Manuel's arm—"how do you store the information that contains the laws? In the particles? But they are made by the fields, and thus by the laws themselves! Circular! How do you convey the information? *What makes the laws?*" (230).

Piet's final supposition is this: "Suppose the artifact is *in* this universe, but is not *of* the universe?" (230). This, however—shades of Lem—is the God paradox all over again, and Manuel refuses to stop here. Ultimately, Piet's vision appears to present the same circular tyranny Bob Wilson rejects in Heinlein's story "By His Bootstraps": "If God created the universe, who created God? Who wrote the notebook? Who started the chain? . . . He knew that he had about as much chance of understanding such problems as a collie has of understanding how dog food gets into cans."[7] Bob Wilson abandons the riddles and paradoxes of philosophy for personal engagement. He realizes that, whatever the nature of this infinite series, for him *personally* its perceived circularity is a "perpetual motion fur farm," and as such it remains a dynamic, open-ended process. For even if its amplitude, past to future, is restricted to a time loop of four hours, the loop itself, as an energy construct, is subject to change, if only in the form of entropy, to its very slow winding down.

Indeed, the idea that the laws of the universe themselves may be local phenomena, different and ever changing from "world" to "world," was far-out physics in 1982 (although today's "string theory" seems to posit something similar). For the Aleph to be truly infinite, it would have to encompass such phenomena. Benford's point however, in a story told from the point of view of a young initiate on the far edge of human advancement, may be that the Aleph is simply unknowable. But for Benford, the powerlessness of theory in the face of the unknown is not treated, as in Lem's *Solaris*, satirically. Nor is it seen as a mark of our tragic human condition. If there is a bit of satire here, it is more in the manner of the Strugatsky brothers' *Roadside Picnic* (1972). In this novel, a mysterious "zone" full of alien objects appears in the middle of a city. Scientists attempt to examine, classify, and name the objects. They gain some sense of how they work, but know nothing of their origin. One scientist, Pilman, tosses off a hypothesis: that aliens traveled through our space and, having neither a notion of us nor care for our environment, had a "roadside picnic" and simply left behind their litter. This is an obvious joke on the Strugatskys' part. But the joke is on Lem's pessimism in the face of the cognitive unknown. For despite all the theorizing, there remain the physical objects. These are not only unknowable, but they pose a tangible challenge to humans, as their existence promises to change their world, for good or for bad. If Pilman rightly remarks that scientists are "hammering nails with microscopes," at the same time he points to the fact that he is not really hammering anything. Pilman is to protagonist Red Schuhart as Piet and his Earth scientists are to Manuel: "*They came here out of duty. Not from a yearning. . . . They're like priests, not explorers*" (190). On the other hand, it is Red who must engage the zone, must physically push the limits of the unknown. And Manuel, entering the Aleph for the second time, has, like Red, the task of apprehending the alien with all his senses: "Yet many of the things he'd felt had not come through sight, but through the other senses, taste and smell and sound and touch, stretching fine and firm as though he was experiencing them for the first time" (229).

The final vision in *Against Infinity* is that of a Manuel, who has come of age in a world where coming of age means facing the unknown frontier alone. The Aleph he thought dead rises up; quakes happen that kill Piet and his Earth expedition and nearly destroy the settlements. Manuel admits he has learned things about the Aleph from Piet. But more important, he has learned from Old Matt, and from a final reconciliation with the memory of his father, why men "hunt" the alien:

> For at the camp in that dusky morning of Old Matt's death he had joined forever the other side—the wilderness, the opening-outward, the undomesticated, the country of old dead time. Perhaps the Colonel had understood that too. . . . The Colonel's words still hung in space in the space between them: *killing everything that's old*—for his father had never meant to kill the Aleph, he had merely wanted to hunt it, to be drawn out by it from the cozy pockets of an insulated life, out from humanity. And in the death of the thing the Colonel had seen, with foreboding, his own end. (244–245)

In the end, the issue is not youth against age, or our young species against an ancient universe. The Aleph is all these things, the whole show. It has taken Old Matt inside it. But if the man is thus contained, his final words are not. *Watch for me,* Matt asks Manuel as he prepares to exit the building and die facing the wilderness. Here he means: "Mount a vigil so that no one stops me." Later, Manuel hears the same phrase as he sees Matt floating inside the Aleph. But now Matt and the Aleph are one, and the phrase appears to have a new function that Manuel now begins to understand: "The swelling ice rose again. He was on his feet now as he understood. . . . Cracks forked from the tortured upthrusting mound. Ice fell away with loud crashes. Manuel smiled. *Watch for me.* All these years, the men and animals running out here, roiling and heedless and joyful, and they never thought maybe it was drawing them out" (250–51). We remember Clarke's Watcher, and Kubrick's dark monolith in *2001: A Space Odyssey,* whose enigmatic presence seemed to serve "to draw mankind out." Though he now knows better, Manuel briefly entertains the possibility of providence, of some form of destiny: "The land ruled now, not men. Its casual rippling had cast down his father into a laser's path, and by doing so had begun Manuel's own journey back to this place. Was it possible that, once the Aleph had stopped boring through the ice crust years ago, the gathering stresses were no longer relieved? So that killing it had brought all this on? Manuel shook himself. That was crazy. Crazy" (248).

Manual's final revelation in the wilderness is that the real, ongoing struggle—overseen by the Aleph—is one between Life and nonlife:

> A sudden silence fell upon the wild and endless territory that stretched quietly in all directions: Ganymede as it had been in the formless time before . . . barren and without life, a stage waiting for the ceaseless struggle between the slumber-

> ing, inert wilderness and the endlessly chewing chains of life—all witnessed by a thing that knew everything, contained everything, perhaps had made everything, yet went on mutely amid all the clash and clamor, immersed in its own creation, running, perhaps pausing but never quitting, leaving a wake of wreckage that was tragedy to men but mere passing drama to it. (250)

Manuel on Jupiter's moon is in the same situation as Huck Finn at the end of his river. He has learned *and* survived, and now stands ready to light out into the unknown: "And as the first of the alabaster blocks broke free of the restraining land . . . he knew he would carry this, carry it on with him in the long decades of rebuilding . . . through the heavy years of toil out in the territory, beyond the ever-reaching hand of man; the thought would come to him each day as he worked for his own undiminished destiny" (251). We saw, both in Faulkner's story and here, that the "hand of man" is as destructive as it is necessary. But both Manuel and Ike McCaslin, if on different scales, have glimpsed something seemingly endless in mankind's relation to nature. Even so, alone on the edge of the unknown, both men have only memory: "At dark moments when memory alone was all he had to sustain him—he would carry the certain sense that it was there, somewhere in the vastness, and he would remember" (252).

Interestingly, there will be a moment like this at the end of Clarke's *3001: The Final Odyssey* (1997), as the same Bowman and HAL (now conflated as "Halman"), who a millennium before at the beckoning of the monolith launched their quest upon the seas of infinity, now prepare for another human adventure into the unknown. Halman proposes to create a new monolith by "downloading" mankind's millennial adventure on a "petabyte tablet," to be stored on Earth's moon at the location of the original "sentinel" that started it all. The purpose once again is to send a signal, when the time is right, to some future evolved humanity, which in turn will see fit to resurrect its past. Until that time, the tablet is to be guarded by the all-too-mortal Poole. Like Manuel however, Halman can only, in his final words, call upon the memory of the reader to be mankind's final repository against infinity: "If we are unable to download, remember us."[8] Benford takes a lesson learned from Faulkner to Ganymede. Infinite nature is the lure, all the more so because infinity, by definition, is unattainable. Mankind's further adventures against the unknown can only be guaranteed by memory. Bowman's first leap into the infinite, in Clarke's *2001* (1968) is from space around a Jupiter moon. But its relaunch will be from Earth's Moon, repository of human memory. Mankind's future, for Benford, seems increasingly rooted in the continuity of its past, and Manuel's task, on a world where few remember anything of their Earth origins, is to learn to remember. The author will develop this same dynamic, on a vast cosmic scale, in his Galactic Center novels.

CHAPTER 4

GALACTIC CENTER ONE
Benford's Space Epic

The works that make up the series of Benford novels commonly called the Galactic Center saga span nineteen years of the author's career. They encompass as well a changing landscape of science fiction, in which space adventure, once central to the genre, becomes a near relic. The first novel, *In the Ocean of Night* (1977), is close enough to the Apollo program and an iconic work like Clarke's and Kubrick's *2001: A Space Odyssey* to reflect the period's spirit of high adventure in the promise of space travel. Even so, on opening this novel, we know immediately that ten years have passed since those glory days. NASA has become an administrative drudge, and Earth's environment and its political situation are, beyond the Cold War equation, on the verge of collapse. In the subsequent novels, produced in the cyberpunk era, Benford seems to take refuge from this trend in the increasingly arcane physics of spacetime. Rather than deal with social, environmental, and political issues cyberpunk raises, he continues to do what he has always done as a *science* fiction writer—pursue the question of mankind's condition in the face of science's genuinely expanding universe. This encounter between mankind and the physical universe remains Benford's core concern across his career. The venues of encounter become increasingly more inventive, indeed wildly so, in the Galactic Center series. But the terms of this encounter do not change; they simply become clearer. For in the end, the ultimate context of human evolution is no longer Descartes's mind-matter opposition. Nor is it some cosmic competition between organic and machine intelligence. It is the vaster, ever-evolving struggle of sentient Life to abide and evolve in a universe of blind, inert forces. The Belgian writer J.-H. Rosny, at the end of the nineteenth century, accorded the possibility of sentient life to iron-based forms. For him, the limits of sentience was the inert mineral kingdom. As we shall see, for Benford's Galactic Center explorers, this limit no longer holds.

Despite the immense sweep of spacetime, the central figure of Benford's Galactic series will remain Nigel Walmsley, the maverick NASA astronaut who dominates *In the Ocean of Night* and its sequel, *Across the Sea of Suns* (1984). He continues to mark his presence as the cosmic landscape expands. He returns, as what seems a series of "manifestations," in the strange timescape of the final novel, *Sailing Bright Eternity* (1996). Nigel's initial adventure is relived by other like figures—Killeen, his son Toby—as individual mankind expands its spacetime horizons across this sea of suns. Benford's transformation of conventional space opera in *The Stars in Shroud* now expands to become a work deserving of the term "space epic." Born in the matrix of Clarke's *2001*, Nigel is a space-age Odysseus—a crafty, restless, forward-looking intelligence for whom the going out, encounters with the ineffable alien, must always remain a coming home. But although Benford's protagonists in the later novels remain avatars of Nigel, there is more to Galactic Center than the adventure of a single individual. The figures who follow in Nigel's footsteps are asked to do something he did not do—to assume the responsibility of the human tribe and community, who are now faced with relentless attempts by machine adversaries not just to annihilate them, but to manipulate them to its own ends. These are issues faced by that other epic hero, Aeneas, on his trek from Troy to Rome, a new place where he seeks, against mighty odds, to recreate a semblance of lost Trojan society. His destination then, analogous to Benford's Galactic Center, is a potentially hostile place of inscrutable gods and forces. The adventures of Killeen and Toby are closer to those of Aeneas than to those of Odysseus. The final novel in Benford's series will seek to reconcile these epic strains in a physical world beyond human scale and perhaps comprehension.

The term "epic" is not used lightly here. In fact, Benford's series seems to corroborate the often-made claim that science fiction is the epic form of the scientific twentieth century. A series like Star Trek follows the paradigm of the Homeric epic as the collective story of a people and culture, the product of many hands that has evolved over time as that culture and society changes. The early "mythic" characters are shaped by the Roddenberry vision; successive manifestations of these figures are reshaped by newer social visions, in the matrix of successive generations of writers and actors responsible for its continuation. Benford's epic, like that of Virgil, is the product of a single hand, thus of a poet free to elaborate a vision based on the actions of individuals of its own creation. Aeneas was a minor figure in the Homeric adventure. Virgil lifts him from obscurity, gives him the mission (fictitious in the sense of "invented") to found an empire based on a "dynasty" such as that which runs from Nigel to Killeen to his son Toby.

Many SF works (and their publicists) lay claim to the epic label, by which they simply mean the vast *scope* of action, instantly and effortlessly bestowed by the space adventure trope. Benford prefers the word "saga" to describe his Galactic Center series. But it is clear that the wanderings and adventures of Aeneas offer the model most apt to confer epic scope to the sagas Benford inherits from Heinlein's glorious juvenile space adventures of the 1950s. Heinlein adds a touch of Calvinist election to the crafty, self-reliant frontier survivor epitomized in Huck Finn. Everyman figures like Max in *Starman Jones* or young Kip in *Have Space Suit, Will Travel* find themselves, thanks to their maverick nature and to instantly revealed special skills, unexpectedly in a position to save a spaceship or planet Earth. Benford's disobedient astronaut Nigel is to some degree a protagonist in this vein. At the end of *In the Ocean of Night*, his quasi-divine revelations of unity emanate from, and center upon, his own being as that being wrestles with the contending forces of a universe far greater than his own insignificant condition. But if Nigel is, via Heinlein, Emerson's self-reliant Man, the Virgilian epic allows Benford to extend this vision of self-reliance across the galaxies. For Emerson, "A man Caesar is born, and for ages we have a Roman Empire." For Benford, Nigel came to be, and for dizzying stretches of spacetime, mankind seems empowered to pursue its destiny.

Benford's six books are an obvious bow to E. E. "Doc" Smith's Lensman series. But if this bow pays homage to pulp roots, it at the same time invites comparison, and contrast, with Smith's conventional space epic, which, insofar as it centers on vast intergalactic warfare between two opposing societies and worldviews, gives us an intergalactic Iliad. Smith's novels are the product of serialization, which, in order to hold a reader, dictates a narrative logic of self-contained, highly dramatic episodes, a logic radically different from that of *In the Ocean of Night*, where a series of seemingly unconnected events are eventually pieced together—and their cosmic meaning finally revealed—only through Nigel's participation in them. There are other, non-epic elements in *Ocean*, and the novel could easily have taken another direction. But it becomes clear, as the novel develops, that Nigel will be the kernel from which Benford's series can organically expand. Smith's first novel in his completed Lensman saga is less the seed from which the series grows than an afterthought, a novel adapted to a project after that project had already been conceived and elaborated. The main body of the Lens novels were published in the early 1950s. But novels 3–6 (*Galactic Patrol* to *Children of the Lens*) were all published in serial form from 1937 to 1948. In 1948, Smith revised an originally very different serialized work (1938) as the novel *Triplanetary*. In this revised form, it became the preface to the series. The second novel in the final series, *First Lensman*, published in 1950, leads into *Galactic Patrol* but was not previously published as a serial. This first Lensman novel was the last to be written and was tailored to an already elaborated epic landscape. Its role is to tie together, after the fact, the complex actions and themes that compose the initial, serialized core—novels 3–6. Smith's epic series therefore has an interesting circular genesis, one which allowed for additions and corrections after the fact of its serialized conception. In contrast, Benford's work seems to spring from the single inspiration of Nigel Walmsley. Each new episode unfolds organically, both from what came before and from what was *written* before. Benford's space epic is truly the lengthened shadow of a single man.

Even so, Smith's space epic remains Benford's forerunner, in the sense that it has scientific extrapolation and a story with genuine cosmic sweep.

Its overarching narrative is the vast power struggle between two contending superforces: the Arisians and the Eddorians. The Arisians are apparently of our universe and were already, a billion years before the series' narrative present, a highly evolved and peaceful race, which had developed mental powers over physical ones. The Eddorians are the exact opposite. They are an aggressive and warlike race whose power is physical strength. They are the Achaeans to the agrarian Trojans. And like these ancient Greeks, they invade Arisian space because (in terms of physical theory of Smith's time) our galaxy is seen as unique among the known cosmos for favoring planet creation. The apparently underdog Arisians go underground. But they use their time in hiding to develop a series of mentally superior peoples on the planets of this universe so coveted by the invading Eddorians. They do so by creating covert breeding programs on these planets. On Earth, there is the all-male line of Kinnisons. These males are the sole bearers of the "Lens." But there is one exception, the red-haired Clarissa McDougal, whose purpose is to breed future "children of the Lens." There ensues a protracted intergalactic war between the forces of mind, and the tool-enhanced Eddorian "mechanists." Smith's struggle takes place along the classic lines of this Cartesian mind-matter duality. Benford will expand this opposition—in light of more recent science—into a cosmic struggle between various forms of sentient existence. Even so, in Benford as in Doc Smith, the underlying dichotomy, at least for most of the saga, remains one of "us" and "it." No matter how great are the forces that seem to engulf us puny humans, we continue to strive. "Doc" Smith makes no bones about it: humanity seems predestined to play a central role in this cosmic All. Nigel's role is more subtly conceived. He is cast as an intergalactic Huck Finn whose resilience and ability to survive and move on secures for the humanity he represents—if still in quite mysterious ways—a prominent place in cosmic evolution.

To reread Smith's Lensman novels in light of Benford's Galactic Center is a learning experience. "Doc" Smith had a doctorate in chemical engineering but worked as a food scientist in industry (the Dawn Donut Company). Benford is a research physicist. Smith's prose is stilted and functional; his characters are space-opera stereotypes writ large. Benford seeks to develop "round" characters and is a consciously inventive stylist for whom style becomes the ultimate means by which scientific mankind is able to probe the physical unknown. Yet despite its "black and white" nature, Smith's work is seminal for later writers like Heinlein and Clarke, who feed directly into Benford. Smith's career, in fact, spans the entire development of American space adventure. He evolved in the climate of Edgar Rice Burroughs (to whose seminal work Heinlein paid homage in his omnibus novel *Number of the Beast*). Smith's work flowered in the early days of John W. Campbell's "Golden Age." It formed a monument to be reckoned with and was recast by writers like Heinlein. The cosmic scale of Smith's work remained a powerful influence in the 1970s on writers like Niven and Benford. It showed them that an SF writer could "think big," could conceive action on an intergalactic scale and still write scientifically.

Smith's work, then, is nothing less than co-extensive with the development of American SF. His career began before science fiction had a name: *Skylark of Space* was written between 1915 and 1920. His Skylark novels remained unpublished until the advent of Gernsback's *Amazing Stories*, which published *Skylark III* in 1928. *Amazing* was the matrix that produced Buck Rogers and the flamboyant work of Edmond Hamilton. Smith, however, aspired to move beyond pseudo science in his Lensman novels and to build space adventure around "real science." Along with the science, Smith sought to shift emphasis from the Buck Rogers space warrior to a more sophisticated sort of protagonist, one who pits mental activity against brute force. The ideal of the Lensman is captured in Hubert Rogers's iconic 1939 cover. We see the Lensman step forth from his gleaming space ship, clad in metallic gray. His ray guns, however, are sheathed. Instead, he holds in his hand the "lens," described as a "pseudo" organic communications device that gives its bearer telepathic abilities, allowing him to weave a web of understanding and purpose among the most diverse life forms. The Lensman stands strong, his demeanor shows resolve. But his face and eyes show intelligence, not lantern-jawed brutishness. Though Benford does not give a complete description of Nigel Walmsley, one can imagine him in his astronaut's suit, walking in the footsteps of Rogers's Lensman.

Smith's work governs the epic lineage that develops in American science fiction. There is, at the center of this epic tradition, the idea that mankind—in the incarnation of the single epic hero—has some special, even chosen role to play on the cosmic stage. In Smith's Lensman novels, the Arisians recruit for their galactic patrol exceptional beings from a great variety of alien races. But ultimately their focus turns to Earth, and to a single human,

Kimball Kinnison, chosen to be wearer of the Lens. Out of all sorts of wonders of organic sentience, a single human being is singled out to carry the struggle against the enemies of life to its end. This is anthropocentrism of epic proportions. And Heinlein, whose vision is clearly shaped by a quasi-Calvinist sense of election, carries Smith's idea of the chosen hero further yet, especially in his later novels which, in strange ways, remain space(time) epics. Heinlein's epic heroes—both in his juvenile and his later novels—are generally unassuming and seem to come from nowhere. Physically, they are not perfect specimens like the Kinnisons. Instead, we have Kettle Belly Baileys and Hugh Farnhams—out of shape and middle aged. Yet this exterior appearance belies both their inner resolve and their cosmic destiny. Like Calvin's elect, they bear no external marks of election. Extrapolating from this, we see the inconspicuous, even insignificant, exterior of humanity as a whole as concealing some predestined role as arbiter and catalyst among vastly more powerful and "advanced" cosmic races. If mankind is a mote, it is a mote in God's eye. Heinlein's protagonists are (predetermined by their very names) both everyman and chosen one—Maximilian Jones the Starman is an example. For Heinlein, "democracy" is the means of keeping the field open, of allowing for the rise of the chosen one, for otherwise mute, inglorious Caesars to take full possession of their destiny.

The development of Benford's Nigel and his epic "children" appears to follow the nonpurposive path of evolution. Yet a shadow of election hangs over them. There are aspects of the Heinlein epic that are visible in Nigel's makeup and destiny. He rejects the sheep mentality of bureaucrats and institutions. He is by no means a perfect physical specimen, and Benford allows him to become middle aged. He does not, like Smith's Lensman, possess superhuman mental powers. More like Heinlein's protagonists, he intuits and acts on his intuitions yet remains a fierce defender of mankind's ability to rebel and to strive, to utter its human "yes" in the face of a cosmic "no." He is also incredibly lucky. This can be seen as a sign that, despite the evolutionary context in which he operates, he has been chosen by some obscure higher force to carry the message of mankind's uniqueness to the Galactic Center. What, in terms of accomplishments, has Nigel actually done to earn such amazing "grace"? In Heinlein's fashion, it is neither by actions nor deeds alone that this epic hero persists to the end.

Yet in terms of sheer scope and of the many technological marvels encountered on the epic journey to Galactic Center, Benford's primary debt is to Smith's saga. Smith was a scientist, and however dated the science he used to extrapolate his alien beings and machines, these retain their sense of scientific wonder even today. Instead of Circe, Polythemus, or the Sirens, Smith's galaxies are "peopled" with strange and wonderfully detailed aliens. There are marvelous worlds and inventions based not in myth but in scientific possibility. There are things like the "Nth space," an alternate dimension where all matter is tachyonic, moving faster than light. Beings survive liquid helium temperatures because they have the capacity to extend their metabolisms at will into other dimensions. Inhabitants of planets with variable suns live by morphing their bodies accordingly. Smith invents the "hyperspace tube," a sort of wormhole comprised of "dureum," a super-dense substance. There is the "inertialess drive" that propels at faster-than-light speeds, not by eliminating mass but by abolishing inertia. The Eddorians use defensive "thought screens," obliging the Children of the Lens to "think over" or "under" them. "Terawatt" power is generated by the controlled matter-to-energy conversion of "allotropic iron." There are all kinds of futuristic weapons—power armor, mind killers, space axes, "macro-beam" guns. These are not, as in Gernsback, simply catchy neologisms slapped on fanciful inventions. They are functioning devices conceived and constructed along principles of science and engineering, however erroneous that science and technology may be. Doc Smith's seminal cosmic epic bequeaths to Benford a dimension Heinlein does not have—a scientific sense of wonder that confronts the human observer at every turn of the interstellar road.

Benford's Galactic Center epic consists of six increasingly hefty novels, each of which is packed with adventure, invention, and often profound meditation on the nature of the cosmos and mankind's position therein. A detailed analysis of each is beyond the scope of this study. I propose to focus on seminal texts and moments that allow me to chart both the fictional voyage and the author's own itinerary as storyteller and stylist over the twenty years of creation that separates the first novel from the last. *In the Ocean of Night* is a fascinating, almost improbable point of departure for a galactic adventure. In itself, it is an excellent novel and merits a close reading for the subtle way it positions its protagonist, and his planet Earth, to play a central role in the evolution of a vast array of cosmic life forms. It seems that Benford began this novel as a near-future scientific mystery and then gradually, organically, found ways to point the various strands of the action toward what eventually emerges as their unique source—Galactic Center. Its direct sequel is *Across the Sea of Suns* (1983). Separated from the earlier novel by six years, it reveals Nigel's resolve to continue his step-by-step advancement into space, beyond the solar system to another star system. The novel ends with a defiant interstellar leap toward the galactic center. Four more years intervene, and there appears in close succession a pair of novels—*Great Sky River* (1987) and *Tides of Light* (1989)—that are (as the advertising blurb tells it) "set on a distant planet at the center of the galaxy and tell of a small band of humans" fighting for survival. The focus now is on the struggle between machine mind and organic life. Nigel wrestled as individual with this dichotomy during his space apprenticeship in *In the Ocean of Night*. Now Nigel has disappeared into this same ocean, but his inner struggle has become an external space battlefield. The narrative focus shifts to Killeen, a future human who possesses the same character traits as Nigel. Benford (or his publishers) show a desire to link these fictional worlds separated by a gulf of spacetime by appending to the 1987 paperback edition of *Across the Sea of Suns*, as teaser and transition, the first chapter of *Great Sky River*, issued that same year. The thread drawn between this and the earlier novels is the heroic nature of the human protagonist. Killeen is a future human being who is physically and mentally "enhanced" yet by the force of things is compelled to revert to primitive tribal conditions. But in this beleaguered and cramped world, he carries on Nigel's struggle against human shortsightedness. He has inherited Nigel's intuitive vision of the vastness of the cosmic mechanism. From his tribal bunker he senses the strangeness of worlds that lie out there, beyond our human present, but that are potentially accessible to human imagination and ingenuity. Of the two Killeen novels, I find *Tides of Light* most interesting. It is a tour de force in imagining alien beings and the extraordinary, even sentient machines by which they harness incredible physical forces. There is once again a five-year hiatus, between *Tides of Light* and the next novel in the series, *Furious Gulf* (1994). Here, the focus shifts to Toby, Killeen's son. Killeen takes his remaining band on a last-ditch journey aboard the spaceship Argo to the galactic center. The novel recounts the struggle between father and son. We discover, however, that Toby has another role—that of messenger for humanity. In his body are implanted memory devices that carry the last record of the human saga into this "furious gulf." In its sequel, *Sailing Bright Eternity*, published a scant year later, Toby meets up with Nigel at Galactic Center. This final novel is a tour de force, where Benford, with renewed energy and startling imagination, seeks to tie together the various threads of his saga. This final novel merits a close reading as a stunning achievement in itself and as a surprisingly satisfying climax to the Nigel Walmsley epic.

CHAPTER 5

GALACTIC CENTER TWO

Nigel Walmsley's Space Odyssey

The first two novels in the Galactic Center series are set in Earth's near future. The dates are from 1999 (twenty-two years after the novel's publication) to 2061, a time when mankind has conquered space in the sense that it can reach nearby stars and thus stands on the edge of "the ocean of night," deep space. By the end of the first novel, *In the Ocean of Night*, protagonist Nigel Walmsley has discovered a cosmic struggle between machine intelligence and organic life that will soon engulf Earth. Through several contacts with alien artifacts and entities that had come to Earth in both prehistoric and recent times, he predicts the coming of the machines, which plays out in the second novel, a genuine sequel to the first: *Across the Sea of Suns*. In this novel, Nigel does battle with the machines with the help of organic life forms he finds on the moon of a planet in distant Epsilon Eridani. As he does so, he reaffirms what he had earlier discovered on Earth: that, in the evolutionary sense, the boundary between machine and organism is not clear cut. But still, in this second novel, the machine enemy seems little more than a descendant of Fred Saberhagen's Berserkers. The invading "Mechs" trick far-distant Earth into a thermonuclear war. Only a few human enclaves are left on Earth to do future battle with the machines. The bureaucrats Nigel has fought throughout his career as a NASA astronaut are now destroyed. He now stands alone on the threshold of outer space. Like his proclaimed ancestor Huck Finn, he launches himself and his small band of survivors into unknown territories. Their destination, apparently programmed into the starship Argo he commandeers, is the Galactic Center.

The stamp of Clarke's Space Odyssey is clearly on these two novels. Protagonist Nigel seems the Clarkean hero. Like Bowman, or like the astronauts who enter the spaceship Rama, he is a man of our very near future who, through contact with alien beings (the Ramans) and/or artifacts (the moon sentinel) finds his "door" into deep space, following the lure of eternity. Nigel however, is a composite character. His origins may be British, but he has immigrated to the United States and adopted America's sense of the space frontier as an open path toward the new and unknown. Nigel's presence will dominate these two novels. And unlike figures such as Bowman and Poole, Nigel undergoes no transhuman enhancements. Cosmic landscapes change around him, the obstacles become increasingly difficult to overcome, yet as with Huck Finn and the eternal youths of Heinlein's juveniles, his spirit of adventure never ages. His body, however, does age in the course of the two initial novels. Despite rejuvenating drugs and medical devices, he, like Heinlein's Lazarus, eventually does grow older and is fully aware of the toll time takes on his mortal body. Nigel Walmsley is a fascinating combination of all these elements—Bowman's mystical journey, Huck Finn's eternal youth, Lazarus Long's struggle with his expanding, ever-aging physical existence. A very different "Nigel" will reappear in the final novel *Sailing Bright Eternity*, many thousands of years later in terms of Earth time. Here he exists in a strange dimension of "solid time" where he is free to recreate——as did Lazarus Long in Heinlein's *Time Enough for Love*—a replica of a long-lost original Earth homestead. Nigel, whose early career was marked by very 1960s group families and partnership experiments, now finds—in this fantastic timescape—family, wife, children, and pets, all in a rural Earthlike setting.

Close examination of these two novels is necessary for understanding how Benford launched his space epic. In terms of narrative complexity, *In the Ocean of Night* is the more interesting novel. A close reading is needed to lay bare the process—almost organic in nature—by which the author modulates from a scientific novel of manners to a space epic in the "Doc" Smith manner, complete with cosmic battlefield and contending super-presences locked in seemingly endless struggles. The gradual and subtle interplay between the contemporary and the cosmic is carefully worked out here. In this sense, Clarke's fiction was clearly a major influence on this novel.

IN THE OCEAN OF NIGHT

Despite the Hamiltonesque title, Benford's novel begins inconspicuously in the near-future year of 1999. The structure is episodic—segments were published in various magazines as early as 1972—and Benford masters it as he works out the parameters of his novel. Subsequent episodes bear dates slightly further into the twenty-first century. They recount the career of Nigel Walmsley as he pieces together the puzzle of several events in which he seems serendipitously involved and which all prove in the end to have been alien "visitations." Nigel is a relatively young man in 1999; he is middle aged in the final episode dated 2019. Throughout this sequence, a series of seemingly insignificant or misunderstood occurrences turn out to yield the key to a mystery that suddenly opens out onto cosmic vistas. The model here, clearly, is Arthur C. Clarke's collaboration with Stanley Kubrick, *2001: A Space Odyssey* (1968). In the Clarke-Kubrick work, signals are detected in a series of humdrum, even boring events that lead astronauts Bowman and Poole—quite unheroic spacemen—to the Stargate off Jupiter, and from here to a sudden leap into the "infinite." In fact, Benford's dating of his sequences in *Ocean*, reflecting mankind's slow crawl toward infinity, may have inspired Clarke—an example of reverse influence—to continue his space odyssey in dated sequence: *2010: Odyssey Two* (1982) and so on. Nigel the Cambridge-educated Englishman has become an astronaut in pursuit of a dream of space exploration that, already by his time, has fallen prey to underfunding, social and political unrest, and bureaucratic mediocrity. Benford was already predicting, as early as 1972, the demise of NASA's Apollo dream. Nigel, significantly, is merely a space shuttle pilot. But when an apparent asteroid inexplicably emits a jet of gas and changes course, moving to collide with Earth, Nigel volunteers to undertake a dangerous mission to intercept and destroy it. Suddenly, in the midst of the bureaucratic morass, Space with a capital "S" becomes the order of the day.

The novel begins with a citation from *The Encyclopedia Britannica* dated 2073 (a date subsequent to the dates spanned in the novel), which has classified and named this asteroid: "Minor planet 1566. Had the most eccentric elliptic orbit of all the known asteroids. . . . The unusual orbit attracted only minor attention until 1997, when Icarus suddenly began emitting a plume of gas and dust."[1] A second citation offers this future's take on the Icarus myth: "The legend is often invoked as a symbol of man's quest for knowledge and fresh horizons, whatever the cost" (14). In Nigel's era of overpopulation, pollution, and resource depletion, artists further see Icarus's fall as "an emblem for the decline of Western cultural eminence." The "Icarus" in question, in fact, proves to be all of the above, and none of them at the same time. As Nigel approaches what appears to be a space rock, he suddenly realizes that it is something very different—a spaceship. Icarus's fall here seems due to a physical accident: "The irony was inescapable: the blowout of gases through the vent made the cometary tail flare out from this ancient vessel, causing him and Len to come here and discover it—but that same eruption deflected Icarus enough to strike the Earth and made necessary its destruction" (38–39). Its arrival in our atmosphere gives Nigel the opportunity to display his own Icarian spirit. Ordered to destroy it, he disobeys. Drawn by the possibility of genuine alien encounter, he boards the ship. His explorations delay its destruction and therefore create a real menace for millions of people on Earth, should the object strike the Indian ocean. He accepts to undertake his explorations whatever the cost. His making such a calculation "for the higher good" ("A new power source. Maybe something with higher efficiency. That would be worth the chance.") is a specialty of Heinlein's characters—one thinks of the Nobel Prize–winning scientist Dr. Cargraves in *Rocket Ship Galileo* (1947), blasting off his nuclear-powered rocket ship in the midst of a Midwest town, indifferent to the effects of radiation on the townspeople. Nigel reasons the same way: "I don't want to kill them, Dave. . . . Stop being melodramatic. But we've got to admit that what we can learn from this relic may be worth some human life" (33).

We rejoin Nigel in 2014. He has survived his insubordination, indeed made himself untouchable as the man who "was there." His calculated risk (we assume the ship was destroyed in time) proved successful, and there were things on Icarus of great value to human technology. And yet all of this remains secondary to the core of his experience, which is a brush with something alien and ineffable. Nigel's summary of the situation seems to echo that of the Strugatskys' scientists as they ponder—and miss—the significance of the alien Zone in their novel *Roadside Picnic* (English translation just appeared in 1977): "Interesting, yes; but not keys to a fundamental discovery. Some odd technical tricks . . . an advanced substrate for microelectronics, resistant alloys, some sophisticated chemicals—but somehow the *alienness* of the thing had slipped through their fingers. None of their haul bore silent witness to Icarus's origin" (44). But there is a deeper significance to Nigel's meeting with Icarus, one that only later emerges. As he moved through the ship's alien space—"rooms that seemed to change their dimensions as he watched"—his presence seemed accidentally to trigger some sort of signal that "wasn't on our assigned frequencies" (31).

This has apparent consequences fifteen years later. The maverick Nigel is again called upon by NASA. The Jupiter monitor is now being jammed by a signal coming from something in its vicinity. There is no explanation for this, except the possibility that another alien object is the source, and that once again it is "coming toward us." Icarus seemed an empty derelict, yet the signal it apparently sent (in the manner of Clarke's "The Sentinel") has awakened something out in space that has changed course toward us. Straightforward narrative now gives way to stylistic experiment. The third-person narrator, without warning, yields to a new voice. *Icarus* did not speak to Nigel. Now Nigel seems to pick up the "interior monologue," rendered in *discours indirect libre*, of the space vessel itself. It reveals itself to be a very special sentient machine: "Though it was carrying out a long and labored exploration of this spiral arm, it had not chosen this particular star at random. Long before, cruising at a sizeable fraction of light speed somewhat below the plane of the galaxy, it had filtered through the whispering radio noise a brief signal. The message was blurred and garbled . . . [a] distress call. Life system failure. A breach in the hull, violation of the vital integrity indices" (50–51). This alien may be speaking to itself. But what speaks can be spoken to. And this Nigel will do. He calls his alien the "Snark," and, as in the poem, he will be sent to hunt it. Knowing the absurdity of such a hunt, he disobeys orders. Once more he makes alien contact. But now what before were only intimations of contact—rooms *seeming* to change dimensions with his gaze—will be real contact and dialogue. Moreover, contact is not only with a sentient machine, but it is with one that appears to be a maverick like himself—a machine-philosopher fascinated with the nature of the organic life forms that are its archenemy on the evolutionary scale of the cosmos.

Lewis Carroll described his poem "The Hunting of the Snark" as "the improbable voyage of an impossible crew to find an inconceivable creature." This description will fit the subsequent voyage of Nigel and his avatars toward the Galactic Center. But in this initial novel, Nigel hunts his Snark in hopes of communicating with it. There are other powers on Earth interested in the Snark as well. Times are troubled, and a new "post-scientific" religion is gaining social and political power. These "New Sons" are reminiscent of the "Cosmochristers" in Clarke's *Rendezvous with Rama*, who see in the arrival of Rama a Second Coming from space. On the other side of the fence, Nigel's future NASA answers to the military, who sees the Snark as a potential threat to Earth. Nigel must navigate between these forces: "Any error could be disastrous. The Snark had probably been silent all this time because it was cautious. If the ExComm reply was unclear or seemed unfriendly, the Snark might simply pass through the solar system and away. Gone. Forever" (131).

At the same time as this alien sighting, domestic complications occur in Nigel's life. His companion Alexandria is diagnosed with a fatal degenerative disease. Nigel connects himself to her vital signs through an electronic monitoring device that operates around the clock. At this point in the narrative, Benford is not content simply to contrast, as might other SF writers, personal distress with cosmic wonder. Instead, he connects them in a most ingenious manner. It is through this same monitoring frequency that the Snark chooses, at the *exact moment* of Alexandria's death, to communicate with Nigel. First contact coincides with the Snark's experiencing human mortality. For Nigel, first contact and personal tragedy occur simultaneously. This marks a profound turning point in his personal quest.

How does this connection come about? Nigel, the only human who has previously experienced a genuinely alien object, is allowed to prepare the message NASA sends to the Snark. At the same time, in order to be continuously connected, he reroutes the channel of communication through the monitoring device that connects him with Alexandria. When the Snark transmits his signal back, Nigel experiences, via Alexandria, alien communication as an electronic *liebestod:* "He felt something dark and massive move through him. There was a bulging surge, a filling— The torrent swallowed his identity" (134). At the same time this moment proves, for Alexandria, to be her moment of "resurrection." Having converted to the New Sons before her death, she is physically reborn, experiences her rebirth as a miracle and the Snark's appearance as divine intervention: "You felt Him, Nigel. My love. Perhaps. You did not. Recognize. Him. To you. For a long while. He was the Snark" (136). The New Sons take Alexandria to Mexico to display her as proof of their doctrine. Nigel's response to this is personal and quasi-mystical. He goes alone into the Mexican desert, and in a Carlos Castaneda moment he experiences a sense of cosmic oneness, as he perceives the stones turning into the "decks of an earthen ship, adrift in this high desert" (145). He now intuits that the alien has used the spent body of Alexandria—and with it "the ruined canvas" inside himself—as the means to "taste this sweet world." But he sees as well that this contact has forever changed him, has opened his doors of perception: "The looming presence sat astride the flood of perception and took it all. Before Nigel could apply the filters of his eyes, ears, skin, touch, smell—before all that, the being sponged up this strange and new world, and in the act of taking altered it for Nigel as well" (146). Nigel grasps that, beyond the way he filters the world, there lies a vast spacetime "ocean." He now realizes that if he as a human being has been forced to experience this vastness through the filter of the human condition, he has now passed beyond it: "There was something more, something larger. He snatched at it but it . . . it brushed by him. He dimly saw the fabric of something . . . and then it was gone" (149).

Nigel realizes that, still, he knows nothing useful about this alien. In the meantime, his friend at NASA, Mr. Ichino, has been broadcasting to the Snark a trove of information about humanity. Ichino's sense of his interlocutor is one of "differentness, of inexplicable immensity, as if I was speaking to different personalities each time. A mathematician, a poet—he even wrote sonnets one day, good ones—and scientist and artist. . . . He is so large, I . . ." (163). The authorities however, headed by presidential appointee Evers, see the Snark as a menace and plan to intercept it with a spacecraft armed with nuclear missiles. For the sake of First Contact, Ichino pleads with Nigel to pilot the craft. With Icarus, Nigel defied authority, and what he achieved trumped his disobedience. It is this same insubordinate nature that ultimately persuades Evers to give him the job of "hunting the Snark." Nigel does not know however that this time Evers has rigged an override. If Nigel refuses to fire the nuclear missile, Evers takes over and fires it. Evers intends to send Nigel to his death. The Snark will later point out to him that the distance between Nigel and the blast is insufficient to shield him from radiation.

Evers's plan does not work, for Nigel makes real contact with the Snark. As he flies to intercept the alien, he suddenly finds himself in telepathic communication with it. What ensues is a genuine philosophical dialogue, where two seemingly incompatible (and adversarial) entities reach common ground, and in the process of doing so they redefine the nature of their very different existences. The Snark hails him as fellow traveler. It knows of his intention not to exercise his mission. As proof of its power, it makes Nigel's craft fire a missile prematurely. It has difficulty, however, understanding the contradictory nature of the human *individual*: "Your race has a stream of tongues. You communicate with many senses. . . . These were difficult for me . . . I did not understand that each man is so different" (190). The Snark tells him that there exist other group entities, more powerful and unfathomable. Yet all these have proved easier to fathom than human diversity: "You are tensed, always moving in many directions at once. An unusual pattern. I have seldom seen such turbulence" (191). Nigel qualifies this human uncertainty as "madness." The Snark replies: "And talent. I am afraid I have already risked too much to come near" (191). Heinlein's characters throw this same sense of human uniqueness-through-unpredictability in the face of the universe. The difference is that here, it is the alien itself that defines this human characteristic. It not only defines it, but it admires it.

This dialogue deepens as just such an act of erratic human behavior prevents the two interlocutors from making physical contact. Evers overrides Nigel's refusal to launch the nuclear warhead, and he fires it. In an act of beneficence, the Snark does not detonate the missile, as doing so would kill Nigel. Instead, it chooses to outrun it, to leave: "I must. I exceeded my mandates when I approached so near. It was a calculated perturbation in my directives. A chance. I lost" (193). The Snark identifies itself as a machine made by machines, a civilization that populates the stars, making organic life more and more rare. Even so, it admits that these machines remain the "descendants of the organic cultures that arose and died" (194). Moreover, if they are immortal, they are only so until "a carbon-based life finds them. Machine societies cannot respond to your strange mixture of minds coupled with glands. They have no evolutionary mechanism to make them develop techniques for survival—other than by hiding" (194–95). For machines, disintegration of structure equals information loss: "But that is only for machines. Organic forms are in the universe of things and also reside in the universe of essences. There we cannot go" (195). Benford's machine reiterates the paradox at the heart of the Cartesian mind-matter duality. Descartes (in his *Passions de l'âme*) defines the paradoxical role of the individual human body as interface, as an entity at once in the realm of things and in that of "essences." Because we both live and think in the same body, subsequent thinkers were unable to resolve this paradox without finally denying the existence of mind (Descartes himself was forced to admit that the mind dies with the body). But the Snark, with the example of Nigel before him, sees this apparently irresolvable quandary as a creative condition. He reasons that machines, by definition, are monists, thus confined to their single dimension.

The Snark is a machine entity. Yet in this process of asking questions and formulating answers, it seems to have changed, to have become an anomaly among its kind. Because it sees the spontaneous evolution of life forms giving it "windows" into new worlds, it is clear that its encounter with Nigel has opened its windows into this strange yet fertile human condition. One is reminded of V-ger in *Star Trek: The Motion Picture*, where a machine sent to explore the universe gathers sufficient information in the process to allow it to return as a sentient being. This Snark machine has a mind. But what it lacks, and what it discovers in Nigel's humanity, are those interface aspects that lie beneath the higher reason—the ability to feel, to smell, to access emotions and dreams. This voyager, on its long, programmed voyage through interstellar space, encounters something new with human beings, and this appears to have changed it: "There, there are dreams. And what I gathered in from you is mine. The flavors. Your art and the set of your minds; only *I* am interested in those. Essences? They did not want it; perhaps the world-minds did not need it. But I . . . it is for my times in darkness" (196). Clearly, the machine civilization it represents is not monolithic. It is capable of dialogue and of evolving. The Snark therefore is a mutant: "If I functioned as my designers intended, I would not need your blessing. I would go through that night blindly. I—the part who speaks to you—am an accident" (196). As a result of this encounter, the Snark is able to embrace a cosmic vision beyond *duality*. In doing so, it foresees the course of the ensuing novels: "I am versed in many . . . animal theologies. Some say you and I are not accidents and that we shall meet again in different light. You are membrance. Perhaps we are all mathematics, everything is, and there is only one whole . . . sum. A self-consistent solution. That implies much." Nigel chuckles at this. And the Snark suddenly witnesses another form of human "mathematics" at work—that of Pascal's reed and the two infinities: "I must study that sound, laughter. There is your real theology. . . . When you make that sound you seem to have a brief moment of what it is like to live as I do, beyond the press of time. Then you are immortal. For an instant" (197).

During Nigel's encounter with the Snark, Earth control picks up a "funny signal" from the surface of the moon near Mare Marginis. The Snark corroborates this: "I have received a recognition signal . . . but you will discover them soon enough" (196). The narrative now shifts from 2015 to 2018. A young selenologist Nikka is surveying the moon near Mare Marginis when her craft loses power and crashes near a strange object half-buried in moondust—part of a coppery dome crumpled against a hill face. In a next (seemingly unrelated) episode, Nigel revisits Berkeley's Telegraph Avenue, a familiar 1960s landmark that, like everywhere in this future world, now seems new and strange and adrift. We learn from his musings as he wanders Telegraph that "the moon was thoroughly searched for the Mare Marginis transmitter," but nothing found. Nigel has once again survived the consequences of his insubordination. Long after NASA had given up, he had kept working on computer codes, trying to get a response from the Snark, all in vain. But now, suddenly, above the university buildings and the Berkeley hills, he sees a "dull yellowish glow," a silent yet portentous phenomenon. A satellite over an unpopulated area of the Pacific Northwest simultaneously spots a mushroom cloud. Nikka, stranded on the moon, awaits the rescue craft when there is a sudden brilliant flash. As she looks at the great dome, the sudden flash appeared to come from its base: "I saw it shoot at something over near the horizon" (210). She is apparently well versed in the Snark story and surmises that what she now experiences may have something to do with the Snark: "That signal the Snark mentioned, something from the moon, remember? Maybe this was it" (211). Benford weaves skillfully back and forth from these various narrative centers, setting forth the disparate threads of a single mystery that Nigel will ultimately bring together. The narrative counterpoints the synchronous musings of several separated beings whose otherwise independent thoughts form a commonly shared gestalt, beings whose efforts finally fuse into a functioning organism. The third member of this team is Nigel's friend Mr. Ichino. It is in discussion with him that Nigel suddenly, in an intuitive leap, pieces together the puzzle: The "Wasco Event" (the flash in the Berkeley sky) was itself caused by an alien object "triggered by the Marginis wreck at the same time that survey craft one oh five was getting snuffed" (233). The wreck in question turns out to be a malfunctioning spaceship. A standing order inside the ship must have made it touch off this explosion. But what was it at Wasco that suddenly caused it to do so? "If the wreck had been there [on the moon] a longish time, there might have been ancient operations on *Earth*" (225). Were some of these operations *still* going on at the time of the blast? The mystery remains, and these three individuals, collectively, will eventually solve it.

Benford the scientist takes a surprising turn here. The "operations" in question are those of "Bigfoot." The irrepressible Nigel, at the urgings of Mr. Ichino, now requests of NASA a job on the moon mission to explore the Mare Marginis vessel. In turn, Ichino agrees to "retire" to the Pacific Northwest, near the Wasco crater, in order to investigate the surroundings. Inside the Marginis ship, Nigel encounters, like Clarke's explorers in *Rendezvous with Rama*, a genuinely alien space. He also finds, among the administrators, members of the New Sons cult. He excoriated them in the past for their belief that "man is specifically wedded to this planet," thus extraterrestrial phenomena are foreign to its existence. These Sons now seek to prevent an objective search of the artifact, which risks revealing a theory of mankind's origins that refutes their geocentrism. Nigel's vision is the vastly broader one of the evolutionary process of life itself: "Life was discrete; nonlinear; a nonzero-sum game; noncommunicative; clearly irreversible . . . events multiplied, compressed, rather than merely adding. The past filtered the present" (250). It is precisely his past experience with Icarus and the Snark, as well as his intuitive sense of the human adventure, that leads Nigel to consider the possible role of aliens in human evolution. It is from his realization of this possibility that he now extrapolates the broader sense of a cosmic conflict, not simply between man and machine but as a struggle between the principles of organic and machine evolution themselves—a dynamic process that seeks its synthesis in what the Snark saw as this mathematical All. Nigel is only half joking when he calls himself "a proponent of Cartesian dualism" (247). His quest for alien contact leads him to a possible cosmic resolution of the mind-body question that underlies the man-machine struggle.

Seeking to crack the computer codes in the Marginis ship, Nigel and Nikka suddenly see images appear on the screen—their "first picture of extraterrestrial life." Nigel however finds this life oddly familiar: "On the screen something in a slick rubbery suit stood against a backdrop of low ferns . . . There were two arms and some blunt protrusions below them, with a helmet on top opaqued partially. Through it a vague outline of a head could be seen. Nigel had a conviction that the site was Earth" (260). There is more: "There was something else, taller and obviously not wearing a suit. It was covered with thick dark fur. . . . It held something like a large rock in massive, stubby hands." Faced with the mind-boggling implications of these visions, Nigel follows his ancestor Axel in Jules Verne's *Voyage au centre de la terre* and retreats into waking dreams that carry him back to prehistoric times. In an evolutionary dreamscape that resembles that of Kubrick-Clarke's Moon Watcher, he witnesses primitive man killing animals. As in Clarke, the rapid evolution of mankind suggests some form of intervention in the natural course of things: "Who taught them to make tribes, kindle fire, form the delicate web of family? So nimble a craft, acquired so quickly. It was hard to believe these creatures were driven by the slow, ponderous hand of evolution" (270). Axel, dreaming in his land that time forgot inside the Earth, conjures an anachronous vision of "quaternary man" as shepherd, and he flees in horror. Nigel envisions his prehistoric mindscape as a place of communication across the void of evolutionary spacetime. His primitive creature appears to greet him: "The palm it held up was wrinkled and matted with coarse hair around the sharp nails. Nigel raised his palm in the same gesture. He opened his mouth to reply and the image drifted away in a curl of smoke" (270). The comparison with Verne's Axel is not farfetched. For several pages later (280–81), Nigel renarrates—as did Axel in his famous reverie in chapter 32—mankind's evolutionary adventure. But Axel's vision is devolutionary—retreating from himself as apogee of evolved humanity back to life's earliest origins. Nigel's vision moves forward, up from primitive life through mankind's ongoing quest for new adventure: "Man would rather kill himself than die of boredom. Thus—novelty, gambling, exploration, art, science . . ." (282).

If Nigel here appears more the visionary than the scientist, his modus operandi proves to be a working synthesis of both. He is, in fact, one of science fiction's great sleuths, with insight that far surpasses that of Asimov's scientific detectives. His is a working combination of what Pascal described as the "spirit of geometry" and the "spirit of finesse"—hard science's rigorous method combined with a quasi-mystical faculty that reaches across reason's barriers. Working with a series of seemingly disparate occurrences, Nigel pieces together the cosmic scenario that will inform the later novels in Benford's series. The reader is witnessing, in Nigel's actions in the final pages of this novel, the organic genesis of the series of adventures that will lead Nigel, and his successors, to Galactic Center.

Nigel begins to make connections. The Snark's path has been traced to the constellation Aquila. Aquila is a small constellation, but one that experienced a surprising number of novas during the period from 1899 to 1936. It is not just the number or size of these novas that is significant: "The important point is that they're all along the same line of sight . . . As though the cause were moving toward us" (286). Following that line of sight, the Snark could be a reconnaissance ship. Or a pointer dog, "the kind that sights the quail" (286). The Marginis ship is proof that other beings—"what the Snark called organic forms, not supercomputers"—came to Earth, far back in our past: "The beings in that wreck were in the universe of essences, too, then. They came here to get something. . . . Or give something" (287). We sense the presence of "Doc" Smith's Arisians and his Children of the Lens. But where Smith remained bound by the mind-matter duality, Benford, through Nigel's agency, is striving toward a broader, scientifically plausible sense of the nature of life at the cosmic scale.

A seemingly fortuitous event occurs on Earth that allows Nigel to put more pieces of the mystery together. Mr. Ichino in his cabin rescues the wounded hunter Graves from the snow. In his backpack Graves has a tubular object and photos of primitive-looking beings he later identifies as Bigfoot. Mr. Ichino does his own intuitive guessing: "Graves had become so engrossed with his pursuit of the Bigfoot that he had lost sight of his original aim. The Wasco event first drew his attention—how did Bigfoot relate to that? Graves had not had time to ask" (290). Ichino now has his own visionary moment. By placing himself in the shoes of the alien, he re-thinks human myth and history from their alien perspective. These northern woods were once "a subterranean Eden for these early men, spilling with food and warmth and mating grounds. A holy place that evaporated one day in a spray of nuclear sleet, leaving one or two foraging bands of Bigfoot in the wilderness, small tribes who had somehow wandered from Eden and perhaps had wished to return but were now adrift in a sea of trees and a world of men, pursued by machines that beat at the air with spinning wings and carried a fanatic hunter, a man born in some place surely far distant from Eden." (291). On his faraway moon, Nigel responds to Ichino's musings. He reasons that one must not merely see the world but become *immersed in it*. By this he means that one must intuitively inhabit the core of these various human narratives—religious, mythical, or scientific—so as to be able to redirect them toward new connections and possibilities. Armed with evidence both from the Snark encounter and from the Marginis ship, Nigel now revisits a realm that is usually seen as pure fantasy—the early alien visitation story told by Lovecraft in *At the Mountains of Madness* and (in a work just published at the time of Benford's novel) in Erich von Däniken's *Chariots of the Gods: Unsolved Mysteries of the Past* (1968).[2] From what is now a broadly cosmological perspective, Nigel re-envisions this visitation as lonely, living aliens seeking animal-to-animal contact in a galaxy of machines. Did they come to warn us of something coming from Aquila? Or to pass something on to us—not to give us technology, as in *2001*, but to accelerate our evolutionary development, to create a human race whose prime specimen will be an upward striving monad like Nigel?

In the final sections of the novel, in a sort of stylistic crescendo, Benford plays with a polyphony of voices that ultimately converge in a single vision. We have something akin to telepathic intercutting between Nigel on the Moon and Mr. Ichino in the Oregon woods. The latter now "clearly realizes" that the tubular object in Graves's backpack is an alien object, "perhaps a talisman given the Bigfoot long ago, a parting gesture, something to help their survival" (294). Nigel responds antiphonically with a supposition: The aliens who crashed on the Moon had possibly a significant effect on human evolution itself. The pieces of the puzzle fall together. The ship came between 500,000 and one million years ago. A coincidence? Thus, if mankind appears an anomaly in evolutionary terms, a species that evolved in the wink of an eye, did these aliens "uplift" our species? Perhaps they "trained" us by manipulating RNA (here using physostigminian derivatives), thus passing on intelligence to our species. Nigel enters a realm of speculation where he directly challenges the dogma of the New Sons. But he concludes his reasoning neither as scientist nor as social reformer, but rather as a visionary in Emerson's special sense of the term—as a man whose sense of things forces the world to come round to it: "From Icarus to Snark to Marginis, he'd been after something he could not define, an element he felt only as a pressing inner tension. It had made him an outsider at NASA. . . . There had been moments of course . . . moments when he broke through to the edge of what he was . . . slipped free to a high vantage point. And straightway came down . . . for the moments passed as a flicker, and the realization of them came after the event itself. For that was the nature of them: they were not states of analysis, but new seas of awareness" (304).

Standing in front of the Marginis ship's "computer," Nigel's culminating moment of alien contact is one of seeming self-annihilation, his entire being literally dissolving into a "sea of awareness." Alien images occur in a frenzy that remind one of the final split screen of Abel Gance's *Napoléon* (1926): "Nigel hunched over and tracked the flow of data. The images flared into being and were erased with blurring speed. The large rat, three different views. Rotating pinwheels of orange and blue. Ancient photographs of Earth. Molecular chains. Chemical arrays. The hairy, shambling creatures. The beings in rubbery suits. Star charts. Indices. Data . . . The screen jumped. Froze. Sputtered an array of dots, lines, ripplings— . . ." (308). The screen is suddenly a faceless, blank space, from which "it came at him . . . like a trembling high shriek, in color, a mottled green blister swelling toward him. It hit him in the face and Nigel Walmsley disintegrated" (308). Nigel's moment of alien contact is a quasi-apotheosis. It contrasts with Mr. Ichino's low-key parallel encounter with Bigfoot back on Earth. Facing the Bigfoot that has come to retrieve the tubular object, Ichino in a flash knows for certain that these creatures are of alien origin: "This weapon was the final argument. It linked the Bigfoot unquestionably with the aliens" (311). As he gives the object back, Ichino becomes one with the alien. All at once he is overwhelmed by the sense of his own otherness: *"Take it. You're just as alone as I am. Neither of us has any use for the madness of man."*

The final chapter, dated 2019, is titled "Epilogue," but it is in fact an antechamber to the stars. Nigel is back on Earth, at Ichino's cabin in Oregon. The "annihilated" Nigel Walmsley is now reborn. He stirs a bowl of orange juice, watching a pit form in the juice. He makes comparisons between the swirling dynamics of the juice and the galactic center—the mundane and the infinite: "The yellow pit rippled and slowed. Flecks of rind whirled in the eddies. Down in the tip of it, in the center of the orbiting juice, a white scum formed. The shiny parabola and the angular momentum died together, dynamical twins" (313). Nigel pursues this contrast. He now sees that true understanding of the world without is to be had only through the world-annihilating voyage deep within the self. Only because he taps this inner world of "essences" can he "return himself to this linear world" long enough to pinpoint the origin of the aliens, their home star, and to understand that these aliens came here to make Bigfoot "a forerunner of us": "The—what did the Snark say—universe of essences. Organic life can have it, machines can't. The aliens came to be sure we got it, in time for the—well, the Aquila thing. Whatever is moving toward us" (318). The reborn Nigel Walmsley's vision of cosmic evolution is worth citing in its entirety:

> It's really a lot of learned tricks, you know, our past. We learned pair bonding, social mechanisms. Then big game hunting. When that ran out—all planets are finite—there was agriculture. From that came technology, computers, an information rate to match our storage rate. But the world isn't just that—there's where the computer civilizations run aground. They're right—we *are* unstable. Because there's a tension in us that comes out of how we evolved. Computers don't evolve, they're developed. Planned—to be certain, safe, secure. . . . But the thing in Aquila is a computer society that opted for the preemptive strike—to

> stop organic forms before they can spread among the stars, find the domesticated computer worlds, and inevitably destroy them. (319)

Nigel's discovery sets the agenda for Benford's epic: "We have to become better than we are . . . By entering into . . . [t]he universe of essences. The place where subjects and objects dissolve" (320). This is to be a place where the struggle between machines and organisms itself must eventually dissolve. Nigel can no longer simply utter metaphors. Physically acting out a figure of speech, he literally incarnates—in curiously Pascalian terms—mankind's role in a universal order now cast on a vast cosmic scale: "As he feels in his pocket for his gloves, he finds a coin. Elated, he tosses it up, carving the air. He catches it between his fingers adroitly and lifts it, a brassy circle. The coin, held to the yellowing sun, eclipses it. Perspective defies the innate order. The handiwork of man blinds even the awesome furnace that hangs in the sky" (320). The new Nigel Walmsley, blotting out the stars with mankind's small "sun," now states—in Zen-like manner—that the sole wisdom gleaned from all his quests is that "the looking is better than the finding." Ichino's story to Nikka about his unfixable motorcycle carries the same message: the motorcycle keeps breaking down, he wheels it home, it starts, then breaks down again, none of the conventional diagnostics apply, the phenomenon remains inexplicable, yet he goes on seeking an answer, even to this day. The antiphonic interplay between these two men continues. Nigel, in a long stream-of-consciousness monologue narrated in *discours indirect libre*, chops wood and feels himself merging, moving "homeward toward the center of the forgiving earth." Time barriers disappear as he "watches the pounding dance of hairy forms in the valley below . . . and at once he dances, splitting wood with a glinting piercing ax and coming down into a rhythmic hammering of leaping soaring flying dying . . ." (322). The passage bristles with Joycean rhythms, coinages such as "erewhonderful isle." Its streaming fusion of run on phrases, rhythms, ideas, literally embodies, as it conveys Nigel's physical being in movement, the great synthesis of organism and machine he will envision, novels later, at Galactic Center. A bit like Hari Seldon in Asimov's *Foundation* series, Nigel becomes, in the instance of this prose-poetry, the center of his own circumference. The center is dynamic, its reach vast. For now, on some new continent of "Euclidian joy," Nigel experiences the transcendent wedding of economical and clean thought to the underlying rhythms of the world, distilling order from the rough jumble of life, yet in that spinning instant to merge with life, not split the world into subject and object but to clasp it, merge, the ax hyperbolically propelled by the atoms of skin his hands as they sink into the molecular lattice of the wooden handle . . . no interface, the old dualities lapping aimlessly at the granite mass of the yea verily one self-consistent mathematical solution that gives the universe. . . ." (323)

As the novel ends, practical reality shatters these visions of mystical unity. Graves returns with helicopter and rifle to reclaim his photos and the tubular object. Nigel overcomes Graves, who escapes in his helicopter and is shot down by Bigfoot wielding the alien weapon. Once again time dissolves. Nigel's mind melds with that of his prehistoric predecessor, as he "imagines how Bigfoot saw it, a mad beating of spinning wings, Graves firing down from the hovering fury." It is the same Bigfoot he earlier saw watching him as he chopped wood, "the two of them pinned to each other along the line of sight as across the millennia an eternal wash of light encased them and fleeting dabs of perception spattered over him . . ." (325). But in the end this Joycean Walmsley yields to Huck Finn the cosmic adventurer. The visionary once again becomes the troublesome gnat in the galaxy's eye: "Above was the galaxy, a swarm of white bees . . . a spinning discus slicing space with its own definition. . . . *le's slide out of here one of these nights* as continents butted against each other *an' get an outfit, and go for howling adventures amongst the Injuns* chopping wood, trisecting Andromeda *over in the territory* Oregon to Aquila . . ." (333).

ACROSS THE SEA OF SUNS

This sequel to the 1970s novel of Nigel Walmsley's formative years, published six years later in 1983, takes him fully into the world of space adventure, as he travels from Oregon to Aquila. If *In the Ocean of Night* was Nigel's spiritual adventure, the subsequent novel moves openly into the world of cosmic adversaries and space battles. Nigel is still the wayward astronaut that nobody likes but everybody knows is the man for the job. He is still doing battle with incompetent administrators and will continue to do so until the end of the book when, with the destruction of Earth, these become irrelevant. During the novel, these administrators are helplessly stranded in space as the mech civilizations (the "thing" coming to Earth from Aquila) plunge Earth into internecine warfare. Nigel is still pursuing sexual adventures, this time with Nikka and a woman named Carlotta, who in the end undergoes a sex change. In *Ocean*, Nigel lost Shirley to the New Sons when his true partner Alexandria died. Here Carlotta, in a moment of weakness, becomes Carlos, a male unsure of himself and thus a dangerous adversary to Nigel as he seeks to lead his band of human survivors outward, toward Galactic Center. In the first novel, it was Nigel's evolutionary vision of mankind that seemed irreversible. Now his physical space voyage itself proves to be irreversible. His Earth home ravaged, the new "territory" he seeks has become a real, not a figurative, place. His is now the classic space exodus, such as we have in Heinlein's *Orphans of the Sky* (original serial publication 1941), or in Poul Anderson's *Tau Zero* (1970). The space Galileo, seeking new intellectual horizons, must now become the captain of a real spaceship, with the responsibility of bringing his crew safely to destination. Benford's *Across the Sea of Suns* is less complex than *Ocean* in the literary sense—there Nigel is a figure of such vast potentialities that he bursts the frame of the single narrative. But *Across the Sea of Suns* offers new adventures in narrative technique and style, and, most important, striking examples of scientific extrapolation, especially the modeling of alien species. In later Galactic Center novels, Benford will continue creating imaginatively stunning yet physically possible alien beings (both organic and mechanical) as he probes stranger and stranger spacetime landscapes.

Across the Sea of Suns turns upon three such alien encounters, each involving the discovery of a scientifically plausible life form that has evolved in seemingly impossible environments. Two of these encounters are Nigel's; they occur as the near-light-speed ship *Lancer*—constructed from information deciphered from the "webbed logic" of the Marginis computer—heads into outer space in search of the home world of the machine entities that menace Earth. The third involves a man named Warren, beneath the seas of an Earth now besieged by mech "Watchers." Warren will stay and fight on Earth. Nigel moves farther and farther across the sea of suns.

The novel opens with Nigel as member of the *Lancer* crew tracking a radio signal that had reached Earth from the vicinity of a star, "the red beacon of

BD + 3602147, renamed Ra," because the word "Nile" is in the transmission. The *Lancer* crew, composed of scientists and specialists, discover that the transmitting world is a planet they name Isis, a "red-tinged, Mars-like world." The date is 2056. Nigel is again in open rebellion against authority, in this case the bureaucrat Ted Landon, who remains his nemesis throughout the voyage of the *Lancer.* One of the stylistic traits of this novel is the collective "dialogue" of astronauts and scientists—an unbroken flow of run-on commentary in Houston-speak and techno-babble—as they comment on the events they observe. There are no cities or roads on this barren planet. But the scientists do pick up EM (electromagnetic) transmissions. These match the interstellar signal they have been tracking, which the scientists identify as lines from a 1956 Arthur Godfrey radio show. It seems that some alien being has received this signal from faraway Earth and has been trying to beam it back to its origin, hoping to make contact with what they believe is another organic species.

Once again, Nigel wants to physically contact the alien, while Ted settles for surveillance from a safe distance. Nigel finagles a slot in one of the "walkers," a teleguided robot that he controls from the *Lancer*. Virtually gliding over the terrain, he encounters one of these "radio beings": "A strange prickly sensation seeps into him as he watches the shadow behind a veil of dust. . . . A crisp microwave pulse bursts from it as the long rectangular head turns, jerking like a wheel on ratchets. . . . Its skin is waxy and rough, cloaking an apparatus of bones so obvious that to Nigel it seems he looks deeply into the radio being, sees the lattice-work, the boxy ribs . . . the stiff long legs that jerk as the thing picks its way among the heat-shattered rocks."[3] This bizarre creature is nonetheless a life form, "a shadow of pale blue that works forward, four legs, yes, the quadrupedal imperative." These creatures prove to be nonvocal and blind, "and sense each other only with the massive boxy radio emitters in their heads" (71). In a description reminiscent of J.-H. Rosny's depiction of his early alien Zipehuz, these creatures merge with volcanic rock ("a sexual image flits through Nigel's mind") and "slowly, their skins begin to swirl, the pale blue blushing and rippling, quick rainbows of color washing over them" (72). Though the creature is found to have many organ systems in common with earthly species, "evolution's firm hand had brushed aside the inefficient chemical kindling that ran Earthside animals. The EMs stored electrical energy in big cylindrical capacitors and discharged it in bursts when needed" (90). Back in the laboratory, analyzing the metabolism of these creatures, Nigel formulates a hypothesis: "Oxygen was in short supply down on Isis, with all the sulfur belching out to scavenge the air. So nature had used an entirely nonchemical method of making a big, energy-squandering animal. Don't lock up energy in chemical bonds and carry the mass around with the body. Instead, eat what food you can find, and then process the chemicals, keeping the energy in separated positive and negative charges. . . . No one Earthside had ever anticipated an electrodynamic digestive cycle" (91). But for Nigel theory is not enough, he wants to know "how did the EMs actually *live*? . . . The only clues would lie down there, in the raw, dim landscape" (91).

This novel, and this episode specifically, sets a running contrast in terms of narrative point of view. On one hand, there is the third-person narrator tightly focalized on Nigel's reflections, on the other, the endless run-on patter of scientists and specialists speaking over some imaginary intercom, what Nigel calls the "busy buzzwork of specialists." Nigel cannot "simply gather facts, he has to inhale the place and see it whole." His boss Ted has no interest in exploring Isis or in physically making contact with the EMs. He faults Nigel for always "nattering about the Snark and machine civilizations," all of which is "unverifiable stuff" to the professional scientist. But, true to form, Nigel defies Ted and goes down to the surface of Isis. Only through his holistic intuitive vision can he fully understand this amazingly different life form in terms of its evolutionary, cultural, and even religious context—a religion that appears to celebrate the undying tenacity of life in a machine universe. He discovers, through such contact, that the individual EM is an isolated being. With its "radio eye" and "whole body antenna," the EM is a curious avatar of Pascal's thinking reed:

> Nigel wonders, watching . . . what effect this way of seeing must have on how the EM thinks—if "think" was the right word at all. To it the world responded eternally with fragments of its own name, like a constant reassuring chorus which both tells the EM what it needs to know and reassures it of its own individuality, its importance in the very act of defining the world. If the EM did not call out its name, the world was a cipher, a silence. Yet if it spoke, the universe itself leapt into being. (97)

Nigel discovers their dwellings and "villages" where, he finds "a few elaborate designs scratched in the walls and filled with superconducting stuff." Acting as a true exobiologist, he asks: Is this art? history? literature? Scientific answers to these questions cannot be given. Yet, as he watches their ritual of joining together, he gathers a sense of how these beings survive in this forbidding landscape: "They seek the volcanoes for *food*, not for warmth." He describes how "the lava flows down thousands of meters of mountainside, a hot metallic conductor falling in the strong magnetic field of Isis," and creates an electrical current that forms a feeding loop, a "blind current following Faraday's remorseless law" (108).

From this observation, Nigel gains a poetical insight into their "electromagnetic condition," as they gather together to send forth a signal he suddenly recognizes is "the long, low tone that is from the old Earth-side radio show. They are joining together to point at the sky and send the slow, mournful impulse that will wed with the other millions of EMs and stretch across the light-years toward the Earth, a mere dot in the sky that so long ago seemed to speak to these time-weary creatures" (108). Via the narrator's tight focus, we share Nigel's new mastery of "scientific poetry," a new, powerful accent in this novel. These EMs have learned to exist on a "sluggish rustworld," "a vast and perpetual generator changing gravitational energy into useful electrical forms, an energy which no other creature but the EMs can tap . . . making possible their radio eye and with it a steady survey of the sky, searching for an answering strum of electromagnetic song, a vigil that had gone on now for aeons without machines or computers or the army of mindless servants men have made to help them. Here these creatures had harnessed the grinding workings of the planets themselves, all to survive, all to call a plaintive note into a still and silent sky" (109). Nigel's observations lead to intuitions that encompass both the physical evolution of this bizarre life form and its spiritual aspirations. Benford strives to be strikingly un-anthropocentric in his creation of a physically plausible, nonhumanoid alien. Yet it appears that he may be simply inverting the human condition as Earth scientists still see it. For in a real sense these EMs are doing what human astrophysicists do today. They persist in seeking out, beyond any simple Darwinian need to survive, some alien voice from the vast heavens in hopes of discovering that they, we, are not all alone after all.

This novel offers two other highly ingenious modelings of alien life forms that have survived and evolved under crushingly superior odds. Interwoven with the narrative of Nigel's interstellar voyage is the story of a mechanic named Warren on Earth, marooned at sea in the Pacific. The date is 2061, and Earth's situation is the following: a Watcher has appeared above Earth and is directing an invasion by aliens called Swarmers. Its purpose in doing so seems to nurture nuclear war between Earth powers. At the same time, there has emerged as counterforce in the Earth seas an alien life form—the Skimmers. As is the case with the Nigel episodes, the third-person narrative is tightly "focalized" on Warren. He is presented (again through *discours indirect libre*) as a man who "knows how engines work." He is therefore an analogue to Nigel, who supplements pure scientific knowledge with practical know-how and intuition. The science here is linguistics. And Warren, though not a scientist, shows investigative acumen when he concludes from the Skimmer messages (an apparent jumble of words in German, Japanese, English) that their lack of syntax indicates that their authors "did not seem to think of things acting but instead of things just being, so they had put down names of objects in long rows as though the things named would react on each other" (165). In an overlong scene, Warren is captured by Chinese soldiers who believe he has knowledge of the Swarmers, whom they hope to co-opt and use against their Earth enemies. This scene is intercut with a long passage in capital letters that presents the Skimmer version of the Mech invasion of their home planet and tells the story (this time with syntax) in the form of a Skimmer epic—a song of their struggle and fall, detailing their cosmology, a vision of the universe that holds organic life sacred. When Warren escapes from the Chinese, he finds himself conveyed to the Skimmer world beneath the sea. These beings have sought refuge from superior force. Their struggle has adopted the long view of the EMs. But short-lived Warren does not have this luxury. He gathers other escapees into this underwater haven. It is to be a "freehold" as in Heinlein, a place where humans prepare to launch renewed combat against their enemy.

With Warren left to fight on Earth, the action shifts to 2060, as Nigel sails interstellar space aboard the *Lancer.* The destination this time is the Ross 128 system, "the ship coming around to rendezvous with the gas giant and its interesting moon" (251). Nigel has formulated "Walmsley's Rule," which posits that any celestial body capable of developing organic life must have a Watcher orbiting it. This planet's moon, which they call "Pocks," seems to break this rule: it has a Watcher circling it, but it seems life never existed here. Like Ganymede, it is a "snowball moon," methane ice, ammonia, little or no water. Throughout his career on Earth and his trek across the sea of suns, Nigel affirms the ability of organic life—even when reduced to its most minimal form and pitted against overwhelming physical odds—to survive and evolve. This could be called Walmsley's real "rule." According to this rule, evolution remains the common denominator between dichotomies like machine and organism or mind and matter. Machines have intelligence and can use it to boost their own power by "adding on new units." Even so, they are subject to the same forces of evolution as organic life: "Self-replicating machines can forage for raw materials anywhere . . . we're hopeless, messy sods. But resources always run out. That will ensure competition" (213). Nigel's example is the Snark, "too long gone from its masters, traitor to the lathe that bore it" (206). Thus, at some level of physical reality, Nigel glimpses the possibility of synthesis of machine and organism. For why, he asks, if Walmsley's rule holds, and all worlds that might possibly bring forth life must have a Watcher, is Earth the obvious exception? He does not know that Earth now has its Watcher. But his musings point to the possibility that, in this cosmic mix, evolution may have given mankind a special role. Finding that role will be the goal of mankind's trek to Galactic Center.

On Pocks, Nigel again senses that, despite all appearances and consensus reality, there must be life beneath this new "ocean of night." The only way to know this, for Nigel, is to make physical contact. Scientific theory is one thing, tangible fact is another, and Nigel again conjures his guiding light Mark Twain ("Nigel recalled Mark Twain's remark that the wonder of science was how vast a return of speculation you got from such a trifling investment of fact" [217]). He again disobeys his "superiors," and like Huck Finn, whose adventures he now re-reads for the umpteenth time, he commandeers a bathyscape device and plunges into unknown "territory." In the depths he discovers more EMs, but different: "EMs. But not the huge-headed beasts he knew. These were slim, tall, graceful in their grave pacing . . . These were what the EMs had been before. Before the asteroid rain crushed their biosphere. Before they had to make themselves into something the Watchers would pass as perhaps machinelike" (322). What he discovers, below the ice of this moon, is a sanctuary, a bubble world that serves as millennial place before the EM fall: "They were inside a vast ball, fully five kilometers across. Inside were hills, streams, dusty clouds, high forests of blue and brown. It reminded him of those childhood toys which, shaken, show a winter scene with descending snow. Only here the liquid was outside, and within moved a trapped world of air and growth" (322). Nigel fires his laser beam, one of the figures looks up: "Had they seen him? Did they know what had happened to their race back on the home world? Deformed, beaten down but still going on. Of course they knew something. They must be the remnants of an earlier age, a time when their world sent out ships and explored the nearby stars" (322).

Nigel's intuitive vision, making links far beyond the reach of the collective scientists and their patter, desires here to span the void: "He knew their descendants, could tell them that the home world hung on still. If he could make a sign, some gesture across the abyss—" (323). It is this desire that confirms Nigel's sense of the continuity of life, and of the unique role of humanity in that continuity. For now he can both include the mechanical Watchers in that continuity and intuit how *his form of life* might have an evolutionary edge. He thus assesses the mechs: "Patient and calculating, in principle like life in their analytic function and in the laws of evolution that acted equally on silicon-germanium as it did on DNA, yet they were not fully in the world as life was, they had not risen from the crusted bonds of molecular law, did not thrive in the universe of essences—as the Snark had put it" (328–29). Again the Cartesian word "essences" suggests a unique quality that sets mankind aside, that protects it from machine extinction. In this light, mankind's advancement can come only from "special" humans like Nigel. Benford is careful here to stress that his special humans are not chosen in any predestined sense. Instead, their edge comes from a talent for empathy, desire to communicate with the alien. Nigel shows such empathy during the first EM encounter on Isis. He is sitting before a console as EM codes suddenly form pictures on the screen: "Nigel watched the picture build on the flatscreen and then . . . he felt the *implied* motion of the water, the sustained layers beneath in which brown currents carried wriggling, fishlike swarms . . . This was Isis, at a seashore unlike any men had found . . . Nigel *knew* he was seeing in some nonlinear way the world of the EMs as it had once been . . . So *this was EM heaven*" (133–34). After the

EMs inadvertently kill Nigel's companion Daffler, there is a long narrative passage that interweaves bits of commentary from the "scientific community" with Nigel's italicized musings, again presented in *discours indirect libre*. Juxtaposed with hard, unsympathetic facts is Nigel's sense of these beings' cosmic loneliness. Beaten down on their barren planet under the Watcher's vigil, they pour their vast yearning into the absurd Godfrey fragment, their sole hope to communicate across the void with another life form. Nigel's is an expression of evolutionary altrusim. This capacity for empathy for the alien could be—in the strict context of evolutionary theory—that "essential" something that gives puny mankind its unique evolutionary advantage in the vast universe. For if the universe does not feel, we humans do.

The novel ends with *Lancer* destroyed as Ted attacks the Watcher. Nigel and a small band of survivors approach the Watcher on their buoy. Ironically, they disarm it by smearing its surface with "mud" from Pocks. They board the machine entity and fight their way through the corridors, "all intensely aware they were like fishermen swallowed by a whale" (349). Inside they discover a starship, as if waiting for them. On its control screens they find a map of the galaxy. They realize the Watcher had another mission than to destroy organic life: "Something had told the ancient craft to notice pulsars and the positron plasmas that spewed out into the galaxy." Nigel concludes that something at Galactic Center is beckoning to them. His band must urgently leave the Watcher. They cannot go back to Earth—again, some predetermined destiny seems at play; but again these humans realize that their destiny depends on the freely willed action of a single man. It is Nigel who opts for going forward, not backward. And it happens: "For there was always the opening-out, and it would always win, *over in the territory.*" Once again, Huck calls, and Nigel answers: "'Let's go,' he said, and pointed at the galactic center" (353). And so ends Nigel's near-Earth saga. In this novel, it is the older man who reflects and feels his way from alien to alien to the up-and-out moment of high adventure. We will meet him again in *Sailing Bright Eternity*.

CHAPTER 6

TO THE GALACTIC CENTER

From Earth to Eternity

The next four Galactic Center novels span vast expanses of spacetime and nine years of the author's career, from 1987 (*Great Sky River*) to 1996 (*Sailing Bright Eternity*). The reader of this human saga wants to know how it will end at a place of such unthinkable magnitudes as Galactic Center. What will humanity encounter there? What kind of "humanity" will it be, and can anything vaguely human survive this encounter? Do the Nigel novels promise some special destiny reserved for humanity at this terminus? Benford delays answers to these questions for the first three novels, as he chronicles mankind's 30,000-year struggle to survive and to advance. These are all fine novels. They offer what the hard SF reader demands—mind-bending environments, plausibly extrapolated aliens, and high adventure. I will discuss these novels as space permits. My focus, however, will be on the final novel *Sailing Bright Eternity*. Here, space opera becomes fiction of a very different order. Nigel, in the first novel, by solving the mystery of alien involvement in our origins, launched mankind on a quest, physical and spiritual, to discover its role in the cosmic order of things. Action yields to dialogue in *Sailing Bright Eternity*, and Benford has the task of giving fictional voice to alien beings of the strangest sort. Doing so leads to dazzling experiments in narrative structure and tone. A good deal of this novel is discussion between "them" and "us." As these various life forms seek to explain and justify their ways to Man, Benford offers his reader philosophical discourse in the grand manner. Improbably, Nigel Walmsley returns here. But now his role is less that of Huck Finn than that of Socrates—the great ironist who turns feigned ignorance into a powerful weapon for "humble" humanity.

The first two novels of Benford's saga follow Clarke's slow advance into Earth's near future, to the year 2061, following Nigel Walmsley through his normal human lifespan. *Great Sky River* takes place some estimated 30,000 years after Nigel's "big jump" (telling time will itself become a part of the scientific adventure as Benford's novels advance toward the mind-bending spacetime of the Galactic Center). The action takes place on a planet named Snowglade. Unlike the planets in *Across the Sea of Suns*, this planet has no known location on mankind's celestial map. We learn simply that it orbits around a black hole, referred to as the Eater. *Great Sky River* is the story of Killeen Bishop, the leader of a band of cyborg-humans who are on the run and engaged in constant struggle with the Mechs. The reader here takes a sudden leap into the world of Doc Smith. Much of the novel deals with fighting, hiding, raiding—with human survivors ever on the run, heroically pitted against the dominant force of mechanical life. It is a world of tactics, weapons, battles. But there is much more. Despite the leap into vast spacetime, Killeen remains a figure cut from the same cloth as Nigel Walmsley. His quest to save his ever-dwindling band leads him to more and more alien encounters. Using the same combination of reason and intuition as Nigel, Killeen finds himself in communication with a new, more complex form of mech entity—the Mantis. Their meeting provokes the manifestation of an emissary of "the one from the Eater," a magnetic entity whose source of vital energy seems to lie in the black hole itself, and to whom the Mantis suggestively refers as "the minister of magnitudes." Killeen senses, as he engages the Mantis, that the Mantis is leading him somewhere. This encounter ends as the voice from the black hole singles out Killeen and his band. It "talks down" to them, designating them as lowly life forms. Yet, mysteriously, it urges them to "find the Argo." In what is by now the familiar ending for these novels, Killeen, his son Toby, and his band discover the super-starship Argo, commandeer it, and light out for new territory closer to the Galactic Center.

There are some very interesting things in this novel. First, there is a detailed presentation of Killeen's "enhanced" humans. Their ancestors on Snowglade, the original settlers, appeared to have had a highly developed technology. They seem initially to have co-existed—perhaps on equal terms—with the Mechs. Orbiting the planet are vast satellites that Killeen's band calls "Chandeliers," which their advanced ancestors apparently built. But now the technology that built these structures, if it was human, has been lost. It is only through oral tradition, passed down from generation to generation, that these edifices are said to be human constructs. The members of Killeen's tribe, the Bishops (some bands of surviving humans have names taken from chess, while others bear the names of baseball teams—also a cerebral game of slow patience), all have functioning electronic sensors. But they have no idea how these were built; they have become users of technology, not makers of it. As such, they carry their scientific and cultural heritage literally implanted in their bodies. Killeen carries this heritage as an "Aspect" named Arthur who appears in the text as a voice—transcribed in boldface—that (often pedantically) intrudes into his thoughts and actions. Arthur's implant antagonist is the "Face" called Bud. Mankind's mythico-religious heritage is conveyed by another officious Aspect named Nialdi—the voice of an ancient priest, whose message is usually diametrically out of line with the situation at hand. Killeen, like Nigel, finds himself frequently in dispute with the dry facts of science, as well as with various forms of authority. He takes what he needs from the past, but his "tilt" (as Benford puts it) is always forward. Like Nigel, Killeen has no time for eloquence or erudition. He and his band speak in a form of agglutinated English—examples are the word "surekill" for "totally dead," a person unable to be resurrected by means of the sophisticated medical treatments still at the tribe's disposal; or the term "mechknow," the advanced technology of the Mechs. Their speech might seem but another example of pulp primitivism. Instead, it resembles Heinlein's "speedtalk." In Benford's novel, it gives its speakers an evolutionary advantage, allowing a band under attack to move information quickly and effectively.

Second, there is the discovery, toward the middle of the novel, of a strange white building of beautiful proportions and inexplicable function, in the middle of a blighted area where Killeen's band had just skirmished with Mechs. Killeen is the sole member of the band who recognizes that this building is not "mechwork": "*Humanity* built this. That's why it's so beautiful."[1] There is another detail that strikes the reader: "On the back of the last marble wall there was a single plate of solid black. It seemed like a dark eye that gazed out on a land inhospitable. Written above it in ebony script was *NW*" (140). As Killeen ponders this edifice, he realizes it transcends the struggle between Mechs and humans that has determined his life. For if his companions dismiss this artifact, Killeen realizes that the fact that the Mechs who dominate this territory have left it standing is significant: "Tugging on his pack, Killeen frowned. If mechs honored this human place, then humans should too. Of that he was sure" (143). Killeen's vision, locked in his place and time, can go no farther: "Arthur kept repeating a name. He turned it over in his mind, trying to make sense of it. It was like no language he had ever known. Finally he gave up. Lost in time, it meant nothing, though he did note that the slow and gravid sound, Taj Mahal, rode pleasantly on the lips" (143). In the first Galactic Center novel, Nigel lost his companion Alexandria. This led to Nigel's meditation that linked her name with that other great human monument—the Library at Alexandria, which once contained all human knowledge and was subsequently burned to the ground. Were it still standing, it would testify to a stage in human advancement now "lost in time." If "NW" were in fact Nigel Walmsley, who stopped here on his way to Galactic Center, and if it were he who rebuilt this other monument to human genius, why did he do so? Did he, at the moment of his passage here, already know more about a possible evolutionary fusion of life forms than Killeen's embattled humans? Such questions remain unanswered here. All we know is that Nigel, like Kilroy, was here, and, after carving his initials in this moment of "solid" time, moved on.

Killeen will meet another "artist," a new and more sophisticated form of Mech called the Mantis. To Killeen's tribe, the Mantis appears designed to hunt human beings. It seems specifically to be tracking Killeen's tribe. But Killeen, with his enhanced intuitive faculty, begins to surmise that, instead of hunting the tribe, it may be leading them somewhere. On Snowglade, over generations of conflict between humans and Mechs, humans are not the only beings who have evolved. There are the "rennies," the renegade Mechs who, despite their origins as a group entity of interchangeable parts, have apparently had their Cartesian moment, wherein they realize that they too have a unique self, and have decided to use their wits to preserve it. The Mantis mentions, even seems to aid and abet, the rennie called the Crafter. The Crafter allies itself with Killeen's party, preying on other Mechs in order to steal the parts that keep it alive. The Mantis reveals to Killeen that the Crafter's "revolt" was part of "higher" plan that he is now called upon to execute: "I discovered the Crafter some time ago and did not report it because I knew I could use it for higher purposes. That is the only moral reason to suffer such an aberrant mind. It wished to retain all its memories, personality, everything. That is not possible when an individual mind is subsumed into the mechmind. . . . A portion of the individual experience propagates, yes. But not the whole. That would require storage space and complication without end." Human beings pack this individual self into a small and highly mobile package.

The Mantis, apparently manipulating these elements in answer to some preconceived design, calls itself an "artist." During a raid on a Mech factory led by the Crafter, Killeen discovers what the Mantis calls "art." Killeen understands that "the Crafter had all along been operating, without knowing it, under a safe umbrella cast by the Mantis. That was why the Crafter had been able to lead Hatchet into so many mech factories without getting caught" (281). But when the Crafter is discovered, the Mantis arrives to escort the humans back to the enclave. Killeen senses why this is so: "Killeen had a good idea of how the Mantis would treat them henceforth: as pets. Clients. Raw material for its art" (281). As Nigel did with his Snark, Killeen engages this alien in dialogue. The Mantis defines itself, in contrast with the human "dreaming vertebrates," by its "artistic" production. It gives an example of its "sculpture" to Killeen. This is an assemblage of human parts in large vats of "creation." The most grotesque aspect of this sculptural group is a series of male and female sex organs, endlessly copulating but ever disjointed from any whole body or person. For the Mantis, such a human being would be immortal because it engenders neither birth nor death: "I—indeed, all mechs—am used to being broken into parts, repaired, and reassembled. That is the natural way. I did not understand that for you mortal, organic intelligences, the iconography of the human body, rendered into parts, would be repulsive" (284). The Mantis evidently has not read *Frankenstein*, nor learned its lesson. For Victor's attempt to create a whole human being from scattered body parts, gathered under the threshold of a single biologically unified body, results in what humans see as a monstrosity. All at once, Killeen realizes he has already seen an example of the Mantis's art in the Mech factory: "'Those *things* we ran into?' Killeen remembered the disembodied legs and arms, the hideous sculpture of human genitalia remorselessly working—" (284). The Mantis claims his art has gotten "inside" the human being, has exposed its "inner workings": "This is one of those valuable aspects which art can capture, giving us an enduring picture of the organic world" (285). Killeen violently rejects this vision: "Those 'sculptures' of yours? That isn't humanity. It's a horror show. A bunch of freaks. You don't know shit about humanity" (285). The language is out of character for Killeen (the far-future human might, through Arthur, know what a "horror show" is, but "not knowing shit" is a bit of a stretch). If anything, this is author Benford speaking here with passion. He is perhaps remembering the protagonist Wilson of C. L. Moore's classic story "Vintage Season," who violently condemns another such "artist" of indifference, the time travelling "composer" Cenbe, whose great "oratorio" is inspired by witnessing a devastating meteor strike on a town, a disaster which he, as future human who knew this past, could have prevented. The spirit of Nigel finally dominates this exchange. Killeen and his band burst into laughter at the Mantis's pedantic pronouncements. For Nigel, laughter is mankind's moment of eternity. Here again the sound utterly confounds the Mantis.

A third entity intrudes into Killeen's discussion with the Mantis. A "voice" now appears in boldface, and addresses Killeen: **"I have searched long and wary for you. . . . You truly are the locus termed Killeen?"** (288). When it "senses a machine mode," the Mantis replies: "Yes, and amply honored to receive you. I hope this does not bode for an early intersection of our world with the massless ones?" (289). The voice rejects this "intersection," and the Mantis as well: **"These matters are dealt with at a higher level, I presume you know"** (289). It becomes obvious that the Mantis and this being speak a same language. It is also clear that the Mechs are subservient to this higher level of being. When the Mantis bows to this "minister of magnitudes," the latter proclaims that it itself is merely the messenger for a "motive entity": **"The motive entity which bade me deliver the earlier message—that in-**

ductance again wishes to speak to you" (289). This "inductance" is a being that **"cannot speak directly, but must drive its meaning through electroflux and arching currents. It lives far further into the Eater than do I"** (290). A struggle now takes place within the mind of Killeen, as if for his soul, between this higher entity and the Mantis tempter: "Into his sensorium coiled a dark presence. It was the Mantis returning, made bold again" (291). The Mantis now speaks to Killeen's inner self in the cool voice of his aspect Arthur. The latter tells Killeen what he is dealing with: *"A magnetic mind. A personality of dimensions unknown in material beings. It lives in the complex warpage of magnetic stresses, with its information content stored in waves which suffer no damping. In its way, it is another facet of immortality" (291).*

But this remains the Mech vision of things. The "messenger" now speaks directly to Killeen. Its message is neither a riddle nor an explanation—it is a call for action: **"Ask for the Argo."** But as this magnetic voice falters, the Mantis regains ground. It now articulates the Mechs' limited vision of organic life: **"The drive to exterminate you comes from higher up in our society . . . One is to *never* allow the organic beings to link up. They are unimpressive overall, but together can be a nuisance"** (293). Through this exchange, Killeen is "charged up" by the glimpsed possibility of other life forms, at the Galactic Center, far into the Eater: "*Other life!* Intelligent, alien, but at least living. Maybe even other humans, around the stars. It was an intoxicating notion" (294). This intuition allows Killeen to defeat his inner Mantis, to defy its sense of finality and closure, to assert his human self, which he defiantly names: "He gathered himself, amped his systems, and bellowed: 'I'm still here! Killeen! *Give me my message!*'" (293). At this, the Mantis withers away, the clouds open, "the voice boomed forth again." The message is an imperative. It purports to be the voice of his dead father Abraham, who now claims to be alive. And it tells him to move on: **"Do not rebuild a Citadel. They will crush you there. Believe you this of me, for I still live, and I am your father"** (294). Between Killeen's band and other humans, there will be a divide, much like J. D. Bernal's "dimorphic split," where one part of humanity stays home to tend the human "zoo" while the other part "gropes unsteadily" into the unknown. The Mantis enlists in the cause of the stay-behind humanity on Snowglade, no doubt in order to hasten its destruction through its treachery. Killeen will discover the Argo, a fabulous starship. He, son Toby, and his crew will take off again. But despite the ship's name, their goal is not the golden fleece but new cosmic adventure. Once again, they are space Hucks, lighting out explicitly for new worlds. The characters change, but the same drive toward new "territory" abides.

The next novel, *Tides of Light* (1989), finds these space Argonauts seeking a planet where Mechs are not present. Benford seems to promise a replay of SF's New Eden scenario. As with Heinlein's Hugh Hoyland and band in *Orphans of the Sky* (1950), or with the crew in Poul Anderson's *Tau Zero* (1970), such a paradise planet is found at the end of a long and arduous spacetime trek. Here the planet Killeen and his tribe find—and which they over-optimistically baptize New Bishop—is instead what the Strugatskys call an "inhabited island," a place full of unexpected and unpleasant surprises. For they not only find Mechs on the planet, but they discover unfriendly humans as well. These two entities have apparently been at war for a long time. The Mechs on this planet have been programmed to compete with humans in a pseudo-Darwinian manner. But "survival of the fittest" has taken its toll on them, for they have devolved, have become less disciplined and less effective. The humans have also devolved. Rather than maintaining the democratic social structure of the Snowglade tribes—a structure wherein Killeen's leadership position must constantly answer to tribal approval—they have fallen under the leadership of a religious fanatic—His Supremacy—who has declared jihad on the Mechs. His Supremacy is a fanatic who is more than willing to sacrifice his precious human followers in the name of a higher abstraction. This is anathema to Killeen and the Bishops, who cherish their individuality and the few, ever-diminishing human lives that remain in their tribe.

There is a third presence on this planet, an alien race called the "Cybers." Killeen and his humans have, over the many years of their existence, become enhanced humans. Not only have they grown physically bigger—when Nigel meets up with Killeen and Toby in the final novel he is a "dwarf" half their size. But they are now "cyborgs"—humans who have incorporated mechanical and medical devices, as well as memory implants, into their fleshly bodies. They are now partly mech themselves. The Cybers offer an even more complicated amalgam of organic and mechanical parts. The life form that is their base is insectoid—a bow to pulp SFs "bug-eyed monsters." Yet their carapace is equipped with numerous mechanical appendages. What is more, they are consummate users of machines. They use "cosmic strings"—Benford imagines in great technical detail a species capable of putting abstruse theoretical entities at work as functioning machines—literally to slice into this planet's core and extract its mineral wealth, collapsing its entire ecosystem in the process. Their purpose in doing so is apparently to convert matter to energy that can be used to further the expansion of organic forms in the galaxy. To this end they have created the Skysower, a massive entity circling the planet; Killeen first thinks it is a machine, but ultimately he discovers it to be a living being: "He could see all of the Skysower now. It curved like a slender snake that smoothly turned head over tail. The far end was just piercing the atmosphere. Undulations ran like waves in a long string, driven by the supersonic collision of this gargantuan living being with its blanket of air."[2] As his ship lifts off, Killeen sees that the real purpose of the Cybers' mining of this planet is literally to "sow" the stars with organic life forms: "The forests of umbrella-topped trees—they must have grown from the Skysower's own seeds. Snatched up on the harvesting vines, they had now been carried aloft. Some deep biochemical command had activated their stores of fuel. Far from being a mech energy resource, as Killeen had guessed, these trees were now expending their stored chemical energy to launch themselves away from their mother planet" (387). Killeen's "grey aspect" comments on this process: "This creature . . . is spreading its progeny. They leave it here, at the top of its arc, with maximal velocity. They can easily reach the outer precincts of this solar system. From there they can drift to other stars. Seeding, pure and simple" (388). We move from string theory to this part mechanical–part organic "string," which serves as a cosmic slingshot to spread its organic progeny to far distant star systems.

When Killeen and his band reach New Bishop, the Argo is taken over by the all-powerful Cybers. On that ship are the "Legacies," a set of documents that record the far-distant history of humans, back before the high period of the "Chandeliers" to legendary origins on a place called Earth. The capture of these documents causes a rift in the Cyber culture. One faction wants to destroy all humans who, under His Supremacy, have become pests. But another faction—that led by the Cyber Quath—surmises from the presence of these Legacies on the Argo that Killeen and his band may be on some predetermined mission, the ultimate goal of which is to destroy Mech dominance and preserve organic life in the galaxy. Quath and Killeen thus become allies. The climax comes when Killeen confronts His Supremacy and is about to be exterminated by him and his fanatical followers. Quath, who has been following the Bishop band, intervenes: "Killeen felt a squeezing pulse of electromagnetic energy hum past his shoulder. It refracted the air with its wake and struck His Supremacy solidly in the head . . . [Killeen] realized in a rush that it was his Cyber who had fired the bolt. He sat up amid cries and shouts" (370). It turns out that when Killeen peels back His Supremacy's skin, he was a Mech: "Mechtech . . . Micro'tronics."

Quath's faction now prevails; their leaders, The Illuminates, decree that the Legacies shall be returned to the Argo, and Killeen and his band shall be allowed to continue their journey toward Galactic Center. Quath accompanies the humans back to the starship, bringing the Legacies. The Magnetic Mind had appeared briefly to the humans on New Bishop; it had spoken of Killeen's dead father Abraham as the key to the mystery that awaits them at the end of their journey. Yet Killeen is left with nothing but mysteries. First, there is the mystery of the Legacies themselves:

> His Grey Aspect droned for attention. Her voice came slowly, as though working across the abyss of time that separated Killeen from the High Arcology Era.
>
> *There were records . . . incomplete . . . from a time long ago . . . before the Chandeliers . . . before even the First Comers . . . from . . . a culture of legendary origin . . . called Earth. . . . In those times, humanity scratched out its destiny . . . in soil . . . under tortured skies. . . . Yet men lived lives of meaning still . . . despite their small stature . . . in the scheme of things. . . . Humanity has found zest and verve . . . before . . . in the shadows of vastness . . . in a place called Greece.* (402)

Second, there is the mystery that surrounds the Cybers. Quath, it turns out, will accompany Killeen on this voyage. But why? Moreover, she is bringing with her the cosmic string, a machine of enormous mass: "That great scythe would follow them toward the Eater, Quath said. So the Illuminates had decreed. They had stopped the gutting of a world to send the ring along with Argo. Halted the building of their gray warrens. Interrupted the labors of millions of Cybers. For what, no one yet knew" (401). Third, there is the "enigma of the electromagnetic being. Somewhere ahead it lurked, tied to the disk of the Eater." And finally, there is the mystery of Abraham himself:

"Perhaps Abraham was a key to all this. Yet how could his father, lost at the fall of the Citadel, figure in the deliberations of a tenuous magnetic mind? Could such a being revive those long dead?" (401).

The key word here is "yet." The vast history of humanity has made Killeen feel small. He is the maverick captain of a ship whose command remains vulnerable, at the mercy of the votes of his tribe. His hold on control remains tenuous. He sees himself as a speck in the cosmic wash of things: "He looked up into the colossal sky. Fingers of knotted fire worked in molecular clouds. Storms frayed against the stars. Tides of light ebbed and flowed with ponderous majesty. Amid it all, Argo sailed on, a mote" (402). Yet, in another Pascalian moment, the long lost example of Greece makes him realize (as had Nigel before him) that humanity's strength comes from its ephemeral existence. This is Killeen's "Nigel moment," when he seems to realize that the strong leader is a combination of vision and instinct to survive, one whose strength is to believe, against all odds, that there is a "yet," a future adventure for mankind.

The next novel in the series, *Furious Gulf* (1992), shifts the narrative focus from Killeen to his son Toby, who comes of age as the Argo carries its crew toward the Galactic Center. In the previous novel, we saw Killeen several times obliged to relinquish his role as leader of the Bishops. We have witnessed his doubts about his ability to lead. We have seen that ability put to the test when he takes on His Supremacy—acting on a Walmsley-like intuition that could have turned very wrong for his clan had not Quath intervened. In *Furious Gulf*, Killeen the captain is now a figure like Tennyson's Ulysses, pushing his men to "sail beyond the sunset." Or, more in keeping with Benford's fascination with nineteenth-century American literature, Killeen is Captain Ahab, obsessed with reaching the Center at all costs, and willing to push his crew beyond its limits to do so. Through his actions, he creates conflict between himself and his son, who will eventually strike out on his own once the Center is reached. Along the way, the Argo appears to be guided by the same electromagnetic entity that set it on its course. Encounters with Mechs are avoided, and the vessel finally reaches port at a sort of space station at the edge of the Eater, the all-consuming black hole at the center of the galaxy. The humans who run this station are space merchants who allow the Bishops to remain, provided they pay heavy fees. These merchants also seem strangely interested in the Legacies the Argo is carrying. We learn of the "higher" intelligences that inhabit the Center. But what are they? Are they highly evolved Mechs, or organic entities, or some combination of both? Mystery remains as to their identity, as it does about the "destiny" that has guided the Bishops here. There seems to be some overarching design that involves reuniting three generations: Killeen's father Abraham, Killeen, and Killeen's son Toby. Resolving these mysteries is put on hold as the Mechs attack the space station and Toby escapes into a strange landscape of "solid time"—the "esty"—where he not only finds temporary sanctuary but runs into a very, very old Nigel Walmsley. Apparently Nigel has survived his adventure on Pocks and lives on, benefiting from cryonics and time dilation at the Galactic Center. Nigel's memory spans the entire human saga. It is his memory, coupled with his now legendary intuitive powers, that appears to hold the key to the Bishop mystery. If this novel began as Toby's novel of formation, it is his discussions with Nigel in the ever-shifting sanctuary of the esty that complete his education and prepare him for his role to come. These discussions—which help the reader bridge the gaps in what clearly emerges as a human adventure—carry over into the final novel of the series, *Sailing Bright Eternity* (1995).

This final novel merits very close attention. It places its human protagonists in the most nonhuman environment modern science can imagine. It also reveals that the true center of this 30,000-year odyssey is not a physical place—Galactic Center—but a single human being—the ubiquitous Nigel Walmsley. In the course of his saga, Benford has evoked a number of science fiction models. There was Clarke's Space Odyssey series in the first novels; then there was Doc Smith's space opera, and even Edgar Rice Burroughs, as Benford's humans revert to a primitive tribal and warrior state. Finally, at galaxy's center, we have the unraveling of a vast cosmic mystery. The reader is reminded of Asimov's Foundation series. Two years after the publication of *Sailing Bright Eternity*, Benford published a "sequel" to Asimov's original Foundation novels, *Foundation's Fear* (1997). In this final Galactic Center novel, the reader discovers that—just as the center of Asimov's imperial saga is the place where it all started, Trantor, and its center the single man who envisioned it all—Hari Seldon—so the center of Benford's galactic mystery proves to be the man who, back in Earth's twentieth century, began the task of deciphering that mystery: Nigel Walmsley. The quest began when Nigel made contact with the Snark; it ends with his dialogue with the "bird" who carries the message from the "Highers." These are beings said to be "beyond comprehension" for all the contending "phyla" of the universe—organic, mechanical, silicon-based, or formed of pure plasma.

In relation to the three previous novels, the fictional form Benford employs here changes radically. Though there is plenty of discussion and dialogue between different entities, human and alien, in the earlier novels, they remain adventure stories whose fictional models range from Mark Twain to Doc Smith, from Melville's Ahab to Heinlein. For lack of a better description, I would call *Sailing Bright Eternity* a philosophical novel. In a formal sense, it reminds me of a work like Voltaire's *Micromégas*, where, in staged dialogues, puny humans are brought to interrogate mighty forces from distant galaxies about the mystery of the universe. In Voltaire's work, in answer to mankind's query as to its role in the cosmos, the extraterrestrial Micromégas presents the human seeker with a large book. On opening this book, the latter discovers the pages are blank. Nothing is revealed except mankind's arrogance in daring to ask such questions. In Benford's novel, even though Nigel does push the human envelope to its extreme limit, he gets answers as to the human condition. For Voltaire, mankind's vocation, in the face of the ineffable, is not to ask useless questions, but to *travailler sans raisonner*. Nigel, in contrast, both reasons *and* works, pushing and finagling his way to insights and answers that lead him all the way to what seems the highest force in the cosmos, but which may only be another link in an ongoing evolutionary chain. He gets answers, even though they are elusive and tentative. But the "book" at the end of Benford's saga is not blank. The book is that of evolution. It has neither covers nor ending, and in its "pages" humanity's quest remains open.

Hard SF proponents often proclaim that it is the sole literature today that deals with the philosophical and social issues raised by the advancement of science and technology. In fact, the major moments in the origin and development of science fiction occur when some scientific discovery causes a radical shift in worldview. Since the Western "scientific revolution," the task of formulating these shifts has fallen to philosophers. Notable examples are Descartes and Pascal in France, Locke and Hume in England, Kant in Germany, Emerson in the United States, the followers of Darwin—Spencer and Bernal—in England. In his Galactic Center novels, Benford assumes this same role, exploring mankind's possible relation to new scientific paradigms. He takes his reader to scientifico-speculative vistas that surpass any that mankind has previously encountered—in reality or in fiction. His protagonists travel through landscapes of massive gravitational fields, of electron-positron plasma—supremely uninhabitable places for humans. But unlike rationalist philosophers like Pascal, for whom there are only two entities in the universe—us and it—Benford's science imagines (and engineers) forms of sentient life that could possibly inhabit such places. If his universe is ultimately uninhabitable for mankind, it is not a void. Bright eternity has many conceivable forms of Life. Here is where Benford's science ends. For if he is to place human beings in this environment and to make the case that, as species, they are most apt to "sail" this vast universe, then he must abandon physics for philosophy. And beyond philosophy, the next step is mysticism. In order to take his reader on this journey, Benford must first make us, as Clarke did with his explorers on Rama, abandon dualistic thinking and embrace a world that opens out into the possibility of an infinite series. If the central struggle of previous novels appeared to be between organic forms (us) and machines, the reader must now abandon this oversimplified vision as well. The final forms of life encountered on this voyage are formed of basic forces—electromagnetic entities, plasma life, the Eater described as a "datavore." For all these possible forms of sentient life, Nigel's role, in this final novel, is to serve as means of communication between them. As Nigel meets—and communicates with—all sorts of alien beings, the reader is offered a vast galactic panorama of what J.-H. Rosny called "pluralistic" evolution, where Life forms are forever blending, fusing, separating, in some new form of dynamic equilibrium. Nigel's final role, in all of this, is to communicate this process to us, the readers.

Thus, despite the enormity of the Galactic Center, Benford's mankind remains at the center of its great tapestry. Though far vaster entities refer to us as "primates" or even "noughts," we still appear to have a unique role to play in the cosmic process. This is a problem that philosophy and religion, not physics, can address. When the Snark refers to Nigel as belonging to the "universe of essences," we think of Descartes. The Cartesian *cogito* places humanity in a qualitatively different realm from the rest of material existence. Materialist science all but eradicates this difference. But rational mankind has other gambits. Spinoza, for instance, declares the universe itself a rational mind—his famous *deus sive natura*—a higher order which imperfect humans no longer fully understand. There is a bit of this in Benford's Phylum beyond all Knowing, a realm of higher order and reason where humans (and to a lesser degree other orders of life as well) remain false notes in some divine symphony. But whereas for the rationalist this universal order is fixed, subject neither to time nor change, Benford sees this higher order as provisional, a dynamic rather than static equilibrium. In such a universe, the sole constant *is* change itself. Ultimately nothing is stable; all must eventually pass, even Nigel. If humans have access to the "essential," it is only as instants of immortality: Wordsworth's spots of time, Proust's involuntary memory, Nigel's laughter and loves. Given this, it seems impossible that any single human could live some 35,000 years, and physically arrive at Galactic Center in order to unravel mysteries of colossal magnitude. No previous philosopher, or science fiction writer, has given humanity such an improbable role in the cosmic working of things. Asimov's Hari Seldon created the design that allowed the world of Foundation to coalesce around his theories. But what designed his destiny? The same can be asked of Nigel. To these philosopher's questions, the only possible responses seem to be two: skepticism or optimism. Voltaire is a skeptic. Benford offers a physically mindbending, alien-multiplying galaxy, operating according to known or conceptually possible laws of science. But given the extreme material hostility of this world to us puny humans, does he in the end do any more than restate Leibniz's optimism, proclaiming that this is the best of all possible galaxies because Nigel is in it? Benford's novel puts his reader at the crux of the problem of SF extrapolation. What, ultimately, is the utility of its speculative reach as vehicle for philosophy?

We remember, however, that Nigel is shaped by another philosophical-literary model, a uniquely American one. All the titles of Benford's six novels refer to bodies of water and/or the act of travelling on it: ocean, sea, tides, river, gulf. This is the author's central metaphor for mankind's relationship to an increasingly inhuman universe. Arthur C. Clarke uses seas and oceans as the mirror analogue of outer space, where exploration of the familiar becomes just as alien as exploring deep space. But Benford's persistent use of water metaphors has another origin. In all of these novels, Nigel refers to or cites Mark Twain, whose journey into the undiscovered territory was down the Mississippi River. This connection between river travel in America's past and space travel in its future is made clear in a passage in *Sailing Bright Eternity*. The situation is the following: Nigel, Killeen, and Toby are all moving through different "lanes" of solid time in the esty. These lanes contain worlds "carved" from unstable "timestone" that reproduce simulated habitats, some from far distant Earth. One of these habitats, which Toby enters, is the Mississippi River in the steamboat era. Toby signs on to one of these boats as navigator. The following description of life on the river is adapted, almost verbatim, from Mark Twain's nonfiction work *Old Times on the Mississippi* (1876): "Under Mr. Preston, [Toby] was coming to see that the face of the wedded water and metal was a wondrous book, one in a dead language to him before but now speaking cherished secrets. Every fresh point they rounded told a new tale. No page was empty. A passenger might be charmed by a churning dimple on its skin, but to a true riverman that was an italicized shout, announcing a wreck or reef of wrenching space-time Vortex about to break through from the undercrust of timestone."[3] By making this explicit parallel between vast spacetime adventure and this specific, parochial experience of American mankind and its river frontier, Benford seems to say the following: if science's galaxy can be compared to a river, mankind's role, as it travels that river, is to decipher its secret story, a story in which humans are perhaps *the* crucial actors. If nature is a "book," it can only exist at that dynamic interface where metal (human technology) and water (nature's material forces) "wed." It is here that the otherwise dead language of physics comes alive, can "speak its cherished secrets." Humans then, if they cannot physically withstand nature's forces, can still operate on a different level—that of nature's interpreters—in other words, its *storytellers*. The realm of science is the river; mankind's realm, in this alien world, is the realm of science *fiction*.

But Benford makes clear with his parallel that, if "every fresh point they rounded told a new tale," then the storyteller cannot be a mere passenger but a "true riverman," one capable of foreseeing the "wreck or reef" ahead in order to avoid it, in order to continue on as explorer and chronicler of mankind. Nigel, the central voice of Benford's saga, speaks with the authority of Emerson's self-reliant man. He is mind in motion, Man doing, the restless center who in an undulation of power and form generates visions that, if they eventually collapse on themselves, create the energy for another projection. Emerson's philosophy describes the dynamic relation between mankind and nature that Huck Finn incarnates. But despite appearances, it is not necessarily a "democratic" vision. For Emerson, there are passengers and there are rivermen. A figure like Nigel corresponds to what Emerson called a "representative Man." These are figures, like Caesar or Napoleon or Goethe, who summarize the most dynamic types of humanity. But even though individual man may be a dwarf of himself, Emerson's dynamic universe cannot, as with Heinlein's Lazarus Long, be the sole creation of a single man. It involves groups of human beings, capable of evolving in spacetime. Thus Nigel has as his progeny Killeen and Toby. As *descendents* of Huck Finn, he, and Toby in this passage, must learn to ply the dangerous tides and waters of space travel, to adapt, survive, and carry on the search for new "territory" where humans continue to act, and—in this novel where Nigel does more talking than acting—take the story of mankind to the furthest reaches of the human imagination. Unlike Micromégas's blank book, Nigel's is the living one of this cosmic river, where the dead language of metaphor is once again made to speak to those who know how to navigate it. For Emerson's representative Men, there are no absolutes, only comparatives. For Benford, Nigel is special because he proves to be a better navigator than most.

Benford's final Galactic Center novel gathers many of the characters from previous novels to orchestrate a grand "syntony" in which the mystery that began with Nigel's contact with the Snark is finally unraveled, if never fully solved. This unraveling is worth tracing. Toby, still separated from his father and the Bishops, meets Nigel again in the "Wedge," and Nigel tells Toby of the 35,000-year-war between the "Naturals" and the Mechs. The Wedge is a vast spacetime habitat at the edge of the Eater that has become a refuge for Naturals, with pockets containing different environments. It bears resemblance to Philip José Farmer's Riverworld but is eminently less stable and is now under a sort of final siege by the Mechs. We learn from Nigel that the Naturals—beings who evolve via Darwinian natural selection—once created the Mechs as war machines (a tip of the hat to Fred Saberhagen's "Berserkers"). He explains that the Mechs have been guiding Killeen and now Toby, using them to find father Abraham, who is alive and somewhere in the Wedge. Their goal is to realize "The Way of the Three," which is done by uniting three generations of human DNA. But it seems that not just any DNA will do. The Argo has carried the Legacies, and the Mechs have been protecting this voyage in hopes of deciphering its scattered archaic data. What they are after, it is now revealed, is the secret of human pleasure, something Nigel has given plenty of examples of, but something their mechanical evolution has denied them. This secret is said to be encoded in the specific genes of Abraham, Killeen, and Toby. They hunt down these three throughout the esty, in order to assemble the genetic code. A good deal of the novel is given over to this hunt and, in the manner of a travelogue, to the various worlds encountered along the way.

In a later dialogue, this time with Killeen, Nigel further explains that the early life form in the galaxy (humans?) that created the Mechs realized the danger involved in their act. Organic forms are slow to redesign themselves, unwilling to give up, because of anthropocentric ideas like "the human form divine," the bodies that evolution created. So, in the manner of Asimov's laws of robotics, these early organics embedded a fail-safe deep in the Mech design codes—The First Command. Once activated by this command, these codes first cause great pleasure, then death—a Mech *liebestod.* But these ancient organics subsequently lost the trigger code. Some clues may be found in the Legacies, but this information seems hopelessly scattered in human DNA. If anywhere, it still abides in human junk genes, because inactive genes pass down intact, without undergoing evolutionary change. But (a bit like the Trinity) no single strand of DNA can contain the whole code. Three generations of a same family are needed, thus the three Bishops. Killeen now has a flash of insight of his own. He sees that, because the Mechs are blinded by the fact that they see humans as enemies, they automatically conclude that we want to stop them from getting the pleasure code. But this proves to be fatal reasoning, as with those who mistake the location of Asimov's Second Foundation because they are unable to think in a social scientific manner. The Mechs are blind to the possibility that humans *wanted them to find the code*, that the code is in fact a trap.

Eventually, in a spacetime maze full of different manifestations of Killeen and Toby, the two real entities finally meet. The Mantis, however, has been hunting them down and now garners the DNA of both. But a higher entity appears, speaking as a voice to Killeen, reassuring him: "Do not think we are neglectful of you. We do hope you live to help." The same voice speaks throughout to the ever-present Nigel through various animal forms—first a raccoon, later a bird. The raccoon tells Nigel of higher orders but can do no more than describe them as what they are not: "Did you think the galaxy was a simple division between organic forms and mechanicals?" (148). It speaks of "Magnetic fields. Collaborations of organics and mechanicals. And inscrutable symphonies of all three, forms that I can but glimpse. . . . They may function outside our conceptual spaces, their acts indistinguishable from natural law" (148). As with the Ramans, we must think in threes and beyond. Then, in what is not or cannot be told, we can glimpse the possibility of four, or five—a possible infinite series.

The structure of this novel, with its series of short, almost staccato chapters, builds separate foyers of action and insight—much in the random manner of the ever-shifting esty lanes, which appear and are invaded and destroyed by Mechs, all in a flash. Nigel, Killeen and Toby have separate adventures, all interspersed with interesting revelations. In one brief scene, Nigel meditates on the Cauchy Horizon: "He remembered the gauzy filaments hanging in that strange sky. And he thought of the Cauchy Horizon, beyond which physics could not see. As if even God had a sense of metaphysical modesty" (152). But now, in a new scene, a voice answers him from beyond that very horizon:

> *So plasma entities of immense size and torpid pace will drift through a supremely distant era. Sure and serene, free at last of ancient enemies.*
>
> *Neither the thermodynamic dread of heat death nor gravity's gullet can swallow them. As the universe swells, energy lessens, and the plasma life need only slow its pace to match. By adjusting itself exactly to its ever-cooling environment, life—of a sort—can persist forever. The Second Law is not the Final Law.* (153)

But this is merely one voice in a polyphony of voices, and its claim of finality is suspect. If physics cannot currently see beyond this horizon, it does not mean there is not a beyond.

In another scene, Toby evokes the Galactic Library, which he had heard about from his grandfather Abraham: "Citadel Bishop had housed a library. One superior to that of any other Citadel. . . . His grandfather had told him once that each point stood for a whole roomful of the old-timey books. . . . He had seen a picture of one of those. 'Our human library?'" (162). Nigel tells him it contained works from all the organic races that came before the Mechs. Because of this, they want it to "complete some pattern they desire."

Once Toby realizes what this library is, it appears right in front of him, in this lane of the esty. Like the Taj, it seems to be made of something more enduring than timestone: "The pyramid was pure stone, not timestone, and so squatted as a dark mass lit by the smoldering glows beneath. Far above, the esty curved over, bounding the Lane" (163). Toby sees it as "a kind of . . . museum," and once it materializes as a seemingly fixed object in this world of spacetime flux, Nigel can claim to be its "curator." This is an example of the riverman reading the depths of the spacetime river. What before was a mere ripple on the surface of time is now claimed to *contain* the story of mankind's relation to the Mechs. Nigel in turn becomes empowered to tell that story, to fix it in narrative time before it disappears again: "The mechanicals obey biological logic, just as we do. They were first made by Naturals, just like our computers on Earth. Later they replaced their parent species, often on worlds made damn near unlivable by some stupidity of their parents" (167). Nigel physically visited such worlds on his trek to Galactic Center, his mortal body is their repository, their library. Abraham also has come in the flesh with his own genetic library. Toby wonders why the library's patriarch and Nigel, as living embodiment of its content, were brought here. Are these perhaps the fixed places where "the Old Ones come to read?"

The mystery is now identified as that of mankind's role in the evolution of the universe. But first more things must unfold. The Magnetic Mind now speaks, and Toby, emboldened, asks where his father and grandfather physically are. The Mind, instead, warns of an impending Mech attack. Nigel sees that the Mechs have made another evolutionary leap: "They've found a way to populate the Magnetic Mind's own field lines. . . . Pried open the magnetic canopy over us" (169). All at once the library is taken, Toby flees, Nigel falls. Yet he returns in later episodes, where we learn that, just as this pyramid is not "real stone," so the Nigels we have met along the way are merely copies of the original. The novel advances by scenes like this, where action interrupts talk, and complex yet apparently random goings-on create a rich tapestry of information that interludes of reflection seek to unravel. In the final pages, these layers of data coalesce to give at least a tentative sense of mankind's role in this cosmic web of forces. Nigel, the man of many faces, now takes on a new role—that of court jester. At each step, appearing to Killeen, to Toby, to the Mantis, and ultimately to the alien Quath, he informs and goads, taunting the higher powers to reveal a true order of the universe—a revelation that, significantly, never comes.

As he moves through this landscape of ultimately incomprehensible forces, Nigel remains the incarnation of *us*—the human monad facing massive cosmic entities. Nigel describes himself as a dwarf to the more evolved Killeen. Yet it is his stability that remains his greatest advantage. For in all of his myriad adventures, he (a bit like the unchanging junk genes that have conveyed the code across millennia) has not evolved. Thus, through all of his travels, he continues to see the vast workings of the Galactic Center *sub specie aeternitatis*, as a human from the late twentieth century would. From this perspective, he understands why three humans of a same family were able to carry the fatal code across an improbable future of genetic randomness—because humans, despite their insignificant life spans, have learned to overcome their mortality through *connection*, the drive to hand down information, to create libraries and build Taj Mahals that defy the ravages of time. When Nigel confronts the Highers through the intermediary of the telepathic bird, he hears them describing the mechanicals as "working on the Grand Problem," which results in millions of "primate" species perishing. He responds with "species-specific sarcasm." He is told by the Highers that "they cannot be partial to primates." Yet he is physical proof that something, throughout cosmic evolution, *has been partial* to his particular species of primate. He sees this human culture, as well as Killeen's and Toby's, as a "warrior culture." He presents its struggle, even in times of peace, as an "intelligent cowardice," conducted in the name of self-interest. He now gives this process a broad, quasi-metaphysical, sense: "To pass on your own precious genes, some would say, but it was for more than that: [it was for] the Self, *lonely and communal both*, and knowing the tension stretched between these two poles" (305). This is not the rationalist self but the onward-striving monad. Here, incarnate in Nigel and the Bishops, this monad defines itself as dynamic center to an ever-expanding circumference that pushes against the Cauchy Horizon, the Eater, and other absolute limits.

Given his moveable position in the order of things, Nigel is able to unzip the mystery. He knows that once the Mechs get the necessary genetic information, their fate is sealed. He knows why Abraham was spared: to be brought here to give his part of the puzzle—a piece of the genetic code which he has carried in a shared piece of song, an example of the cherished and preserved "Mose Art." Through his dialogue with the Higher Orders, he learns that they began as clay—a ceramic-cellular life form—that evolved into a Phylum whose central property (it claims) is its unknowability. In a Voltaire-like comparison, the higher entity sees Nigel's type of organism as unaware of this ceramic life form as our own genes are unaware of the organism that carries them. If our organisms evolve through genes and memes, here—on this larger theater of self-replicating ideas—evolution operates through "kemes." These intergalactic clays claim to have transformed the "entire crust of their worlds" into integrated lattice-minds. Theirs is a realm of self-aware data, one that feeds on the "conceptual fodder" of the mechanicals. This information is conveyed by voices from above. Nigel however, in a chapter entitled "Conceptual Spaces," derives his own lesson about the Higher Ones by looking inward, by exploring the "poetic" spaces of his subconscious mind. The chapter is subtitled "In Silico." Nigel imagines memes evolving much faster than genes. The organized constellations of information in computers evolved faster yet, so fast that they learned how to leave their silicon substratum. Replicating data, they propagated far beyond their silicon origins, seeking out their domain in various fields—electric, magnetic, gravitational—beyond "the grinding embrace of matter." Generating "filigrees of thought," they used ideas as substrata for "abstractions of a higher order" (372). Their problem begins, however, when they decide "to play in the raw rub of worlds," in hopes of uniting magnetic intelligences, mechanical forms and Naturals.

It is on this plane that Nigel, the "dreaming vertebrate," engages these Highers. Significantly, he does so through the intermediary of the ghost of the Mantis. This ghost offers him its postmortem view of the struggle between the Mechs and humans. Its language is the indifferent one of evolution: humans are "makeshift constructions, built by random time without foresight" (373). Their evolution may lead to higher forms, but "the intermediate stages, which would function more poorly than the original design" must pay "the cost of rearranging," of being "selected out by evolutionary pressure" (373). The Mechs, as the beings "selected" to do this "rearranging," take the Nazi excuse for their "harvesting" of human beings. They claim that they do not know who or what pulls the strings: "I am part of something but I do not know what it is." Nigel may have a "partial vision" as well, but it is one informed by personal passion and anger, which causes him once again to burst out: "You killed my friend Carlos!" (373). When the Mantis tells him that "the careful application of terror is also a form of communication," all he can do is laugh at this "unintentional joke." His laughter proves once again to be the supreme act of defiance. But now he is directly challenging the higher power communicating through the dead Mantis. He, puny human, dares to accuse this power of causing humanity untold suffering. To hell with whatever higher ends are at play; his reaction comes from the gut: "You Highers nearly exterminated us." Like Kip facing the higher bar of cosmic justice in Heinlein's *Have Space Suit, Will Travel*, Nigel wants no special treatment. He opts for his puny humanity: "I suppose I'll stay anchored right here, in my primate point of view" (379).

Yet in some mysterious way, because of Nigel, this same puny primate seems to be at the center of things at the Galactic Center. The Mantis allows him to witness, through the eyes of Besen, a human long thought lost and now miraculously found, the horrors of the Mechs' own collective pleasure-death: "All those mechs. Screaming now in sharp frequencies. Broken and used and not being gathered into the higher orders at all. Not what they had been promised" (376). Besen returns to the Bishops, Toby is reunited with his father, the survivors gather around the fire. Nigel meets a Quath manifestation. In this key dialogue he learns that he, personally, has played a key role in the evolutionary process that brought this band of survivors to this place, where they regroup for possible further adventures of humankind in future places even stranger than this one. Quath tells Nigel that the Mechs "lose creativity because they overcontrol . . . Chaos theory teaches us that any well-defined system will show unpredictable behavior if allowed to run long enough." Even so, it continues, "To avoid chaotic results, control is necessary" (381). But what is this control to be? Nigel "had never favored arguments for control of himself . . . He was not the team-effort type, no" (381). Quath generalizes: "The disadvantage for you—and for us, the Myriapodia—lay in people who went awry" (382). But Nigel, unpredictable and proud of it, somehow did not go awry. Yet there was a price. He now learns that his various manifestations throughout human history were the agent of much evolutionary winnowing: "You had to make human societies who resisted the memes which the mechs had introduced." We learn of an *über*-Nigel (he admits naming himself thus, but of being "afraid of this *him*") who worked with the Earthers to build the

Chandeliers on Snowglade and who presided over the Hunker-Down period of nomadic tribes on the run. As Quath puts it: "Your method was Natural. A few would survive, thrive, resist the mechs—their machines, their memes, everything" (383). But unlike the Mantis, Nigel is able to condemn his *über*-manifestation: "He had brought enormous suffering upon untold millions." Now, however, he sees the result of this winnowing sitting around the fire in front of him: "And finally, the Hunker Downs had yielded up the Bishops. Tough and hard and implacable: Killeen. Able to shrug off the addictive superstitions that beset all humans in groups, the mob mind that led finally to predictable behavior, and then oblivion" (383). Yet Nigel, with his long view of things, reminds us that victory here is only temporary: "A few mechanicals shall prove immune to the pleasure plagues . . . so they shall return. . . . There will always be a struggle, no final equilibrium" (384).

The reader learns, in this tour de force of a novel, that this multitude of Nigels has presided over this vast span of human history. He discovers at Galactic Center a "syntony, a wedding of all forms." But now a new voice intrudes from "the Phylum Beyond Knowing," telling him that the "wedding" is an ongoing, open-ended process, a "dynamic equilibrium, not a stasis" (385). Beyond the naturals and the mechanicals are the clay forms, the "datavores." Yet he is told that "they are the mere base of the Highers. Above this boundary of the knowable towers a realm beyond investigation, exceeding the grasp of serial sentences to describe" (385). And yet it seems that, if anything or anyone is to investigate this realm beyond investigation, it will be Nigel or his progeny: "Conflict will return. It must. But for now, rest. You may be used again" (385).

The final lines of the novel offer the reader a series of graves—of Killeen, of Toby, of the other Bishops. Nigel is there too: "Always slightly distanced, alone and apart, Nigel Walmsley is buried on a separate knoll, in full view of the ocean of night" (400). And indeed, in a final discussion with the bird that claims to speak for these Higher powers, Nigel is allowed to glimpse the future his grave faces toward. The bird tells him "That destiny shall unfold on a truly immense time scale. The decay of all large particles—'baryons' in your terms—will be slow." Nigel replies: "But there's a finite lifetime to it all. Stars run down. The center cannot hold. Nobody's going to be sailing bright eternity" (401). He receives an answer that is a consummate reaffirmation of Emerson's dynamic of power and form, now validated on a cosmic scale: "You are doing it now, primate. There will never be more time ahead than at this instant. And infinities are a matter of taste" (388). Physics now comes to the rescue of the philosopher's sense of an undulating dynamic of center and circumference: "The presumed quantum mechanical ground state of this universe is not in fact a ground state. It is metastable. . . . Metastable conditions could decay at any time" (388). Nigel is given a glimpse of this process, a look perhaps into his own future: "It sent into his mind a flash-image: a gray, seamless wall. Onrushing. Germinated at a point by a nanosecond's handclap, then swelling, engorged on energies of the vacuum, snowplowing out. Behind the front, sparkling births of blank specks, a blackboard fresh for God's writing. The Tumult" (389). Nigel is told that the fundamental science of the future "may apply to surviving the Tumult." One can gloss Nigel's vision with Emerson's famous lines from *Nature*: "Standing on the bare ground,— my head bathed by the blithe air, and uplifted into infinite space,—all mean egotism vanishes. I become a transparent eyeball. I am nothing. I see all. The currents of the Universal Being circulate through me. I am part or particle of God."[4] Applying Emerson to the bird's general statement, we put the human element—Nigel—back in the equation. For in order to observe this process of tremendous energies generated in a nanosecond out of a single physical point, there must be an "I" present—Emerson's transparent "eyeball." This presence, in the context of the Tumult, must physically approach the state of nothingness if it is to do what the bird said—glimpse "in a nanosecond's handclap," the "all." Behind this energy front as it moves to its cosmic circumference, there are "sparkling births of blank specks." These are perhaps new dynamic centers being born. These could be new Nigels, beings who dare to name themselves parts or *particles* of God. What remains in this maelstrom of physical forces is an undulatory process. Because of this, the currents of this clearly named "universal being" can flow through them, allowing future entities, as did Nigel with his rebuilt Taj Mahal, to write their name on this new blackboard of God. I am reaching with this comparison with Emerson, but it highlights the fusion of physics and philosophy, hard science and mysticism, that rounds off Nigel Walmsley's journey to Galactic Center and beyond.[5] Nigel unites Emerson's Man acting with Heinlein's Man surviving, "hunkering down" at the brink of survival, but "going on still," specks born in the wake of endless Tumults, taking the human adventure to galaxies beyond galactic center.

One should read these Galactic Center novels all at a sitting, for they are eminently sequential. The final novel founds a dynasty. But we have neither a celestial Rome nor Asimov's Empire. Instead, the reader witnesses the founding of a dynasty of mankind itself via Nigel, its representative epic Man, at the far edges of physical probability. By any models or standards, Benford's work is an extraordinary achievement. During two decades—the 1980s and 1990s—when both space exploration and science fiction downsized their expectations, Benford has continued to upsize them, working toward the grand union of spacetime, evolution, and human destiny in *Sailing Bright Eternity.* If science fiction is a creative composite of its two components—science *and* fiction—Benford's epic succeeds admirably. He dares to think big, daring to take scientific extrapolation to epic proportions. In doing so, he renovates the noblest of literary forms. As science fiction builds its own canon, Benford's space epic will be hailed as a classic work, perhaps the purest expression of what the genre is, and by definition ought to be.

CHAPTER 7

THE SCIENCE FICTION NOVEL OF MANNERS

During the late 1990s, after the completion of his final Galactic Center novel, Benford produced a series of novels that could be classified as "science thrillers." These are novels where some strange and often menacing occurrence (such as the approach of an alien object to Earth) triggers conflict between scientists, government interests, and global politics. Benford here is writing the kind of fiction—science-based but involving international intrigue—that will be later produced by writers like Neal Stephenson (*Cryptonomicon*, 1999) and Howard Hendrix (*Spears of God*, 2006). But Benford's scientific thrillers—*Cosm* (1999), *The Martian Race* (1999), and *Eater* (2000)—in their detailed descriptions of how science works, how it is conducted in the laboratory, and how this interacts with personal conflicts and institutional politics—hearken back to an important current in Benford's fiction that began with *In the Ocean of Night* and was perfected in a work many consider Benford's masterpiece—*Timescape* (1980). These two early novels—like the three works of the later 1990s—are all set in the near future of their time of publication. They elaborate a social context which is either minimally extrapolated—*In the Ocean of Night* projects twenty to eighty years into the future, in a polluted but recognizable California—or frankly personal and nostalgic, as in *Timescape*, where one time track returns the reader to Benford's own graduate student experience at UCSD in the 1960s. In both novels, the flavor of the 1960s and its social experiments dominate: there is free love and triangular relationships, mention of the Beatles and the Grateful Dead, drugs and Castaneda-like experiences in the Mexican desert. It is this attention to social detail, and especially to big government's role in science, that was much lauded in *Timescape*. Benford returns to this portrait of scientific manners in *Cosm* and subsequent novels.

In the 1990s, however, the times have changed. If the matrix of the 1960s could plausibly allow a freethinking character like Nigel Walmsley, the geopolitical stakes in big science at the turn of the millennium offer a very different social context. Nigel turns his attention to deciphering alien sightings. Despite his social life, he directs his attention to communication with the alien. He leaves behind his life and times to pursue the path set forth in messages from alien sources. His pursuit, though rooted in plausible science, is ultimately metaphysical, even quasi-mystical, in accordance with the *zeitgeist* at the time of its writing. Likewise in *Timescape*, both the British scientist Renfrew and the American scientists Gregory Markham and Gordon Bernstein are ultimately more taken with the mystery of faster-than-light communication than they are concerned about politics or even with preventing an eco-disaster. In Benford's more recent novels, social conflict as related to international intrigue and the question of private enterprise versus government involvement clearly dominates the action. An example is the novel *The Martian Race* (2000). On one hand, there is the scientific mystery of a possible Martian "race," a form of extremophile life that has developed on Mars and which would have been the sole focus of attention for Nigel Walmsley. On the other hand, what comes to dominate the action is an international conspiracy—this time a literal race by superpowers to exploit new energy resources on Mars. This race is ultimately won by a private entrepreneur. By the time of this novel the grand period of NASA and the American dream of space are over. Even so, the entrepreneur is an American. American superiority shifts back to the old Heinlein ideal of privately backed space travel and conquest. Benford comes full circle with the hard-line ideology of SF's Golden Age.

Benford's later novels remain scientifically fascinating, and the extrapolation from current scientific theories is often stunning. But their social discourse—now shaped by issues such as political correctness, public ignorance, official corruption, and the vapid nature of popular culture—readily veers toward the didactic, allowing the author to excoriate tendencies he abhors surrounding his own professional activity as scientist and writer. I wish, however, to focus mainly on *Timescape* as a fully formed example of what a science fiction novel of manners, as Benford conceives it, can actually be. Such a novel, as seen in *Timescape*, offers a seamless weave of everyday scientific activity with the social customs and conventions of a given (thus dated) place and time.

Science fiction is often dismissed by critics as a literary form that develops ideas, not characters. This is the way it is presented in the many review comments cited in the 1992 Bantam edition of *Timescape*. For example, the *Washington Post Book World* reviewer sees Benford "managing the extremely difficult feat of conveying not only the meaning of his speculations in physics and cosmology" but also "giving us a cast of well-developed, strong characters as well." Benford does succeed in doing this. But he is not writing a mainstream novel, as many of today's critics conceive it, where science and the scientific vision of things is seen as an intrusion on humanist issues such as life, love, and death. In *Timescape* Benford brings the two activities separated by these critics—doing science and living life—into a symbiotic relationship. And yet Benford's novel remains a distinctly science fiction novel. Not only does its central narrative focus remain scientists engaged in the daily activity of doing science, but the reality that informs this fiction—the presence of tachyons and the possibility they offer of bifurcating timelines—gives a whole new meaning to the question of how human beings live their lives. The three protagonists of the novel are all working scientists—the American Gregory Markham, the Cambridge physicist John Renfrew, and the UCSD scientist from another timeline, Gordon Bernstein. Even though much of the action and theoretical discussion take place at cocktail parties and around dinner tables, the plot and its resolution involve scientists doing science.

Timescape, at its core, offers a brilliant variation on the SF theme or trope of the time travel paradox. Benford's alternating timelines are an Anglo-American affair. The ease with which each culture engages time travel points to the fact that, historically, this is a common concern of British and American SF writers. Time travel appears to be the terrain where these (for Benford) otherwise divergent national visions of SF most interact. The roots of the time-travel narrative are found in Wells and U.K. writers like John Wyndham. Its elaboration is found in American writers as diverse as Heinlein and Robert Silverberg. The uniqueness of Benford's novel is its focus, not on time *travel* (something physically impossible for humans) but on transtemporal communication, possible once we accept faster-than-light particles as a physical reality. Time travel has continually offered the SF writer the possibility (if illusory) of freedom from biological time. A number of its most serious practitioners, such as Heinlein in his classic "By His Bootstraps," have shown, however, just how limited (and nightmarish) this freedom really is. Despite such warnings, time travel remains for many writers an exercise in Zeno's paradox. This leads to another seemingly unbreachable juncture: that which exists between "mentalized" time and the real time of evolutionary process. Benford, in *Timescape*, confronts this dichotomy head on. The result is a resounding attempt to synthesize what remain two major divergent currents in modern fiction itself. On one hand, there is scientific optimism, offering humans the possibility of overcoming the barrier of temporal paradox, which sets a limit to human activity in spacetime. On the other hand, there is species-driven pessimism, which says that human beings, at the level of self and their personal biology, remain prisoners of time. At this level, there is no paradox to "paradoctor," as Heinlein puts it. Each individual timeline must end. The aggregate of these individual timelines comprises mankind's evolutionary history. And when these timelines, due to environmental forces, and ultimately to entropy, all finally run out, we arrive at the Last Man scenario. Benford's novel not only brings together these two seemingly incompatible visions, it explores ways to unite them. On one hand, the discovery and use of tachyons does result in communication across timelines, with mind-boggling consequences for mankind's sense of time, as it stands on the threshold of a many-worlds timescape. On the other hand, this breakthrough does not obviate the fact that *each individual physical timeline* must run its inexorable course. Benford's novel ultimately recreates, in a spatiotemporal landscape never imagined by Mary Shelley and other writers of this subgenre, a compelling Last Man narrative. His reconciling of the Last Man's terrible sense of finality with the physical possibility of a many worlds universe wherein each instant offers myriad potential timelines, is a narrative tour de force.

To get a sense of just how difficult it is to achieve this balance between the scale of theoretical time and that of human time, let's look at several of Benford's recent attempts to achieve it. In the wake of the conceptual and narrative pyrotechnics of *Sailing Bright Eternity*, Benford's novel *Cosm* (1998) returns to the near future, to institutionalized science, and to the alien visitation scenario of *In the Ocean of Night*. Here a scientist, working on a particle collider, actually creates a baseball-size miniature universe in her lab. For his speculative cosmology, Benford extrapolates from then current scientific papers by Alan Guth and others. The idea is that time runs much faster in this mini-universe (the idea finds SF antecedents in works like Theodore Sturgeon's "Microcosmic God" and James Blish's "Surface Tension"). Given the physical reality of this pocket universe, Benford's researcher, Alicia Butterworth, must make her observations quickly, and academic politics and other factors get seriously in her way. We have the makings of a science thriller, and Benford develops this intrigue skillfully. And yet, in this voluminous novel, there is plenty of room for authorial commentary and polemics. First of all, Alicia, the female protagonist, is black. Second, she rails against Afrocentrism and tokenism, refusing to see her success as due to anything but her own efforts and talent. This is fine, but in the novel her disclaimers have the ring of a staged attack on the political correctness reigning in the academic establishment at the time. What is more, she is no Nigel Walmsley. On the contrary, there is a tone of built-in failure that surrounds the talented and imaginative scientist here, as if Benford were replaying the scenario of Sinclair Lewis's *Arrowsmith*, fueled by a nostalgia for the epoch of the lone genius. Some of Nigel's quasi-religious awe—his sense of scientific discovery as momentarily "living the infinite"—remains with Alicia. But it soon gives way to lamentations on the state of science and scientific research. For Alicia, particle physics remains the only pure science today; the other sciences have sold their integrity to special interests and government regulation. Moreover, she sees science in this last decade of the twentieth century as grossly misrepresented in the media. Because of this, the general public has little or no knowledge of its real practices and goals. Once science—and the drama of doing science—lose their luster in the eyes of the general reader, there is no way forward for the hard SF writer except to make science and doing science the center of political intrigue, or occult mystery, as in *The Da Vinci Code.*

The title of Benford's next novel, *The Martian Race* (1999), offers a significant *double entendre*. The novel is primarily about a literal space race to get humans on Mars. If the NASA ideal was already tainted for Nigel Walmsley, now it is totally dysfunctional. Other governments are launching Mars missions that risk being more successful than ours. But the day is saved for America by the Sir Richard Branson–variety entrepreneur John Axelrod, a name quite appropriate for a latter-day "quantum mechanic." Axelrod bankrolls an expedition that wins the race and puts its scientists on Mars. The subterranean life forms they find on Mars, however—the "Marsmats"—prove to be formed of different chemical compounds than our form of life. Were this to constitute the metabolism of a Martian race, that race would be biologically alien. The myth of life on Mars—from Edgar Rice Burroughs's romantic affirmation, to post-Apollo realist denial—is now turned in a new direction. Mankind might at long last be confronted with an alien being (assuming it were sentient) that does not answer to its anthropocentric sense of the universe. Benford could be parodying his entrepreneur Axelrod in the same way Jules Verne parodied Barbicane and Nicholls in *De la terre à la lune* and *Autour de la lune* (Benford's novel, in fact, has a like situation—Axelrod did not put any means of an emergency return to Earth on board his vessel, and it appears for a while they might remain stranded on Mars). Yet given the author's recent comments about the superiority of private enterprise in pushing forward the dream of space, he may be deadly serious about Axelrod's feat. The reader senses in this novel a disjunct between the scientific and the narrative implications of "extremophile" life forms. Their alien chemistry makes them of greatest interest to science. Pure Mars science more than suggests that sentient life is not necessarily modeled on human chemistry or its sense of organic time. But this possibility, at the same time, tends to make the marsmats irrelevant to the human story. This is one Mars story we cannot end with a Bradbury-like conclusion; there is no more looking down into Martian waters and seeing the new Martians in our image. Marsmat Martians are chemically alien;

they do not relate to our biological existence. The only way to make them interesting then is to make them potentially menacing to humans. Benford skillfully suggests this possibility at the core of his thriller. But the two "races" ultimately belong to different temporal narratives—scientific description on one hand, action-adventure on the other. Many recent SF novels face this narrative dilemma. The science they deal with is so abstruse, like the many-worlds postulate so alien to the human experience, that it can only be described yet cannot plausibly generate narrative structures that have meaning for humans. This disjunct seems to imply that, for these writers, science no longer has a human story to tell. Benford would never admit this is true, but his novel points in this direction.

Benford's millennial novel *Eater* (2000) is a vast elaboration of the scenario set forth in Benford's 1981 story "Exposures." In fact, it looks even further backward to *In the Ocean of Night*, where Nigel is confronted with an alien-invasion event. In *Eater*, Benford returns to this SF trope on a grand scale. But now the intruder is neither an alien space vessel nor a meteor or asteroid. Here (post–Galactic Center) what appears in our skies is nothing less than a small black hole. This black hole (shades of Nigel's Snark) proves to be a sentient entity, thus one that can change its course at will. The black hole is headed for Earth. It establishes communication with a trio of scientists (an American; his astronaut wife, dying of cancer, who volunteers for a Nigel-like act of heroism by physically going to meet the intruder; and an Englishman). Harkening back to Nigel again, the narrative spends much time on the complicated, love-triangle relationship between this trio. But the scientific shocker comes when the scientists discover that this small black hole (large mass, small diameter) is an "eater" of civilizations. It has become sentient (and increasingly intelligent) as it "devours" various planetary cultures on its voyage across the galaxy, in each case storing information about these advanced cultures in its magnetic field. This is the V-ger scenario once again. Yet the difference is that, in Benford's novel, humans have nothing to do with the Eater's origins. For some higher reason perhaps, this entity wants to store Earth's best minds in its database (the Snark had the same mission). Among these are the minds of our two scientist-protagonists. This novel fleshes out in great detail the nuts and bolts of what was only hinted at in "Exposures": a possible distant threat, so distant, in fact, that, if it occurs, it will be so far in the future as to be irrelevant to present and even future humanity. Here, beyond the possible threat, there is the possibility of a cosmic mystery, one again beyond the ken of the scientist-protagonists. The characters in *Eater* are well drawn, to the extent that they reveal themselves to be real people in a difficult situation and not just mouthpieces for commentary. Even so, to heighten the suspense of the novel—a suspense the millennial reader now seems to demand—Benford again turns to international intrigue, with governments and the military in the mix. This is the same conflict between authority and individual initiative Benford develops in the Walmsley sequel *Across the Sea of Suns*—only here it is projected on a massive scale. The science is exciting; the intrigue is compelling. But there is still a lot of commentary, and the love triangle, even for a diehard Benford reader, is a bit tedious. There is a sense of *déjà vu* here. And if the various narrative elements are skillfully handled, they do not seem to coalesce into a successful narrative whole.

Timescape, on the other hand, seamlessly integrates social activity and scientific research. Unlike these later novels, it relies on showing, not telling, to use an old but trustworthy distinction. We do not hear the author's voice (behind that of his characters) making social criticism. Rather than hearing overt commentary on big-government science and academic politics, the reader witnesses these processes in action, sees them invading private lives, hindering the possibility of doing creative science. Nor are all the characters pre-typed. For example, if Gordon Bernstein predictably runs into vicious departmental rivalries and short-sighted superiors, Peterson on the Cambridge timeline proves to be a much more flexible and creative scientific administrator. Not all administration is a bad thing. We have a range of individual characters. All are subtly drawn, and all are allowed to define themselves and their limitations with their own words and actions. They are (to use another old-fashioned distinction) "round" characters, the very sort the novel of manners, in the tradition of Jane Austen, cultivates.

The novel begins with a domestic episode in the household of John Renfrew, a Cambridge physicist. The year is 1999. A diatom bloom has occurred in Earth's oceans, and the planet is essentially dying from this eco-disaster. Renfrew's partner is an American scientist—Gregory Markham—who is working with him on a possible solution. Markham is somewhat stereotypically presented as the American boor. Even so, he is articulate and intelligent and functions well in British society. He has written a brilliant paper on tachyons, faster-than-light particles. What the Cambridge scientists are debating is the possibility of using tachyons to make contact with the past at a point in spacetime where it is still possible to pass information that will result in a reversal of the processes and policies that lead to the death of the world of 1999. Much of the discussion of this project takes place, not in the scientific laboratory, but at cocktail parties and in pubs. The doing of physics is literally surrounded by domestic activities. In a "Special Acknowledgement" published in the 1992, Bantam's re-edition of his book, Benford cites the contribution of his sister-in-law Hilary Foister Benford: "She contributed significantly to the manuscript, bringing to it her special qualities of interest in people. . . . As a native of England and a graduate of Cambridge University, she gave invaluable help in developing and maintaining a consistent British idiom."[1] The detail given to English speech and manners owes its source to her. On the other hand, the world targeted by the tachyon emissions is that of 1969 La Jolla, the time and place of Benford's own graduate studies in physics at UCSD. The attention to details of everyday life here is due to the fact that the author himself lived it. He admits many times that characters in his novel are modeled on identifiable figures. The anchoring of two disparate cultural worlds in sharp detail is grounded to lived experience. It could be said that Benford is as close to the speech and manners of these worlds as was a Jane Austen to hers. Whether he rendered their social dynamic with equal acumen is a matter of opinion. But manners are an integral part of the narrative, and this accounts for much of the mainstream praise for the novel.

Even so, what emerges from this social discourse and causal conversation is a highly sophisticated variation of the SF trope of time paradox. Markham, in his quantum-mechanical explanation of time, openly makes fun of the idea of time travel. It is a naive idea born of Wells and his Time Machine. It is impossible for someone to travel physically through time, for being physically in two places at a same instant of time invariably triggers paradox. The horns of this dilemma were neatly outlined by Robert Silverberg in his novel *Up the Line* (1968)—we can travel anywhere we want in abstract Time; but we can travel nowhere in our own biological timeline. Markham further points to the absurdity of Wells's Traveler leaving 1895, jaunting through evolutionary time far beyond the year 801702, then returning to 1895. For where, he asks, *is*

1895? How can we ever locate any single spacetime point of origin given the complex mechanics of plotting its "whereabouts"? Instead, Markham envisions the possibility of *information* being conveyed to past worlds by means of tachyons. To do so, however, the information must get around the famous grandfather paradox, the barrier of causality which states that an event in the future cannot influence an event in its past. This is the enigma of the famous flower from the future that Wells's Traveler gives to the narrator in 1895—a flower that will wither *before it blooms*. Markham explains that this barrier might be overcome if we adopt a different, quantum view of time: "There's even a sentence in the original Wheeler-Feynmann paper—'It is only required that the description should be logically self-consistent.' By that they meant that our sense of the flow of time, always going in one direction, is a bias. The equations of physics don't share our prejudice—they're time-symmetric. The only standard we can impose on an experiment is whether it's *logically* consistent."[2] Markham follows with his description of the "time switch": "Think about sending messages, instead of shotgunning grandfathers. Everybody assumes the receiver—back there in the past—can be attached to a switch. If the signal from the future comes in, the switch is programmed to turn off the transmitter—*before* the signal was sent. There's the paradox" (92). But the flaw in this logic, he continues, is that our conception of the switch is wrong, especially if we assume that there is a "switch that has two settings—off and on—with nothing in between" (92). He asks his interlocuter, Peterson the administrator, to "think of all these times [messages are sent] being in a loop. Cause and effect mean nothing in this loop. There are only *events*." The solution then is to get the message through before the past turns off the switch: "That's it. The closer it gets to 'off,' the slower it goes. There's an information wave traveling forward into the future and—like a reflection—the tachyon beam comes back into the past. . . . Well, say, the switch gets near 'off,' and then the tachyon beam gets weak. The switch doesn't make it all the way to 'off' and—like that toggle controlling the lights—it starts to fall back toward 'on.' But the nearer it gets to 'on,' the stronger the transmitter gets in the future" (93).

Markham has devised a localized time machine by which messages might get through to 1969. But as he rides a plane back to the United States—a plane that will crash before arrival—he seeks to expand his local "timescape" into a unified theory of time. Here he runs into Gödel's theorem, by which "even simple systems of arithmetic contained things which were true, but unprovable" (308). Gödel, by forcing arithmetic into describing itself in its own language, "had trapped it in its own box, deprived it of ever proving itself by reference to things outside itself" (308). He now asks: What would happen if indeed a message did get through to the past? "Some critical volume of spacetime had to be tweaked, and then the disturbance would propagate outward instantaneously, with enough amplitude to matter. You could change the past at will, yes, so long as you didn't make paradoxes that had large amplitude. Once you exceeded the threshold, the tachyon wave would have a signficant impact on the whole universe. But if so, how could you tell that had happened? . . . How did the universe pick a way to resolve the paradox? They knew they had reached the past—Peterson proved that. But what more could happen?" (308). For Markham, this question is left unanswered, at least in this timeline. His plane crashes, his theory gone with it.

The reader will soon learn what happened, at least to a degree. Benford's reader is privileged to move between the worlds of 1968 and 1999. The message in fact did get through. It was deciphered by Gordon Bernstein in La Jolla, and the cause of the eco-disaster is revealed in time to prevent it from happening. But in what world does this event occur? Another switch seems to have been activated when Gordon learns that the assassin's bullet did not kill President Kennedy after all. From this spacetime event, a new American timeline opens out, into a world where a Markham exists, but this is not the same Markham of 1999. With this bifurcation, each world goes its own way, 1968 to an alternate history, 1999 to its apparent doom. But an even more troubling time event occurs for Gordon. He is given the Nobel Prize for his discovery. But during the acceptance ceremony, he looks out into the audience and sees his own mother sitting there, who in the world he inhabited before the Kennedy event had been dead for years. Apparently the initial tachyon wave *did exceed* the threshold as Markham had predicted, and there was a significant effect on time in the larger universe, one that reaches far beyond two bisecting time lines. If the world of time has no clear on-off switch, then what does occur in this in-between zone?

In any event, for the two worlds involved here, what is clear is that 1969 must continue on, now following a different, yet-to-be-determined track, and

1999 must go on to its end. This latter is a dying world that ultimately must have its Last Man, just as in Clarke's *Childhood's End* Jan remains on Earth in order to chronicle its physical death. As we have seen, Benford may follow in the footsteps of Clarke, but his goal in this exchange is always to find ways to go *beyond* Clarke's endings. In the world of 1999, however, he faces Clarke's final ending, but now it is that of an entire human timeline, one that does not know that other timelines exist—and has no means of contacting them even if they did. Clarke, in *Childhood's End*, has a strategy to go beyond the terminal moment: he lets Last Man Jan and his Earth die, he but allows Jan's (our) story to be captured by the Overlords and preserved in their cosmic "museum" for some possible future use. The logic of time, in *Timescape*, denies this escape hatch. In terms of many worlds physics, 1999 is a *localized* situation, with no means of locating its position in the larger timescape. Theoretically, there is no one "out there" to hear the story of this dying timeline. At this juncture, Benford opts for *individual* action rather than passive storytelling. To the degree this action succeeds in opening a window into new spacetime worlds, Benford offers a Heinleinian solution to the Last Man problem.

The final chapter of Benford's novel returns to Cambridge in 1999, and to John Renfrew who is conducting one final, desperate experiment with tachyons. By choosing to end his narrative here, with the death of *this* Earth, Benford signals the reader that he is consciously taking up the SF trope of the Last Man. This might seem illogical, given the fact that the science Benford deploys—faster-than-light communication and the physical possibility it raises of an infinite number of world lines—would seem to abolish the need for a Last Man. For the many-worlds theory postulates that there are as many "last" men as there are "last" worlds. We are comforted by the fact that if one of these world dies, there remains an infinite number of possible world lines. The need for a tragic end of the entire human race, in evolutionary time, is therefore abolished. If Wells's Traveler could not abolish the iron laws of causality, here in the many-worlds universe election and evolution alike become localized phenomena within a larger timescape. But this is theory. As Markham pointed out in his final moments, any real knowledge of this timescape is beyond the apprehension of any single temporal instant. Whatever unified field vision he perceived was at the moment of his death, its testimony lost forever in his ending. And so it is—even in this highly flexible spacetime structure, with its infinite number of doors and escape hatches—that each of these many worlds remains doomed to end. Localizing the Last Man problem does not make it go away.

This situation seems humanly intolerable—the end of all ends. Even in that grimmest of Last Man novels, *La Mort de la terre* (1910), where author J.-H. Rosny allows no sentimental deviance from evolutionary process, the last human being on that Earth still seeks to transmit his human information—genetically—across the barrier of finality. Be the situation the end of evolutionary time or, as with Benford's timescape, the finality of a closed, self-consistent system, science-fiction mankind, it seems, always seeks to move beyond closure, to go on. And so it is, in the final scene of *Timescape.* Benford suggests that tachyons themselves, if cleverly used, may offer a way out of the closure of localized time lines and systems. Benford's vision of the timescape itself, despite the spatializing metaphor, proves to be an unstable system: "Time and space were themselves players, vast lands engulfing the figures, a weave of future and past. There was no riverrun of years. The abiding loops of causality ran forward and back. The timescape rippled with waves, roiled and flexed, a great beast in the dark sea" (238). The reference to the timescape as a "great beast in the dark sea" implies that this timescape "beast" itself—is this a reference to Clarke's Jan reenacting the resurrection myth of Jonah in the belly of the whale specimen the Overlords carry from dying Earth to their distant planet?—may offer the means for a single last human to enact its own individual destiny, even in the dizzying flux of tachyon reality. It further implies, as possible reference to Ahab pursuing *his* whale, that the timebeast itself may be hunted down and, perhaps, ultimately defeated. We remember the importance of hunting with Manuel in *Against Infinity*, and more significantly with Nigel's hunting of the Snark, where hunting becomes a means of joining with the forces of life *against* those of a physical nature that would obliterate it. Renfrew remains the Last Man in the dying world of 1999 Cambridge. Yet he takes action against this process. In one final experiment, he tosses what seems a last bottle in this roiling sea of time, as if to test the inflexibility of this "weave of future and past" that appears to imprison his world and its fate. He seeks to make tachyon contact with some other spacetime location. And, among what seems an impenetrable maze of sleeting lines of tachyon flow, he suddenly receives a decipherable message, in English. The message is not from Bernstein's time world but from what Renfrew believes to be 2349, a location ever so close, yet forever separated by an unfathomable gulf of noise. He realizes that he somehow stands, in his dying world, at some tachyon junction, a cosmic way station with messages coming from all spacetime directions: "He shook his head. All form and structure was eroded by the overlapping of many voices. A chorus. Everyone was talking at once, and no one could hear." (392) We are far distant here from Benford's serene vision of the cosmic artist and its timescape. Renfrew suddenly sees that his world is an impossibly insignificant speck, lost in a maze of world lines, a babble of temporal possibility. As this tumult of voices modulates to a terrifying cosmic silence, he remains suspended between a spacetime infinity Pascal could not have imagined. All the generators shut down in Renfrew's laboratory, all buildings and streets fall empty. And yet, in the same breath he realizes, now in his sole body, that however complex this "riverrun" of worlds he has just experienced may be, his own personal time-river still flows. Its path is singular and inexorable: "Causality's leaden hand would win out."

And yet it is only at this moment of personal tragedy—as with Markham in the finality of the individual ending—that Renfrew at last can take comfort in knowing, physically in his body, that his world is not alone but part of an infinite weave of temporal *voices*. His vision here is another personal breakthrough, a Nigel Walmsley moment. It comes from an instant of intuitive contact between mortal human and immortal nature, in which he suddenly sees that, even if in the cosmic weave of things these many worlds remain tragically separate from each other, these worlds are also, by the same token, forever safe from one another. Once again, Pascal's cosmic aloneness is turned on its head. What emerges once more is Huck Finn, whose actions allow the individual to survive to act another day: "The soothing human world of flowing time would go on, a sphinx yielding none of her secrets. An infinite series of grandfathers would live out their lives safe from Renfrew" (393).

Personal tragedy is now seen as the general romance of Time. For despite it all, Renfrew *has* received a message from what is apparently another human being, originating from a measurable, if only approximate, date of 2349. There is apparently a human future out there for some receiver. A message beyond Renfrew's last moment did get through to someone. This is perhaps what he means when, openly accepting that his world is lost, he paradoxically feels "elated, free." He has a message, and he responds to it by retreating to his own domestic world just down the road, where his family still awaits him, with those famous preserves on the shelf, which can keep them alive for a long time. Things in the end shrink to the measure of manners. For Renfrew now retires to his family arcadia. This is not the defiant place of Heinlein's Farnham's Freehold, a survivalist bunker. Instead, it is a muted, civilized space, where he can wait in hope that some other message, some serendipitous twist in the spacetime fabric, may yet save his family, if not his world.

In Benford's opus, *Timescape* represents a moment of supreme balance between the demands of science and of fiction. *In the Ocean of Night* begins Benford's quest for narrative and stylistic effects that convey the sense of wonder encountered as his human protagonist moves through physical worlds beyond physical possibility, if not beyond imagining. *Timescape* quietly brings the astonishing effects of quantum temporality into the labs and bistros of everyday human life. Nothing in this novel exists for sheer effect alone. Science is masterfully integrated into the workings of everyday life. Premature death cuts Markham's unified theory short. The astute administrator Peterson retires to his country house to die. Renfrew accepts his role as Last Man. In this novel, we do not travel to an alien world of tachyons and timescapes. That world appears in our midst, we greet it with modest dignity and veiled hope. Benford, in *Timescape*, is not simply resurrecting the novel of manners; he renovates it by creating a genuinely *scientific* version of this form, proving thereby that there need not be an either-or divide between literature and science fiction.

CHAPTER 8

BENFORD'S SHORT FICTION

Since his first published story "Stand In" appeared in 1965 in *The Magazine of Fantasy and Science Fiction*, Gregory Benford has published a large number of short stories in magazines and in anthologies. He collected many of his best stories in two landmark volumes—*In Alien Flesh* (1986), and *Matter's End* (1990). These were followed by three more recent anthologies—*Worlds Vast and Various* (1999), *Immersion and Other Short Novels* (2002), and *Anomalies: Collected Stories* (2012). The short story is often seen as the essential form for science fiction. Indeed, many of the most revered SF novels have their beginning as an idea-packed short story, which the author subsequently elaborates (often with less success) into a larger narrative. Orson Scott Card's "Ender's Game" is an example, where a story generates not just a single novel but a series of novels. Benford has followed this process. For example, his novel *Eater* (1999) is clearly an expansion of his classic story "Exposures." Indeed, in the introduction to his most recent e-book anthology, *Anomalies* (2012), Benford openly admits to writing "concept stories": "Here . . . are stories written to size, mostly for the science journal *Nature*, whose Futures page each issue is the most read item in the magazine. Generally, you have time to deliver only the idea, a tight constraint."[1] In fact, Benford is such a good SF short story writer precisely because so many of his stories have this "tight constraint," in the sense that they skillfully present a big idea in a small space. Generally, however, Benford the short story writer is less interested in sketching "concepts" than in the craft of the short story itself, whose essence, whatever the genre, is to present a crucial situation that calls upon the reader to imagine its elaboration beyond the boundaries of the narrative. The best of Benford's stories are stand-alone classics in this manner.

In a sense, American science fiction, with its publishing roots in magazines and digests where most major writers got their start, has kept the short story form alive, even contributed to its development, across the twentieth century. SF has produced many masterpieces of short fiction, both in terms of speculative content and experimental form. Notable examples are the stories and novellas produced by Robert A. Heinlein from 1939 to 1944. Great SF stories—again attempting to narrate situations born of advanced scientific speculation—continue to be written at the end of the twentieth century. Striking examples are Robert Silverberg's "Enter a Soldier. Later, Enter Another" (1989) and Ted Chiang's "Story of Your Life" (1991). Generally, many of the best SF stories avoid the perceived trap of mainstream literary "exhaustion" by demanding that their readers take a speculative or hypothetical situation as literal reality. The experiment here is that of a protagonist actually living in a world that is new and untested. Many of Benford's stories are benchmark examples of this sort of experimental science fiction storytelling.

To conclude this book, I first look in detail at two stories—one from *In Alien Flesh*, the other from *Matter's End*. The stories are "Exposures" (1981) and "Mozart on Morphine" (1989). Both have a working scientist as protagonist, whose activity in the narrative is the professional one of doing science. Both have strong autobiographical elements. But, though a scant eight years separates these stories, they move in very different directions. "Exposures" looks back to Nigel Walmsley and the Benford of the 1970s, fascinated with alien sightings. "Mozart on Morphine" takes its direction from Markham's inner musings in *Timescape*. In each case, these stories are philosophical tales, that pursue the human implications of the new—and supremely alien—worlds brought forth by modern physics and mathematics.

"Exposures" is considered by many to be Benford's paradigmatic narrative of scientists "doing science." By this is meant the mundane work of professional scientists, working in the modern context of an institution, a university or a private laboratory, in contrast to the "lone genius" figure who continues to appear in Golden Age science fiction. An example of this latter figure is Heinlein's Waldo. Even so, American SF during the 1950s seriously clipped the wings of the lone genius. Growing cold war fears of atomic holocaust led to works like Walter M. Miller's *A Canticle for Leibowitz*, where irresponsible science is seen, in a clearly theological context, as the bringer of apocalypse. In post-cyberpunk SF and the SF of the "information age," either because of such stigmatization or for political and social reasons, the scientist as protagonist tends to disappear altogether. Even in a recent neo-Heinleinian novel like Cory Doctorow's *Makers* (2009), whatever science is present is now envisioned from the point of view of the user (and manipulator) of new technology, not from that of the experimenter who created it. Benford's approach steadfastly differs from all of the above, at least on the surface. Benford the professional scientist creates his scientist-protagonists in his own image, as men or women working within the boundaries of the government laboratory system a Heinlein so abhorred. Benford in this sense is a realist writer, for he recognizes that these boundaries, however constricting, remain necessary, as money and grants are needed to fund research and build the radio telescopes and supercolliders modern science must have if it is to get results. His scientist, then, is subject to department heads, government priorities, boards of review for whom the middle road is always best. His scientist is a small cog in a larger gearwork. Here, by the very nature of things, there can be no "eureka" moments, no world-changing breakthroughs wrought by a solitary genius. Instead, his scientist's daily activity consists of gathering data, working with teams of researchers to form hypotheses, verifying, correcting—a process that is tentative at best. One can, of course, given the reality of institutionalized science, blame the institution and not the science. This is the way of Sinclair Lewis's Arrowsmith and (to some degree) of Benford's later Alicia Butterworth as well. In "Exposures" however, Benford simply gives a realistic portrait of how science is done, both in current conditions, and in the sense of it being a supremely tentative activity. His nameless scientist in "Exposures" describes the act of making experiments as an ever-inconclusive engagement with physical phenomena: "You never get it right beforehand, really. Sure, some features lie this way, others have a luminous spectral grace similar to what you imagined. But the thing itself inevitably bristles with specifics, knotty pimples, splashes of irregular and unconforming life."[2] When all romanticism and anti-scientific bias are stripped away, this is the way science works.

This portrait of the modern scientist at work has an insider's feel. His statement of method cited above is what we would expect from a CalTech (or a UCI) scientist, a well-equipped cog in the wheel of big science. But the matter is not so simple. For in "Exposures," this standard portrait of the modern scientist's job of work is a clever façade. Beneath this façade, the dream of the lone genius—the myth of the individual and its big discovery—remains active. Despite the Cal Tech setting and talk of shared laboratory time, the reader is struck by the fact that it hears only one voice—that of a narrator immersed in his own thoughts. This scientist is essentially *alone.* His solitary condition is subtly, almost subliminally, revealed to the reader through certain slips, in statements inadvertently made that somehow don't fit the profile. For example, the narrator describes the experimental scientist as one who always works outside the "convenient, ordained maps," as one whose "only true guide is an eye for the graininess of the world." This statement about *the only true guide* being an *eye* for the graininess of the world suggests a scientist both interested in absolutes and going his own way to discover them. The ghost of the lone genius stirs in the depths of what is significantly a scientist's *monologue*, from which the collective voice is absent. (We remember the contrast between Nigel's monologue and the collective patter in the slightly later *Across the Sea of Suns*). Benford's narrator may extol the rigors of scientific method and the need for judgment by one's peers. But in the next breath, he speaks of these safeguards as if they were the products of a personal imperative, to which he alone adheres. He asserts that "the standards of science are austere, unforgiving." Yet he does not seem to be referring here to institutional guidelines but rather to his own personal, quasi-existential standards.

His reference to "things in themselves" conjures scientific attitudes that would appear to have no place in a modern laboratory. For a rationalist like Descartes, such a term would refer to the innate quality of clear and distinct ideas, not to the product of inductive reasoning. For a later thinker like Kant, this *Ding an sich* represents the material limit of human understanding. And for Guy de Maupassant, the "thing in itself" is the Horla—an object of research that is not simply unknowable but unnamable, "grainy," inscrutable—ultimately the menacing and even monstrous "thing" from "out there." Benford's modern experimenter sees himself as one who has "to hedge, to take one step back for each two forward, to compare and suggest and contrast, always sticking close to the data" (244). Yet as his description of what is clearly his own private experiment unfolds, we find him in a position very much like that of Maupassant's protagonist, facing the possibility of a phenomenon that is unknowable and terrifying in its unknowability. Here is what he recounts. In the midst of routine fact checking, he discovers a series of facts that simply shouldn't be part of the experiment. The data that mysteriously appears in this researcher's "slots" does not pertain to galaxy NCG 1097, which he has been studying. His reaction to this data, odd for an objective observer, is telling: "*Someone* had co-opted my space." The naming of an agent, and the attributing of a design to "co-opt" to this agent, seems strange for a scientist who has just finished talking about "impartiality." He could simply see this as an error in measurement, an unverifiable anomaly, thus something to be rejected. Yet he rushes to interpret, all too willing to see agency involved in what should scientifically be dismissed as an observational error: "There was no explanation for the Sagittarius A data. It had been received from the station in orbit and duly processed. But *no command* had made the scope swivel to that axis" (242). All at once, we are not listening to an objective scientist but to someone imagining invisible forces "commanding" things to happen. As he tells us, these are things *only he* observes. His next step in this internalized logic is to imagine that these aberrant phenomena are directed *specifically* at him, that only he, for some unknown reason, is destined to observe them.

Some "data" breaks into this scientist's routine process of observation. And he rushes to judgment in a personal, unscientific, and perhaps paranoid manner. He rashly envisions disaster and catastrophe, in the form of an escaping black hole rushing toward our galaxy. If, as he says, this phenomenon appeared to him in the objective language of numbers, his description of it is far from objective: "The hammer of time was a set of Dopplered numbers, blue-shifted because the thing rushed toward us, a bulge in the sky. Silent numbers" (242). There are accents of finality in this statement that are more in tune with a disaster filmgoer than with a modern scientist in an institutional setting: "There were details to think about, calculations to do, long strings of hypotheses to unfurl like thin flags. I did not know the effect of a penetrating, ionizing flux on Earth" (242). He suddenly becomes aware that he must work outside the institutional framework. The NGC 1097 data, he muses, might make a good academic paper. But for the Sagittarius A data that has mysteriously co-opted its space, "there was no crisp professional path" (243). I mentioned above Maupassant's "The Horla." The parallels between this story and Benford's—both first-person accounts by figures who claim to pursue a scientific method of investigation of an unknown and (to them) menacing phenomenon are striking. Benford's scientist now begins to see his "compact" Caltech campus, the "varnished perspectives of its tiled hallways," as a modern version of the asylum that enclosed Maupassant's protagonist, as an institutional space that closes off out-of-the-box thinking.

Benford's scientist recites the doctrine of empiricism. But here, faced with this unlikely data, he resorts to something more like Cartesian intuition: "I would have to look, try to find a bridge that would make plausible *what I knew but could scarcely prove*" (242). Increasingly, his discourse has unmistakable accents of paranoia. He sees this data as something that "had to be placed in context, beside NGC 1097." His musings go from claiming that "*someone* in high orbit had fed data into our satellite's scope" to making the quasi-paranoid remark that he alone was *intended* to see the data, that the data was "keyed to a connection that *another eye than mine could miss*" (243). Finally, he openly asserts, "*Only I* could have made the connection to NGC 1097, and guessed what an onrushing black hole could do to a fragile planet" (243). Benford's story of doing science all at once drops its mask and veers toward the SF catastrophe scenario. His institutional scientist now takes on overtones of the old "mad scientist," where, in the final step in his chain of logic, scientific method begins to resemble insanity: "But to convey this information in this way was so strange, so—yes, that was the word—so alien. Perhaps this was the way *they had to do it*, quiet, subtle, indirect" (243). Given the generic overtones in this narrative, one might think Benford was rewriting a "mad scientist" story, where what first appears to follow strict scientific method gradually turns out to be the discourse of a madman. But Benford may be teasing his reader here. For that reader remembers that a similar sort of intuitive vision—one that both accepts the existence of aliens, and believes that they are attempting to contact us through a single individual—is proper to Nigel Walmsley as well. Nigel's specialty is thinking outside boxes, putting odd and uncommon occurrences in a personal context that may at first seem madness but which eventually leads to advances in knowledge well outside the routine process of institutionalized science.

But none of the voices suggested above—that of the dutiful modern scientist, or that of the "mad" lone genius, or even that of the intuitive maverick Nigel Walmsley—entirely encompass Benford's narrator in this story. Instead, the author seems here to play off various types of scientific behavior against the reader's expectations. If a realistic portrait of the institutional scientist doing science seems too boring, details in the text let the reader glimpse the shadow of the lone madman lurking under this façade. But if this goes too far in the direction of pulp fantasy, other details pull the reader back to a vision of the scientist as synthesis of rational method and intuitive imagination. In the concluding pages of this story, Benford skillfully modulates between these different visions of doing science. On one hand, his story is finally revealed to be much more than just another SF story of impending disaster. In fact, if there is to be a disaster, it is one for which neither science nor humanity clearly has a solution. And even if the reader comes to believe that disaster will occur, that the scientist (à la Philip K. Dick) is not paranoid but in fact "right" about alien involvement and about his being chosen as messenger for this event, all this proves ultimately to be meaningless. For a black hole event has no human time frame. And just who is the protagonist going to warn? Finally, what difference does it make if he does issue a warning, the event is on a time scale so vast that it is of no immediate concern to anyone in his world or in future worlds. The reader can see this as speculative terror and leave it at that. But the whole narrative consists of more than lonely scenes in the laboratory. It intercuts between these and vignettes of private family life. Given this narrative rhythm, it presents Benford's scientist-narrator as another Nigel Walmsley, as the improbable mediator between human finiteness and the vast universe of things like black holes. The narrator's activities weave back and forth between the microscale of individual family life and the grand scale of cosmic forces beyond human control. His musings on NGC 1097 are contrasted with scenes of his domestic life. On one occasion, he remarks upon going to bed: "I went over to my chest of drawers . . . across which I had tossed the residue of an hour's dutiful parenting: a scrawled essay on marmosets, my son's anthology of drawings, his reading list, and on top, the teacher's bland paragraph of assessment. It felt odd to have called these things into being, these signs of a forward tilt in a small life . . . the angles appropriate to cradling my children still lived in my hands . . . Now my eye strayed to his essay. I could see him struggling with the notion of clauses, with ideas piled upon each other to build a point, and with the caged linearity of the sentence" (240–41). If Benford's story is about scientific method, in the end this proves to be Nigel's method. The scientist works to "pile up ideas," to generate open-ended clauses. But these must not lead to the "caged linearity of the sentence," either in the sense of bowing to institutional authority or of rushing to personal judgment. As the reader itself crosscuts between extreme views of doing science—institutional hack or mad scientist—it finds a via media. This, once again, is the taking things in phases/phrases that underlies mankind's open-ended search for understanding. This scientist's final vision comes during a church service. Here a different kind of ritual—one based in basic human activity ("Take, eat. Life calling out to life") yields to meditation on the path of the scientific investigation ahead: "I remembered my son, remembered that these events were only pieces, that the puzzle was not yet over, that I would never truly see it done, that as an astronomer I had to live with knowledge forever partial and provisional, that science was not the final results but instead a continuing *meditation* carried on in the face of enormous facts—*take it in phrases*—let the sentences of our lives pile up" (245).

"Mozart on Morphine" (1994) is in many ways a scientifically updated version of "Exposures." The scientific discipline here is no longer astrophysics but mathematical physics and string theory. As the first-person narration of a working scientist, it again weaves back and forth between incompatible scales of activity—personal events and abstruse excursions into the theoretically infinitesimal. Even more seamlessly than in "Exposures," it is the scientist's discourse—describing firsthand the personal and theoretical events that intertwine in the making of a scientific discovery—that modulates between extreme conditions. This story further differs from "Exposures" in the fact that there are no overtones of stock SF plots such as the "foreign object" threatening to strike. In that story, Benford seems to enjoy tweaking the stock plot, making his colliding object a breakaway black hole, thus shifting the emphasis to complex physical speculation, rather than simply evoking the "imagination of disaster" that marked the SF films of the 1950s. "Mozart on Morphine" has no such alien overtones. Its focus is straight scientific theory. The question it poses is clear: If the universe depicted by string theory is the real universe, can humanity have any meaningful role in it? The story begins with the protagonist's addressing an unnamed audience. It is an audience of professionals, for he speaks of the "unspoken rhythms of our trade." But at the same time he promises to address "matters scientists usually avoid." This is personal experience, the story of the life behind the theory. The epigraphs chosen to preface this story set the register in which this personal narrative will operate. The protagonist is searching to formulate a unified theory on the level of multidimensionality. He thus engages areas beyond human experience, where only abstruse mathematics can reach. There are no aliens like Quath here, who construct vast mining machines out of "cosmic strings." The focus now is directly on mankind versus a hypothetical physical world beyond the reach of human experience. As there are no fictional aliens to act as intermediaries, this is an existential narrative in the strictest sense. If these strings have a "landscape," it is one of invisible entities far more mysterious than a Nigel Walmsley could imagine. The first epigraph, from physicist Freeman Dyson, echoes the riddling mirror Voltaire held up to the universe: "As a working hypothesis to explain the riddle of our existence, I propose that our universe is the most interesting of all possible universes, and our fate as human beings is to make it so."[3] This offers little hope for mankind's ever understanding its place in the universe, but it promises along the way interesting (and perhaps futile) theoretical maneuvers such as string theory. The second quote, attributed to Goethe's Faust, bids us push aside theory and simply live life: "All theory, dear friend, is gray, but the golden tree of life springs ever green." But if the speaker here is Mephisto, can we trust his call for humanity to abandon theory? Interesting philosophical parameters are set for the "scientific" discourse to follow.

The narrator tells us he is working on the mathematical implications of particle theory: "I had been pursuing a model for the universe which did not begin with any assumption about its dimensionality. We are used to our cozy three spatial dimensions, plus ever-flowing time—four dimensions in all. When God made everything, was this choice forced? Could the deep laws governing matter work well in, say, six dimensions? Twenty-six? The question reeks of arrogance, of course. Just *what* or *who* could force God?" (11). In the narrative, this comment is bracketed by two personal experiences, both of which involve near brushes with death. In one the narrator is shot at as he jogs on the beach, at a moment of respite from his theorizing. The second is a near-fatal automobile accident that occurs while the narrator is visiting his parents in Alabama (Benford's own childhood home). These are encounters, not with Goethe's tree of life springing ever green, but with hard, unyielding laws of matter: "This impossibly sharp world, and my persistence in it, demanded equally hard-edged explanations" (12). But what relevance can theory have at this level of experience? Here is the narrator's profession of faith: "The spirit of Einstein moves us still: we try to find the unifying principles behind the universe by looking for symmetries hidden in the laws that govern matter. The greatest scientists are unifiers . . . and indeed nature often begins its grand works with a simple, unified start. . . . A common ancestry of apes managed to break their smooth symmetry into such as we, with our complicated symbol-scribbling languages and cultures. It is a recurring theme: diversity from unity" (13). But the issue here is not the nature of reality; it is how far our minds can reach into the multiple layers of reality that separate our lives from ever apprehending any such thing as a primary unity: "Each step downward in scale is by twenty orders of magnitude. That is how remote our theories have become" (13).

A third brush with death, paradoxically, will bring the narrator closer to these depths that only mathematical theory is said to reach. He suffers a burst appendix. Gangrene sets in, antibiotics seem not to work. Almost at death's door, the narrator puts on headphones to listen to music: "They had me on demand morphine. Every hour or so I called for an injection and lifted off the sheets and spun through airy reaches. Mozart on morphine, skimming along the ceilings of rooms where well-dressed people looked up at me with pleased expressions . . . I kept flying along softly lit yellow ceilings, above crimson couches. . . . Toward the blue geometries. Mozart had understood all this and had seen in this endless gavotte a way to loft and sweep and glide, going, to have ample ripe substance without weight" (17–18). "Substance without weight" is exactly what this theoretician needs in order to undertake a *physi-*

cal, bodily exploration of the intangible abstractions of super-strings so as to convert these mathematical entities into "blue" geometries: "That was what I saw in the days that followed. It was all there. Abstractions, yes—but I also felt strumming kinesthetic senses, taking me where the mathematics led. I could tie the superstrings in knots, make of them what I wanted. Unimaginably small, they still had to follow the same logic of mathematics. I *knew*" (18). Knowing, in this case, is not a Cartesian abstraction; it is a case of physically *being there*. This experience brings with it "a strange new sense . . . the calm acceptance of mortality." He will now not allow theory, he says, to "deflect me from life itself" (19).

Thinking and the mathematical vehicle it uses are now apprehended as an existential act. This leads the narrator to a new take on the mind-matter problem of the rationalists. He asks: "What is it that breathes fire into the bare mathematics and makes a new raw universe for them to describe. Now that we have achieved a unified model, we have in a sense answered the question first posed by the Greeks: *What* is the universe? My answer is that we experience events in a higher dimension. Our perceived universe is the shadow of a higher realm. Now we should turn to a grander issue: *Why* is the universe? To attack this question is to ask to know the mind of God" (20). In the light of such a question, the narrator finds recent scientific discoveries, the catalog of four forces, as something "comfy, domesticated": "Gravity can cause matter to collapse to infinitesimal size. In my theory, *no exact solutions are available for anything*." This seems to place us once again between Pascal's two infinities: God and the void of matter: "Even the most lovely of all models gives us, in the end, a set of equations. But now these squiggles describe events in higher realms, in vast vector spaces where imponderable entities move to their own differential waltz" (20). But the waltzing world of mathematics brings the narrator back to his Mozart on morphine experience. There it was not mathematics but rather the flesh-and-blood individual sailing above the equally inscrutable realm of his personal death. It is same existential link between his mortal body and mathematical theory that takes him to India and the Taj Mahal to contemplate this human place where the "serene eternity" of its mathematical proportions coexists with the brute fact of death in a land where "death just happened." The story ends with the author's own musings on mathematical beauty and life: "I thought of Mozart and heard a faint light rhythm, felt myself skimming effortlessly over a rumpled brown dusty world of endless sharp detail . . . and watched the buzzards and the bathers and felt the slow sad sway of worlds apart" (23).

But just how "apart" are these worlds of theory and life? The narrative flashes back to the present of the narrator's discourse. This, it turns out, is his acceptance speech to the Nobel Committee for a prize in physics. He tells them that if his approach seems "odd," its focus is the "human experience of science"—in other words, a focus on the insurmountable distance between us and the natural world we pretend to study: "We contend endlessly against pale immensities." Benford's mathematical physicist directly takes on Pascal in his concluding remarks. His glance at the human condition through the lens of superstrings adds an interesting dimension to what seems to be Benford's abiding concern in all of his fiction: "We seem so small. Yet we have a common, perhaps arrogant impression that we matter, somehow" (21). We are matter that "matters"; however, we are so *now*, not because we are the only thinking thing in a universe of unthinking matter, but because we possibly share this property of thought with the universe itself: "Consider the tiny processes governed by quantum mechanics. There, matter is not inert. It is active, continually making choices about probabilities. . . . Mind is present, at least in the sense that nature makes choices. Let us go one level higher, to our own brains. These fragile vessels amplify the quantum choices made in our heads by molecules. We apply the lever of size to underlying probabilistic events. We are magnifiers" (22). His conclusion is striking: "Still, there emerges evidence of mental processes at work on many levels of physical reality. We may be part of some larger act. For example, perhaps we contribute remotely to the universe's thinking about itself" (22). We think here of Emerson's famous remark, that man is the dwarf of himself, not just a "magnifier," but physically *part* of some larger act, a being that, by "applying the lever of size" to events on its tiny scale, insures the galvanic circuit between center and circumference, be this on the scale of the infinitely large or (as in this case) the infinitely small. True, our "besieged brains" are tiny; we cannot know anything about the higher order "with anything approaching scientific certainty." Yet we are given "a glimmer of perception" of this order "through the godly language of mathematics." We remain finite, mortal creatures—the lesson of India teaches us this in a natural process we must accept. Yet once again, as in all Benford's work, there remains the forward tilt. Here, this comes from the intimations of immortality the protagonist gleans from his "Mozart moments."

"Matter's End" ties together a number of Benford's abiding preoccupations in a significant manner. Also, what returns here is mention of the eternal human monuments—the Taj Mahal, Mozart's music. We rejoin here Benford's fascination with messages—enduring monuments both cultural and physical—by which humans pass information to far future inhabitants of Earth or to unknown spacetime locations where human culture and humans themselves no longer exist. This is the subject of Benford's book *Deep Time: How Humanity Communicates across Millennia* (1999). We have seen examples of such communication in the reproduction on Snowglade of the Taj Mahal, signed by Nigel, a monument that has apparently communicated something to the ruling Mechs, as they leave it alone. There is as well the "Mose Art," passed from generation to generation down to Abraham. Finally there is the genetic "library," replacing the Great Library of Alexandria, the three human generations—Abraham, Killeen, and Toby—that preserve the genetic code that destroys the Mechs, allowing further human participation in the ongoing process of cosmic evolution.

Benford also has stories where the right message is sent to the wrong receiver. "Of Space-Time and the River" is a good example. It is a story about ancient Egypt and archeology. Author Benford, in the afterword to the story, talks of his contact with this ancient civilization as an "experience of crawling through subterranean caverns" among the material vestiges of a lost world.[4] In contrast, Benford's protagonist, a UCI professor of comparative literature, takes the high-culture road to this ancient civilization, seeing it through the eyes of English Romantic poets—Shelley, Blake, and others. These poets have abstracted too quickly from the pyramid's stones, seeing "the world in a grain of sand . . . and eternity in an hour." In fact, eternity in an hour is literally what the alien "archeologists" in the story, the Quarthex, extract from ancient Egypt. From the chaos of a near-future overpopulated Egypt, they will physically recreate their idea of the world of the pharaohs. Through feats of space-time engineering, they encompass monuments and people in a symmetrical and impermeable spacetime bubble. Within that bubble, they reinstate what they see as the "glory" of Egypt. But this proves to be a slave world. Inside it, modern humans regress to the primitive "bicameral mind," a closed system where the gods seem to talk to man within the confines of his own brain. Benford's protagonist, a man of letters, has chronicled this operation in his daily diary, the ideal Romantic vehicle for solipsistic self-examination. Caught up in the bubble, he abandons the writing of words, the only means left for mankind to toss its message in a bottle into other seas of thought.

For Benford, the possibility of deep time depends, ultimately, on the persistence of matter, for (Western) physics the substance that underlies all material reality. But what would happen if matter were to "end"? In the final paragraph of "Mozart on Morphine," the narrator goes to India and stands before the Taj. Here, chaos and order appear to find resolution in the dance of matter: "By the glimmering dawn radiance, I watched buzzards pick apart something on the flats . . . The Taj coasted in serene eternity behind me . . . its cool perfect dome glowing, banishing the shadows below. Somehow in this worn alien place everything seemed to fit. . . . From this simple fact came India's inertia" (23). Interestingly, in Benford's story "Matter's End" (1991), it is Indian scientists, in India, using Western particle physics and its modes of measurement, who make the discovery that matter itself has an end. All at once, the physical bedrock of all our theories falls away. The mind-matter duality that underpins Western thought simply dissolves. This is the situation of Clarke's story "The Nine Billion Names of God." Here computer scientists succeed in "naming" these names, and "overhead, without any fuss," the stars of Benford's Galactic spacetime journey, "were going out."[5] To rephrase this in Emerson's terms, a situation is created where there is no longer a subject and an object, thus no longer the possibility of creating the "galvanic circuit" that defines the dynamic of power and form that underlies Western science and technology. Matter is the source of energy, the "power" that fuels the activity of the self-reliant man. Self-reliance involves the individual's defining its unique space-time of action. Without matter, no such definition can occur.

The Quathex time bubble effectively removed the Nile from our physical spacetime, causing it to flow over and under the bubble in a circular, self-contained manner. What is at stake with matter's end is Huck Finn's riverrun and Nigel Walmsley's great sky river. These dynamic processes now yield to India's "inertia," as even the Taj Mahal is plucked from the course of spacetime. In Benford's story there is no matter-energy conversion, as in Clarke's *Childhood's End*. The Indian scientists see its "end" as lifting the veil of illusion, in this case Western science's *belief* in the permanence of matter. Once this is gone, there remain only interpretations of reality. This seems a quantum situation: the stars go out because there is no longer a consensual "reality" to perceive them. But this itself could be merely another Western mask, one that conceals a radically different physical condition—eternity.

Emerson, with his dual vision West and East, may have intuited the possibility of physical eternity, brought into being as reaction to self-reliance's excessive individualism. To restore dynamic connection between these extremes, Emerson presents his "representative Men," men who represent a category of mankind, whose task is to restore connections within a field of action potentially fractured into its individual parts. Benford, in this story, presents his protagonist as Emerson's representative Man. As such, Robert Clay, in this post-matter world where opposites are seemingly abolished, retains the freedom to choose the point of view of his class—that of the Western scientist.

Logically, when matter and mind become one, narrative time—time as a function of states of matter—must end. In contrast to the previous three stories, Benford here uses a third-person narrator. By convention, third-person narration carries the expectation of general knowledge, if not omniscience—an impossibility after matter's end. If we play with Benford's "net up," then in the post-matter world, narrative as we know it would disappear. But Benford's narrator, significantly, remains highly focalized, intimate with the mind and thoughts of Professor Clay. This allows fixed point of view and no point of view to intersect in one and the same man, where Clay, the representative of Western science, confronts the demise of that science. If we follow this reasoning, the narration itself, in the act of narrating the impossibility of narration, positions its subject—Clay—as a new dynamic center that in turn must generate its own circumference, forming a "circuit" that appears to hold, even as the Western concept of order breaks down.

Clay is an establishment man. He is sent to India by the NSF to report on a proton experiment conducted by Indian scientists who claim they have measured the lifetime of matter. The Indians have hard numbers, and Clay confirms them in the Western manner. Clay sees this as Nobel Prize work.

The Indian scientist Singh sees much different consequences: "*This world*—this universe!—labored long under the illusion of its own permanence . . . We might die, yes, the sun might even perish—but the universe went on. Now we prove otherwise. There cannot help but be profound reactions" (238). Clay's name grounds him in the earth. Yet at the same time he is potentially a mobile center. Benford surely has in mind here, four years before the publication of *Sailing Bright Eternity*, those "clay" or silicon intelligences whose evolutionary path is the transformation of matter into information, but who "remember" their origin. Clay is likewise decentered. He is a black man, by his origins not quite at home in the world of the European science he professes. From the outset, he is an odd spokesman for Western reason, for his initial contact with an India ravaged by Western technology is intuitive and sensual, not coldly rational. He is thus an individual of potential mobility, physical and intellectual. It is this mobility that allows him to secure a new galvanic center when the old order vanishes. Clay, a new version of Benford's essential representative man Nigel Walmsley, now faces the ultimate challenge to his human class—Brahma awakening, eternity in the now.

It is fascinating how Emerson's text glosses this story. Clay here is Man relocated. As such, he fits Emerson's definition of a "great man": "I count him a great man who *inhabits* a higher sphere of thought, into which other men rise with labor and difficulty."[6] Emerson thinks in terms of comparatives, not superlatives. Thus Clay's "evolutionary" name seems to prepare him to move from great to greater as he negotiates the worlds of Western science and Eastern religion. Matter may end, but his nominal origins allow him to physically withstand the dissolving of substance. If he is able to recapture his material origins in the midst of breakdown, he will learn to speak and reason anew. For Emerson, the sole condition whereby matter may be transformed into mind is when mind in turn remembers its material origins: "Man, made of the dust of the world, does not forget his origin, and all that is yet inanimate will one day speak and reason. . . . Shall we say that quartz mountains will pulverize into innumerable Werners, Von Bachs and Beaumonts" (4).

Clay's Western belief in the mind-matter duality is dismissed by the Indian Singh: "That word we use—'thing'—it means something *we* are not, yes?" (273). All dualities related to matter will be abolished in a final, apocalyptic fusion of entities. Yet Clay will retain his position as *active* intermediary between worlds—East and West, time and no time. As such, even in his final moment of seeming transcendence, his presence as intermediary between worldviews preserves the means of forming a new galvanic circuit, a way human beings can hope to communicate with the ineffable, rather than being passively subsumed by it. His personal moment of fusion is a sexual union with the Indian scientist Mrs. Buli. Mutual cultural contamination occurs here. Clay speaks of Brahma; Mrs. Buli evokes the Westerner Plato: "'It's good to see that some features remain. Perhaps these are indeed the underlying Platonic beauties.' 'What?' Clay cried. 'The undying forms,' Mrs. Buli said abstractly. 'Perhaps that one Western idea was correct after all'" (287). Two different worlds—"underlying" is not "undying"—may fuse in this union of two *representative* figures. But Mrs. Buli's mention of Plato suggests human agency, not the pre-Socratic world of undifferentiated atoms, nor Brahma ascending. And Clay—through the medium of Benford's focalized narrator—is given the last word here. It is a vision that speaks of energy and dynamic change: "Time that was no time did not pass, and he and she and the impacted forces between them were pinned to the forever moment that cascaded through them, all of them, the billions of atomized elements that made them, forever" (288).

Matter has not ended here. Through Clay, its power has been magnified. Something great has become greater. But if this is a new Clay, he has not lost contact with his representative condition. The telephone that connects East and West has no meaning post-matter's end. Yet as he prepares to move to a new plane of reality, he restores connection with the old: "Somewhere far away his wife and daughter were in this too. *G'bye Daddy. It's been real*" (288). The hip slang of the old divided world takes on greater meaning in Clay's new, transmuted world. But it is the connection that forms a new galvanic circuit, where time that is time may once again pass at some new plane of human endeavor. From Clay's new dynamic position, acceding to timeless perfection is but one possible circumference. If the old consensus world is abolished, might not Man create a new one, born of greater power, with greater reach? With one foot in each world—the old and the new—Clay incarnates the process of undulation whereby the striving monad will continue to create "freeholds" in this quantum landscape, just as Killeen and his band did on Mech-occupied Snowglade, or Nigel and Toby in the esty. These human monads will continue to invest "representative" forms, using them to move on and up, subject to

Emerson's law of "rotation."[7] It was Emerson who proclaimed: "Within the limits of human education and *agency*, we may say great men exist that there may be greater men" (7). These are the agents of Benford's "forward tilt." Benford's short stories, at their most complex, do not simply deal with single incidents. They take on major philosophical, even religious, issues raised by modern science.

CONCLUSION

There are many other aspects of Benford's work which, alas, cannot be studied in detail because of space. One particular aspect—which has been part of Benford's approach to fiction from the start but which has intensified in his later career—is an open process of creation. By this I mean not only his interest in collaborating with other writers, but in actually writing sequels to their work, in which he continues a story they started, and *in the manner of a creative dialogue*, blends his vision skillfully with theirs. One notable example, his rewrite of Clarke's *Against the Fall of Night* (1953) is significantly titled *Beyond the Fall of Night* (1990). Writing this novel seems to have spurred him, in turn, to write a sequel to his own sequel, the novel *Beyond Infinity* (2004). We remember that Benford earlier wrote *Against Infinity*. The new novel, *Beyond Infinity*, makes no reference to the earlier novel. But in Benford's afterword to this novel, he explains that the scope of *Beyond the Fall of Night* was constricting, that he needed a broader canvas in which to meet the challenge of Clarke's novel. And in a very real sense, in all of these rewrites, it is clear that "against" is no longer enough. Benford, in rewriting Clarke, is at the same time rewriting his own vision of things. Again, we see an author at work who always needs to go beyond earlier ideas and fictional forms as they stand. The process of creation remains ever open to access to new data. Written works, like the work of science, are never fixed but are always ready to be revised, rethought. We see this creative intellectual restlessness clearly in Benford's recent reprints of *The Stars in Shroud*, and in his recent reshaping of his scientific mystery novel *Chiller*. Each work has been substantially revised. *Chiller* was originally published under the pseudonym "Sterling Blake." Benford now, in an updated work that continues the story of cryonics, drops the mask and publishes the novel under his own name.

Throughout Benford's career, collaboration has always been an act of expansion. Collaborative work, in fact, is a hallmark of science fiction in general. Its presence is a tacit sign that the expanding universes of SF are too big to be the exclusive purview of any single writer. SF writers share what have become collective tropes or worlds. No writer can write about Mars, for example, without at least a sideways bow to Ray Bradbury and Edgar Rice Burroughs. Borrowings from other writers are seen not as plagiarism but as building on a shared tradition, in which a community of writers literally creates a functioning fictional landscape, one that remains potentially open to future comers. Among SF writers, Benford is somewhat unique in his willingness to write co-signed collaborations. During the 1970s, he had a number of collaborations with Gordon Eklund, a prominent Seattle fan and author primarily of space opera and Star Trek novels. The collaboration began with a series of stories ("Westwind, Falling" [1971 *Universe* 1]; "The Anvil of Jove" [*Magazine of Fantasy and Science Fiction*, July 1976]; "Hellas Is Florida," [*F&SF*, January 1977]), and produced two novels: *If the Stars Are Gods* (1977) and *Find the Changeling* (1980). The effort garnered him his first Nebula Award (for "If the Stars Are Gods") and thus may have firmed his desire to continue writing SF. Benford wrote one novel with another well-known fan—artist, filmmaker, and sculptor William Rotsler—*Shiva Descending* (1980). During this decade he collaborated on stories, and on one novel—*The Heart of the Comet*—with David Brin, a writer with a PhD in space science from UC San Diego, who later came to prominence with his Uplift Novels (*Startide Rising* [1983]). In the late 1990s, Benford participated in the project known as the Second Foundation Trilogy, a series of novels written by Benford, Greg

Bear, and David Brin (the "killer Bs") that proposed to fill in gaps in Asimov's original Foundation cycle. This Foundation project is a declared act of writing in someone else's universe. Asimov's creation is perhaps the most mythic of the world-structures of SF, overshadowing even Frank Herbert's Dune. It is a world so compelling that it cries out to be supplemented. Benford's *Foundation's Fear* (1997), the first novel in this "Second Foundation," takes freewheeling liberties with Asimov's original world, camping simulations of figures like Joan of Arc and Voltaire alongside Hari Seldon. Each of the three authors takes off from the original text on his own tangent. Benford does likewise, but clearly here with a desire to supplement Asimov's creation, seeking to examine new scientific possibilities in fictional structures otherwise set by the spatiotemporal limits of the original books. Asimov himself worked all his life to elaborate and evolve his original Foundation vision. Benford carries this task beyond the life and work of the original writer, freeing writer and concepts alike to evolve freely, always the forward tilt.

But Benford's most fascinating example of such rewriting of a previous script is with Clarke in the novel *Beyond the Fall of Night* (1990). This work is nominally a collaborative sequel (Clarke was alive at the time and his name appears as primary author on the book's cover). In fact, Benford (the real author) is rewriting Clarke's *Against the Fall of Night* (1953). If Clarke was the writer who started it all for Benford, it has become increasingly clear throughout the author's career that Clarke's vision needs to be expanded. As early as 1988, an elderly Clarke began to franchise his Rama world. There was a series of such franchised works signed Clarke and Gentry Lee (*Rama II* [1989], *The Garden of Rama* [1991]) but essentially written by Lee. The last novel signed solely by Clarke, *The Hammer of God* (1993), revealed a hopeless recycling of prior ideas. There followed a series of novels, each based on an idea of Clarke, but written entirely by Stephen Baxter (for example, *The Light of Other Days* [2000]) and others. Finally, there was *The Last Theorem* (2007), signed Clarke and Frederik Pohl, but again written by the latter. Looking therefore at Benford's Clarke novel—and subsequently at the author's own sequel to this sequel, *Beyond Infinity* (2004), that conflates *Beyond the Fall of Night* and his earlier *Against Infinity*—it becomes increasingly clear that his primary purpose in writing these fictions was to address Clarke's ambiguity as to whether—once placed in the broader scientific context of planet-wide biome organisms in which sentient humanity has effectively become extinct—

Alvin's dying humanity can be effectively revived, and how this might occur. In *Beyond the Fall of Night*, Benford introduces Cley ("clay" or "clé" the French word for "key"), an early or *ur* human (possibly a Neanderthal) who has been regenerated from DNA stored in an interplanetary library. In Benford's novel, Alvin cannot be allowed to die until he has resuscitated the moribund humanity against whose extinction he stands as barrier in Clarke's novel. *Beyond Infinity* is the story of Cley's struggle to restore the spark of consciousness to life forms that have flourished with the extinction of mankind. In the Gaia world of the novel, Cley's task seems to offer a reworking of the role of Mother Maureen in Heinlein's final novels. For she assumes the role of individual genetrix of life forms—among them humanity—that are otherwise faced with cosmic extinction. She offers an extreme example of Benford's forward-striving monad, facing and overcoming Clarke's muted fatalism.

Such analysis is all too hasty. But it points to the author's desire to continue, into the new millennium, the ongoing dialogue between individual human tenacity and cosmic processes in which mankind no longer appears to have a role. If Benford recently seems to have sidelined fiction for commentary and scientific research in the new (for him) field of genetics and life extension, this has proved to be only a temporary pause. The appearance, in late 2012, of the novel *Bowl of Heaven* marks Benford's return to collaboration, this time with Larry Niven. Here, the stated idea is to "redesign" Ringworld, to take this legendary space habitat, and re-engineer its massive construction as a space vessel that draws upon the power of suns to propel it and its alien stewards toward unknown destinations as inhospitable, and possibly more so, as Galactic Center. There are sequels announced. The spirit of high space adventure is rekindled in an age when space travel itself needs rekindling and when science fiction is turning away from science and toward social dogma. As these ongoing collaborative works and revisions indicate, Benford's mind remains ever restless, ever searching for answers to the same question of mankind's place and role in science's vast universe. His recent work offers hope that a new science fiction, rooted in future scientific discovery, will continue to emerge, to create and to address new challenges for the reader and for the future of narrative.

INTERVIEW WITH GREGORY BENFORD

GEORGE SLUSSER: Greg, the definition of SF I find challenging, and yet vague, is that of Robert L. Forward: "Science writes the fiction." Could you tell me how you, as scientist and writer, see this definition? How do you see you must nuance it?

GREGORY BENFORD: I often begin by imagining how a scientist will confront a new scientific result, discovery, or idea. I then use what I know from long observation to elicit how scientists think, which may be my central theme—even when writing of events distant in time and space, as in the Galactic Center series. Long ago I realized that I had one great advantage in fiction, since few write about scientists, yet science is the driving force in modern times. Writing SF seemed natural because I knew its genre labyrinths and could serve my apprenticeship within it while I learned. If I had chosen to write conventional fiction I doubt I'd have been accepted; even now, scientists seldom appear in ordinary fiction.

I took Bob Forward's *science "writing" the fiction* definition of SF as a short truth, though of course the method has many nuances. I usually start by roughing out a scientific idea, then let my unconscious play with it to see where it leads.

I've always wanted to render how scientists think while in their most characteristic mode—facing the unknown, that is, doing research. Vast steps forward, like the invention of quantum mechanics a century ago, show us that physics at least has a unique method. To make truly breakout discoveries, you can use elements that seem far from the old positivist ideas. For example, the aesthetics of equations (Dirac), the building of simple models that capture some of the ideas but miss many (Bohr), *gedanken* experiments (Einstein), and pure imaginative leaps encased in mathematics (von Neumann, Hawking). The same can be true in other sciences, and depicting how this can happen seemed an exciting way to make SF explore avenues other literary forms don't even imagine doing.

GS: Let's turn the question around: Can you see, in a work of fiction that adapts and extrapolates from scientific concepts, fiction acting to write the science?

GB: The SF genre does serve as thought experiments useful in anticipating the accelerations and swerves of our times. *Gedanken* experiments come from physics, after all. The SF that emerged from the scientific/technological culture opening out in the nineteenth century was a natural, intuitive outgrowth. Novels to be truly novel at all must be experiments.

That said, I think the central deep question SF can address is *What meaning does human action have, if any?* Existentialists root all meaning in what we decide matters, as though we just made up things to care about—but that seems to me to ignore our biological origins. We're the only form of chimp that got out of Africa, so rooted deep in us is a desire to expand human horizons. I think that's a fine, great mission, for through us the universe finally gets to fathom itself. We manifest that well in SF. Such longings to comprehend our world come from natural selection and so arise from the world itself. Doing this gives us meaning because that's how evolution shaped us. If this universe is an experiment, we're the ones pushing it forward, trying to comprehend it. The experiment wants us to understand it.

GS: The next question deals with the possibility of science outpacing fiction. Do you see a danger of science and fiction going in opposite ways? Is there the risk of today's readers finding the scientific description itself more interesting than the story vehicle?

GB: Being provisionally true until the next, deeper description comes along, science is intrinsically more interesting than the arts, since it can and must evolve. This is seldom shown in fiction, though it is in SF. People often need a human entry into the sometimes-austere lands of science. If readers start going after books on science, all to the good—and surely that's good for SF too. Alien life is different, though—its mere existence implies so much. How we react to such knowledge is the core emotional arc.

Against Infinity is my favorite novel because it comes from my own growing up—a coming-of-age story with Faulknerian overtones that resonate with me, a southerner. It rode on its own melting, as Frost said of his poems. So easy to write!—and I could resolve the emotional issues intuitively, almost without thinking. Science is sometimes like this, a struggle with hard problems and niggling detail that suddenly breaks through to a new understanding. The moment of realizing something true and sometimes even beautiful, being the first to see it, is a deep satisfaction. I often try to convey that in fiction as a way to fathom what drives scientists and why they think rather differently.

GS: But have we reached a point in scientific speculation where the worldviews implied by scientific theory are no longer narratable? You are on the cutting edge of science. Do you have any new strategies for telling science's new worlds?

GB: Certainly arcane fields like string theory and cosmology are hard to bring down to the human scale. So is mathematics; consider how Borges for example managed to use such concepts in his mannered, petite poems to cool reason.

My strategy often begins with a scientist meeting a problem, following a linear plot structure that opens up at the climax. A recent example story is "Bow Shock," which I had floating in my imagination for a decade. Another tack is to start in a strange situation and let the reader infer what's happening. This is risky, because I sometimes use extreme cases—such work is for the hard SF fan, mostly, just as the locked room problems were for mystery fans.

There is nothing especially hard about the quantum world if you see it as a mathematical theory and learn new intuitions from that. It's the substrate of our gross world of particles and waves. Using that particle-wave duality to describe quantum mechanics is just an analogy we can grasp; the actual quantum world is not remotely like ours, after all. I often sense a thinness in contemporary fiction about the way the world operates, making the conventional world primary when it's not. That's just a lazy habit. The universe that science reveals to us is comically unrelated to what our primitive senses report, after all.

GS: On to the question of anthropocentrism in SF. Science describes life forms chemically different from ours, and places we can never physically go. In dealing with these, is SF doomed never to cross the anthropocentric barrier?

GB: I draw a parallel to quantum mechanics. Led by aesthetics, early TwenCen physicists groped their way to an understanding of the quantum world that no one could have fashioned without the guide of science's great dance—the waltz between theory and constraining experiment. That's how we may reach larger perspectives in fiction—trying in fiction to convey perceptions at the limits of our comprehension. Try out new ideas, see what it's like to walk around inside them.

SF thinks about such grand scales—humanity as a species, not just a bunch of interest groups, cultures, faiths. Surely this is a grander prospect than class, race, sex, and death as riddles for the thinking animal. In a century or two technology will have had more to say on these issues than our literature. Further, any writer's opinion on what everyone thinks are the big issues of our time is inevitably coarser than the texture of the writer's conjuring up of life as it comes at him or her. Writers often say more than they mean, thank God. To me, imagining the alien is "Effing the Ineffi ble." You always fall short, but notable successes like Lem's *Solaris*, which also has deft satire of science at its core, show that it can be done.

GS: Here is a related question, which has to do with limits of the SF genre. SF has become a label under which to explore identity politics, race and gender issues, issues with little or no relevance to science. What does this bode for the future of SF? Genres have thematic and formal limits. Do you think SF as genre is dying?

GB: Not dying, but changing. I like that some writers are increasingly concerned with making books that are not sloppy, that can be reread. But young writers are fools to follow a trend or theory. Sure you can illuminate indirection; even *Star Trek* did that. SF is a big tent. I doubt most readers go for it as a mask over current social comment, though.

GS: To change direction, let's talk about style and narrative form in SF. What are your thoughts today, after forty-plus years of writing, on the future potential of SF, in terms of narrative innovation?

GB: Plato noted in *The Republic* that bad characters are volatile and interesting, whereas good characters are dull and always the same. Definitely a literary problem for realism!

I like space adventure blending into epic, and without setting off to do so, wrote the six-volume Galactic Center sequence because ideas kept coming forth. Space was the central image of the twentieth century, and I suspect its true emergence is coming only now, with commercial firms readying hotels in orbit. The long-range future of humanity will be bleak without the resource reservoir of the solar system to tap. That's a fundamental truth, and SF was the first to see it; most don't even see it now. There are no truly strange places left on this world, and for a roving, over-the-horizon species, that's a troubling problem. But imagination can solve it.

GS: Let's turn to the short story. I would like your thoughts on the role of the short story, both in the development of SF and in your own writing experience. Do you feel that short stories offer you a "lyrical" dimension, as opposed to "philosophical" vistas of space epic?

GB: Of course short stories in their compression and focus can have great power. They're fine for trying out ideas. I was amazed to find in one of my first fanzines, written at age fourteen, a two-page story which clearly prefigures the concerns of *Timescape*! Plainly, my unconscious has been mulling on these questions of time for a long while. I thought my interest came from a paper I wrote on tachyons while a postdoc at Livermore, published in *Physical Review* and one of my most referenced papers.

So short stories are like experiments; novels resemble military campaigns, especially in the long, hard marches in the middle. You can indeed wax lyrical in them at small cost; it becomes an "atmospheric" story.

I especially like short stories because I often wrote them in one sitting. Once I deliberately wrote a story in one hour just to see if I could. They resemble surfing, which I still do—forcing you to be in the moment.

GS: Now to your "worldview." You often refer to Pascal. Your reflections on mankind's role in the universe occur in a scientific context far "advanced" beyond Pascal. Do you believe his idea of the "human condition" remains relevant today? Or will this forever be our limit?

GB: I am suspicious of definitions of the human condition that focus on our limitations, since we keep transcending them. I also suspect genetics will make possible this century directed evolution of a nonhuman hominid, an epic moment. (I founded some genetic companies devoted to longevity, mostly because it's now possible to deliver results.) But I can see coming potentials that will test our definitions of ourselves through direct technological methods.

Still, our species has limits, though we know only vaguely what they are. My conservative side says, learn from these limits. My liberal, SF side says, transcend them. We amplify our abilities artificially, from eyeglasses to implants (my left shoulder is artificial) to the coming possibilities of mind/machine interfaces. It's hard to see how our exploding frontiers of the mind will ever fade; we're far too early in this game.

GS: A couple of final questions. First, throughout your career there is continuous interest in the question of human longevity and scientific solutions to this question. The problem is one of mythic proportions. Your thoughts today?

GB: SF strives against limitations, and death is the big one. I founded Methuselah Flies LLC and Genescient to use genetics based on long-lived flies, all to ferret out human longevity genes. It's working so far, we have products that work, derived from genomics—and this is just the beginning of applying the genomic revolution to the real world.

Moral persuasion has done little to improve human nature, though education is the best way to do it. You learn as you age, after all. Longer-lived people make better, longer use of their education, particularly the hard-won fruit of experience—and bring wisdom to the table, then. Educating women improves society generally, for example, so Muslim societies see it as too radical an idea. Extending human mean lifespans has done wonders; the longest-lived nations are the most advanced, liberal, and educated. We don't much notice the steadily expanding lifespans and healthspans around us, as they're gradual. We've seen a 50 percent increase in mean lifespan per century for two centuries now. If we continue that, in 2100 the *average* person will live to 100. People might work productively into their eighties. This means a longer healthspan, too, because genomic processes can up-regulate genes that carry out repairs.

Beyond that, cryonics is the ultimate act of faith in the future. The odds are low but the rewards immense. It's a gamble that will probably fail, but it does allow people to die with hope. Yet so far every major SF writer who wrote about cryonics—Simak, Pohl, Heinlein, Asimov—has turned down a free freeze. Hard to explain.

GS: Second question. You have sharply criticized today's society for abandoning the space program, for abdicating the "sense of wonder" it generated. But very recently, with *Bowl of Heaven* and promised sequels, you return to space engineering and cosmic mystery. What is your reason for this? Nostalgia? Or sensing a need for big projects today?

GB: My larger aims are already accomplished. I've written novels about how scientists live, love, and work (*Timescape, Artifact, Cosm, Eater, Chiller)* and a space epic (Galactic Center), various fun novels, over one hundred short stories, three nonfiction . . . I have no desire to write a mammoth book; my longest, *Chiller*, was a mere two hundred thousand words. I think we are rushing toward terrible times, with all pressures rising: climate chaos, resource depletion, overpopulation, the rats-in-a-cage frenzy of maddened crowds. So maybe pointing out ways we can best solve these problems by looking large is the best use of my time. I'd urge more geoengineering, which is inevitable, use of space resources, a hard push for education in oppressed societies, and bringing down the remaining tyrannies.

Mostly, though, as I turn seventy and look forward, I want to have fun doing whatever I choose. Writing allows a craftsman's intimate satisfactions. I've always written because I liked to, and if people read me, even better.

GS: Greg, now that the book is finished and you have read the manuscript, is there anything you would like to add?

GB: I found it surprisingly slow reading. Immersing in books and stories written decades ago draws one back against the currents of inexorable time. Revisiting those works returned me to ideas and emotions felt long before and very nearly forgotten. I also saw patterns I did not consciously construct but clearly are there, welling up from my unconscious. I found myself *living through* the process of creating them, a dense process I had not engaged ever before.

The centrality of the Galactic Center series in my work became manifest here, and its themes and leitmotifs surfaced again for me. Because I wrote the series over a quarter-century, I deliberately did not reread the prior novels, for reasons I knew intuitively but cannot state even now.

Your treatment of a few short stories was insightful. Some surprised me: "*Eater* (1999) is clearly an expansion, on a massive scale, of his classic story 'Exposures.'" Yes, but I didn't know that until you said so. "Of Space/Time and the River" and "Mozart on Morphine" both came directly from my scientific life and began as notes written to get my experiences down before they faded, with no prospect of being fiction. Only later, awakening from dreams which used this material, did I see that I had somehow warped them into fiction.

I liked your connections to philosophy, especially French, Descartes, etc. I've read a lot of philosophy, especially the Germans—though I'm not really a metaphysics type—and like Heidegger, whose ideas influenced me; and as well, "Man acts as though he were the shaper and master of language, while in fact language remains the master of man."

Seldom is a writer an expert on his own work. I'm certainly not. Generally, I found your insightful readings quite on target, and have now a different sense of my own work. I do not know what others will make of my writing, which has always been an embracing sidelight in my life, and I appreciate this attempt to see it whole.

A Gregory Benford Bibliography

Benford is a highly prolific writer, with a long and intricate bibliography. I have chosen to present his major fictional works—novels and story collections—in chronological order of publication. In addition, to help the reader, I attach to each entry the currently *in print or electronically available edition.* Given the nature of mass-market publication, many SF works, including classics, go out of print. Benford has developed strategies to keep virtually all of his important works available in one format or another. Benford's complete bibliography can be found at his official website: http://www.isfdb.org/cgi-bin/ea.cgi?Gregory_Benford.

Deeper than the Darkness, as "Greg Benford," 1970 (Ace). No current in-print edition.

Jupiter Project, 1975 (Thomas Nelson). Paperback: Harper Collins, 1998.

In the Ocean of Night, Galactic Center One, 1976 (Dial). Paperback: Hachette, 2000.

If the Stars Are Gods, with Gordon Eklund, 1977 (Berkley/Penguin). Paperback re-issue: Penguin U.S., 1979.

The Stars in Shroud, re-write of *Deeper than the Darkness*, 1978 (Penguin). No current in-print edition.

Shiva Descending, with William Rotsler, 1980 (St. Martin's). Mass paperback: Doherty, 1992.

Find the Changeling, with Gordon Eklund, 1980 (Dell). Paperback: Wilder, 2010.

Timescape, 1980 (Simon & Schuster). Paperback: Random House, 1992.

Against Infinity, 1983 (Ultramarine). E-book: Lucky Bat, 2013.

Across the Sea of Suns, Galactic Center Two, 1984 (Simon & Schuster). Paperback: Hachette, 2009.

Artifact, 1985 (St. Martin's). E-book: Harper Collins, 2009.

Heart of the Comet, with David Brin, 1986 (Bantam Spectra). Paperback: Random House, 1995.

In Alien Flesh, story collection, 1986 (St. Martin's). Paperback: Doherty, 1988.

Great Sky River, Galactic Center Three, 1987 (Bantam). E-book: Grand Central/Hachette Digital, 2009.

Tides of Light, Galactic Center Four, 1989 (Bantam). Paperback: Hachette, 2009.

Matter's End, stories, 1989 (Cheap Street). Mass-market paperback: Random House, 1995.

Beyond the Fall of Night, with Arthur C. Clarke, 1990 (Putnam). E-book: Rosetta, 2012.

Chiller, as "Sterling Blake," 1993 (Bantam). Revised e-book, signed "Gregory Benford": Lucky Bat, 2011,

Furious Gulf, Galactic Center Five, 1994 (Bantam Spectra). Paperback: Random House 1995. Paperback reprint: Grand Central, 2009. E-book: Grand Central, 2009.

Sailing Bright Eternity, Galactic Center Six, 1995 (Bantam Spectra). Mass-market paperback: Random House, 1996. Paperback: Grand Central, 2006. E-book: Grand Central/Hachette Digital, 2007.

Foundation's Fear, vol. 1 of the Second Foundation Series, 1997 (Harper Prism). Paperback: Turtleback, 2000. E-book: Harper Collins, 2009.

Cosm, 1998 (HarperCollins).

The Martian Race, 1999 (Warner Aspect). Paperback: Orbit, 2000. E-book: Grand Central/Hachette Digital, 2008.

Deep Time: How Humanity Communicates across Millennia, nonfiction, 1999 (Bard). Paperback: HarperCollins, 2000. Hardcover: HarperCollins, 2001.

Worlds Vast and Various, stories, 2000 (HarperCollins).

Eater, 2001 (EOS/HarperCollins). E-book: HarperCollins, 2009.

Immersion and Other Short Novels, novellas, 2002 (Cengage Gale).

Beyond Infinity, 2004 (Warner Aspect). Mass-market paperback: Grand Central, 2008. E-book: Grand Central, 2008.

The Sunborn, sequel to *The Martian Race*, 2005 (Grand Central). Paperback: Grand Central, 2006. E-book: Grand Central, 2007.

Anomalies (stories), 2012 (Benford Press). E-book: Constable and Robinson, 2012.

Down the River Road, "chapter book," 2012 (Lucky Bat).

Bowl of Heaven, with Larry Niven, 2012 (Doherty).

NOTES

INTRODUCTION

1. "Why Does a Scientist Write Science Fiction?" *Challenger: A Science Fiction Magazine* 23 (Winter/Spring, 2005–06).

CHAPTER 1. THE SCIENTIST AS WRITER

1. *Challenger: A Science Fiction Fanzine* 23 (Winter 2005–06). Available at www.challzine.net.
2. Robert L. Forward, "When Science Writes the Fiction," in *Hard Science Fiction*, eds. George E. Slusser and Eric S. Rabkin (Carbondale: Southern Illinois University Press, 1986), 2.
3. *Challenger* 23.
4. Claude Bernard, *Introduction à l'étude de la médicine expérimentale* (Tours: Garnier Flammarion, 1965), 305.
5. *Challenger* 23.

CHAPTER 2. BENFORD IN HIS OWN WORDS

1. George E. Slusser, George R. Guffey, and Mark Rose, eds., *Bridges to Science Fiction* (Carbondale: Southern Illinois University Press, 1980), 53.
2. See Samuel R. Delany, *The Einstein Intersection* (New York: Bantam, 1967), 122–23.
3. James Gunn, "The Readers of Hard Science Fiction," in *Hard Science Fiction*, edited by George E. Slusser and Eric S. Rabkin (Carbondale: Southern Illinois University Press, 1986), 75.
4. See Ursula K. Le Guin, "American SF and the Other," in *The Language of the Night: Essays on Fantasy and Science Fiction* (New York: Putnam, 1979), 97–101.
5. George E. Slusser and Eric S. Rabkin, eds., *Aliens: The Anthropology of Science Fiction* (Carbondale: Southern Illinois University Press, 1987), 13.
6. George E. Slusser and Eric S. Rabkin, eds., *Mindscapes: The Geographies of Imagined Worlds* (Carbondale: Southern Illinois University Press, 1989), 273.
7. George Slusser and Eric S. Rabkin, eds., *Styles of Creation: Aesthetic Technique and the Creation of Fictional Worlds* (Athens: University of Georgia Press, 1992), 48.
8. Bishop Thomas Sprat, *The History of the Royal Society*, 1667, facsimile edition, edited by Jackson Cope and H. W. Jones (Whitefish, Mont.: Kessinger, 2003), sect. 2:20.1, 113.

9. George Slusser and Tom Shippey, eds., *Fiction 2000: Cyberpunk and the Future of Narrative* (Athens: University of Georgia Press, 1992), 223.
10. Gary Westfahl, George Slusser, and Eric S. Rabkin, eds., *Science Fiction and Market Realities* (Athens: University of Georgia Press, 1996), 151.
11. George Slusser and Jean-Pierre Barricelli, eds., *Genre at the Crossroads: The Challenge of Fantasy* (Riverside, Calif.: Xenos, 2003), 35.
12. Gary Westfahl and George Slusser, eds., *Science Fiction and the Two Cultures: Essays on Bridging the Gap Between the Sciences and the Humanities* (London: McFarland, 2009), 230.

CHAPTER 3. FICTIONAL DIRECTIONS

1. Gregory Benford, *Deeper than the Darkness* (New York: Ace, 1970), 9.
2. Gregory Benford, *The Stars in Shroud* (New York: Berkley, 1978), 212.
3. I wish to make an important point. Benford was interested in my readings of these two novels, which have had little critical attention. Some sources he mentions, others are obvious. Some others he described as "subliminal," notably Heinlein and the Strugatskys for *Against Infinity*, which he admitted he was reading at the time. His sense, and I agree, is that the word "source" has little meaning for SF writers. They (and their readers) have read a great number of books. They recall situations, landscapes, scenarios, but they cannot identify author and title in many cases. All this becomes common property for the writer, and the word "subliminal" has real meaning.
4. Gregory Benford, *Against Infinity* (New York: Pocket, 1983), 168.
5. William Faulkner, "The Bear," in *Go Down, Moses* (New York: Vintage, 1973).
6. Robinson Jeffers, "Hurt Hawks," in *Selected Poems* (New York: Vintage, 1965), 108.
7. Robert A. Heinlein, "By His Bootstraps," in *The Menace from Earth* (New York: Signet, 1959), 87.
8. Arthur C. Clarke, *3001: The Final Odyssey* (New York: Del Rey, 1998), 238.

CHAPTER 5. GALACTIC CENTER TWO

1. Gregory Benford, *In the Ocean of Night* (New York: Dial, 1977), 13.
2. The German title of von Däniken's book is: *Erinnerungen an die Zukunft: Ungelöste Rätsel der Vergangenheit* (Memories of the Future: Unsolved Mysteries of the Past).
3. Gregory Benford, *Across the Sea of Suns* (New York: Bantam, 1987), 70.

CHAPTER 6. TO THE GALACTIC CENTER

1. Gregory Benford, *Great Sky River* (New York: Bantam, 1987), 141.
2. Gregory Benford, *Tides of Light* (New York: Bantam, 1989), 386.
3. Gregory Benford, *Sailing Bright Eternity* (New York: Bantam, 1995), 236.
4. Ralph Waldo Emerson, *Nature, in The American Tradition in Literature*, vol. 1 (New York: Norton, 1967), 1067.
5. William J. Patterson Jr., in his monumental biography of Robert A. Heinlein (*Robert A. Heinlein in Dialogue with His Century,* vol. 1 (1907–1949): Learning Curve [New York: Doherty, 2011]), offers much testimony of a strong fascination with Emerson on the part of Heinlein and other Golden Age writers. Benford is in this current.

CHAPTER 7. THE SCIENCE FICTION NOVEL OF MANNERS

1. Gregory Benford, *Timescape* (New York: Bantam, 1992), "Special Acknowledgment."
2. Gregory Benford, *Timescape* (New York: Simon and Schuster, 1980), 92.

CHAPTER 8. BENFORD'S SHORT FICTION

1. Gregory Benford, *Anomalies*, Lucky Bat Books (e-book), 2012.
2. Gregory Benford, "Exposures," in *In Alien Flesh* (New York: Tor Books, 1986), p. 246.
3. Gregory Benford, "Mozart on Morphene," in *Matter's End* (New York: Bantam Spectra, 1995), p. 9.
4. Gregory Benford, "Matter's End," in *Matter's End,* p. 238.
5. Arthur C. Clarke, "The Nine Billion Names of God," in *The Other Side of the Sky* (New York: Signet Books, 1959), 15.
6. Ralph Waldo Emerson, *Representative Men*, I, "Uses of Great Men" (www.gutenberg.org/ebooks/6312), 2.
7. *Representative Men*, I, 7: "But nature brings all this about in due time. Rotation is her remedy." "Uses of Great Men" abounds in sentences that gloss Benford's Clay, and his Nigel Walmsley for that matter. An example: "We are as elastic as the gas of gunpowder, and a sentence in a book, . . . sets free our fancy, and instantly our heads are bathed with galaxies, and our feet tread the floor of the Pit" (6). An occasional reader like Benford need only "dip in" and find a watery aphorism on every page.

INDEX

GEORGE SLUSSER is a professor of comparative literature and the curator of the J. Lloyd Eaton Collection of Science Fiction, Fantasy, and Horror Literature at the University of California, Riverside. His books include *Science Fiction: Canonization, Marginalization and the Academy*.

Modern Masters of Science Fiction

John Brunner *Jad Smith*

William Gibson *Gary Westfahl*

Gregory Benford *George Slusser*

THE UNIVERSITY OF ILLINOIS PRESS
is a founding member of the
Association of American University Presses.

Designed by Kelly Gray
Composed in 10.75/14.5 Dante
with Univers display
by Lisa Connery
at the University of Illinois Press
Manufactured by Sheridan Books, Inc.

University of Illinois Press
1325 South Oak Street
Champaign, IL 61820-6903
www.press.uillinois.edu